Crying in The Wilderness

Jack Sayers: a liberal editor in Ulster, 1939–69

Crying in The Wilderness

Jack Sayers: a liberal editor in Ulster, 1939–69

Andrew Gailey

The Institute of Irish Studies
The Queen's University of Belfast

Published 1995
The Institute of Irish Studies
The Queen's University of Belfast

Grateful acknowledgement for financial assistance is made to the Cultural Traditions programme of the Community Relations Council which aims to encourage acceptance and understanding of cultural diversity.

British Library Cataloguing-in-Publication Data. A catalogue record for this book is available from the British Library.

ISBN: 0 85389 540 6

Printed by W & G Baird Ltd, Antrim
Cover design by Rodney Miller Associates

To
Shauna and Emily

Contents

Foreword

When in 1963 James Chichester-Clark became Chief Whip of the Unionist
Party, he was advised to consult the editor of the *Belfast Telegraph*, Jack
Sayers. Sayers, he discovered, was a bespectacled man of medium height,
rather sallow in complexion and distinctly anglicised in accent and demean-
our. Accustomed to the rough-and-tumble of Unionism in Co. Londonderry,
he found, somewhat to his surprise, that to many people Sayers was 'something of a god', courted by government ministers and young aspirants for
office alike; while for many others, both Protestant and Catholic, he was
regarded as a beacon of decency, courage and conviction amid the political
turmoil of the 1960s. This was a time when people asked 'What does the
Telegraph say?', and at border crossings hoardings would welcome visitors
to '*Belfast Telegraph*land'. Yet Chichester-Clark can remember nothing of
his meeting with this deity, and to this day Sayers rates barely a mention in
any of the histories which have poured out on the Ulster Question. The storms
that have swept the province since 1969 have left hardly a trace of his world
and what he stood for. Not surprisingly, perhaps, our appreciation of the
past has been overwhelmed by the awfulness of the present. The tendency to
judge is instinctive in all of us, and after more than twenty years of troubles
post-war Ulster has been judged harshly. But to understand the 1950s and
1960s we must put them in their own context. In particular, we must rid our
minds of the impending catastrophe and seek to recapture the prevailing
sense of triumphant optimism in the face of 'ancient hatreds'. If this is a
world we have lost, it was a world that lived in faith that it had everything to
gain. And few reflected this better than Jack Sayers.

Sayers always fondly described himself as a liberal, a representative of
that radical dissenting tradition that had fomented revolution in Ulster in
1798 in the name of patriotism and liberty. Yet such romanticism aside, he
was never a revolutionary and was much more a constructive Unionist. At
first glance, to describe Ulster Unionism as constructive appears almost to
be a contradiction in terms. The 'Ulster Says No' banners that sprang up in
the wake of the Anglo-Irish Agreement may now look a little bedraggled.
Yet in contrast to constructive Unionism, they represent a Unionism that is
instantly recognisable and whose pedigree goes back to Carson and the Ulster revolt of 1912, if not before. However, constructive Unionism was itself
part of a tradition that was as old as the Union itself. For all its adherence to
the myths of Grattan's Parliament and the Protestant radicalism of the 1790s,
its roots lay in the political legacy of 1800 in which Westminster reasserted

its will, only to abdicate its responsibilities. Rejecting that the polarisation of Irish society was irreversible, constructive Unionists were Unionists for whom Ireland was the first love but who saw Ireland's social and economic development as only feasible within the larger sphere of the British Empire. Within Ireland they sought the reconciliation of all patriots around this goal and attempted to draw out the conservative middle ground of Irish politics. Such ideals enthused Orange Young Ireland, the contributors to the *Dublin University Magazine*, and Butt's Home Government Association. They were at the core of the acute analysis of Ireland's problems of the 1850s and 1860s by Lord Dufferin, the Ulster Whig peer. The re-emergence in the 1880s of Catholic nationalism in the shape of Home Rule stimulated in turn an imaginative response after 1890 from Unionists such as Ross of Bladensburg, Horace Plunkett, George A. Birmingham, Lord Dunraven, Lord Monteagle, and Standish O'Grady. Although the tide ran against them after 1905, it returned again in the 1960s with the liberal policies of Terence O'Neill. These, in their love of country (Ulster), the pursuit of reconciliation through economic development and prosperity and the desire to broaden unionism into a 'national' creed, were wholly in the tradition of nineteenth-century progressive Unionism.

However, O'Neill's conversion to liberalism was always a little ambiguous. At that time the most coherent exponent of constructive Unionism was Jack Sayers, the editor of the *Belfast Telegraph* (the largest-selling paper in the province, with a readership that uniquely spanned the religious divide). A firm believer in the Union, he returned to the province in 1945 after serving on Churchill's staff during the war, convinced that Unionism as well as Ulster would have to modernise; especially if it was to survive in the post-war economic order and contribute effectively within the United Kingdom. He urged, therefore, the diversification of Ulster industry, the encouragement of new businesses and the education of the workforce. He was forever advocating that Ulstermen look beyond the province to the wider opportunities of the UK, EEC and USA. At the same time, he felt that Ulster's devolved status gave her greater freedom to advance her interests and that Unionists should do all they could to make this governmental experiment work as a model for the United Kingdom. If this was to be achieved, he recognised that Ulster could not afford to leave a third of its workforce disaffected. Economic efficiency as well as social justice (he was a fervent Methodist) necessitated the mobilisation of Ulster Catholics as well. And this meant the transformation of Ulster Unionism into an inclusive, supra-class political movement. These ideas, emanating as they did from a traditional Unionist organ, won considerable support in the late 1950s and 1960s. As Sayers's articulate assault left traditional Unionism floundering, he quickly became the confidant of the Prime Minister and was widely regarded as the guru of O'Neillism (in much the same way as Plunkett and Dunraven had been seen as the moving spirits of constructive Unionism in the 1890s and 1900s).

Thus the primary purpose of this work is biographical and intended to rescue, largely through his own writing, a leading political figure from the oblivion that overwhelmed his ideas and reputation after 1969. At the same time this study seeks also to present a range of documentary material highly relevant to a critical period of Ulster's history for which the official record will largely remain closed for some years to come. These sources comprise not only Sayers's published work in the *Belfast Telegraph* and *The Round Table* but also a selection from his private papers, which include appointment diaries, letters and transcripts of his radio broadcasts for the BBC. Given the collaborative nature of leader-writing, it has proved impossible to attribute conclusively particular leaders to Sayers. Consequently, I have restricted my selection of 'his' leaders to the few cuttings that he had kept for his private records and which also reflect his literary style or for which I have supporting evidence of his authorship. There is also (in the possession of his sister) his war correspondence; but it is the run of letters to Conolly Gage, now in the Public Record Office of Northern Ireland, that form the core of this book, particularly for the period after 1959. On Sayers himself there is very little save for the obituaries and a radio programme, 'Proud Thy Name', produced by the BBC on the first anniversary of his death. However, these are supplemented by a series of interviews and correspondence with almost seventy of his contemporaries conducted while on sabbatical at the Institute of Irish Studies in 1990. While much of the Sayers material has had to be edited, largely in order to sustain the narrative flow and to avoid (where possible) repetition, every effort has been made not to distort the central thrust of his arguments or his use of language. Hence phrases that seem clichéd today have been retained, as they struck a resonance with Sayers and his contemporaries. Inevitably, in such a collection of source material the vagaries of quality and survival can tend to determine the structure of the book, and this partly accounts for the size of Chapter 5. But then, there were few in Ulster in 1966 who did not believe that they were living in interesting times.

This work is primarily intended to be a study of one man's ideas. As a result, the linking passages between the documents seek to place them in the context not only of his own development but also in terms of the political world of the 1950s and 1960s in which he moved. In doing this I have drawn heavily on the work of many scholars; my greatest debts are to the writings of Paul Arthur, Jonathan Bardon, Paul Bew, Andrew Boyd, Steve Bruce, Patrick Buckland, Sydney Elliott, Michael Farrell, W. D. Flackes, Eric Gallagher, Peter Gibbon, David Gordon, David Harkness, Rosemary Harris, Alvin Jackson, Keith Jeffery, Dennis Kennedy, David Miller, Amy Miracle, Ed Moloney, Sarah Nelson, Liam O'Dowd, Henry Patterson, Andy Pollak, Bob Purdie, Richard Rose, Joe Spence, A. T. Q. Stewart, Jennifer Todd, Charles Townshend, Martin Wallace, John Whyte, Sabine Wichert, Tom Wilson, Stanley Worrall and Frank Wright. I am also extremely grateful to the following for the time they gave to answer my inquiries: Lord Ashby, Anne Lawlor, Malcolm Brodie, Walter McCauley, the Rev. Dr John Turner, Roy Lilley, Denis Barritt, Rt. Hon. David Bleakley, Sir Charles Brett, Tom Caldwell, Rev. Eric Gallagher, Sir Charles Carter, James Hawthorne, Paul

Bew, John Lewis-Crosbie, Brian Garrett, Alf McCreary, Dennis Kennedy, W. Stratton Mills, Martin Wallace, Sir Kenneth Bloomfield, Thomas Brown, Professor J. F. Pantridge, Professor J. C. Beckett, Rev. Dr Hedley Plunkett, Sean McDougall, Jim Malley, Phyllis Moore, Desmond Neill, Professor Rex Cathcart, F. J. G. Cook, David Cook, John Boyd, Mary Hurley, Hugh Shearman, Rev. Canon Dr S. E. Long, John Fairleigh, Sir Robert Porter, Rt. Hon. Basil McIvor, W. D. Flackes, Rafton Pounder, Dr John Robb, Paul Rose, Rt. Hon. Dr Robert Simpson, Andrew Stewart, Arthur Green, Lady Wakehurst, Stanley Worrall, Maurice Shillington, Edith Taggart, Cecil Taylor, Frederick Owens, Fred Jeffrey, His Grace the Duke of Abercorn, Sir Ewart Bell, Sir George Clark, Anne Dickson, Richard Ferguson, David Gilliland, Lord Grey of Naunton, Sir Patrick Macrory, Lord Moyola, T. W. Mulryne, Col. T. E. Field, Roy Foster, Joe Spence, and to those who wish to remain anonymous. My thanks to the Institute of Irish Studies, and especially Brian Walker and Kate Newmann. I also thank Colm Croker who was copy-editor. Nicky Braddell's help in the preparation of the first draft was simply invaluable. So too was Emma Lee, who came to my rescue when the first deadline was imminent. However, without the typing skills and cheerful forbearance of Lois Sumner this book would never have appeared at all.

I would like to express my gratitude to the following people and institutions for permission to quote from manuscripts in their possession: the *Belfast Telegraph*, the BBC, John Pim, *The Round Table*, Shirley Bourn, Sir Kenneth Bloomfield, W. M. Gage, Lady O'Neill, Betty Wilson and Daphne Sayers. I would also like to record my appreciation of Daphne Sayers and all the Sayers family for having encouraged me in this project.

My initial interest in Sayers was aroused by my mother, who succeeded in turning the reading of the *Telegraph*'s leaders into a family ritual. I would like to thank Jimmy and Marjorie Wilde for first drawing to my attention the existence of the Sayers collection and also, together with my sisters, for sustaining me on my many visits to Belfast. However, my greatest debts of hospitality are as usual owed to my parents-in-law, and for their support I am extremely grateful. To Shauna, mere gratitude could hardly be sufficient acknowledgement of her contribution. Her tolerance in the face of her husband's latest obsession never wavered, and, although she had cause enough over the last five years, she never let anything intrude on my pursuit of Sayers. It is by way of poor recompense that this book is offered as a small token of my boundless appreciation. With an eye to the future, this work is also dedicated to my daughter Emily, so that she may come to know of a time when hope was last in the ascendant in Ulster.

1 'Only a Poor Wee Chap From Belfast'

Recording his reminiscences for the Northern Ireland Home Service towards the close of 1960, Jack Sayers chose to begin with an admission that 'sometimes I call myself a child of the revolution'. Despite the flurry of qualifications that followed, for any Ulsterman born in 1911 there was no escaping from the fact that they had lived in 'troubled' times. Less glamorous but perhaps of more immediate importance was his being a native of East Belfast. The Sayers family lived at the Beersbridge Road end of Cyprus Avenue, just above the Holywood Arches. Later pretensions aside, this had not quite the respectability of Knock. Instead one's attention was led in the other direction, down the Newtownards Road and through the heartlands of Belfast's Protestant working classes. For all its vigour and traditions, this was a world permanently in the shadow of depression. And worshipping every Sunday at Mountpottinger Methodist Church, the Sayers' young frequently witnessed the various humiliations that poverty bestowed on their fellow-parishioners. As with many Methodists, the Sayers household held a practical faith encouraging a mission of active service to the community and a belief in social justice. To them the chosen maxim was Wesley's, that 'the gospel of Christ knows no religion but a social religion, no holiness but a social holiness'. For its relevance the young Sayers had but to open his eyes.

Sayers's father, as a journalist, was himself by no means well paid. But as deputy editor of the *Belfast Telegraph* he had a certain social standing, and it was only to be expected that his son should trek every day across the city to Methodist College at the foot of the fashionable Malone Road. There he won history prizes, performed heroics on rugby and cricket pitches (representing the province in the latter) and eventually became head boy. In the debating society he was to be heard deploring both professionalism in sport and submarine warfare. The 'flip-side' of this moral righteousness came to the fore in the 1st XV concert, where he led the way in the high jinks, building a 'Super-Six Chrystal Set' from a packing chest, a piece of coal, a live cat and innumerable coils of wire. Amid piercing shrieks and blinding flashes, Sayers stunned his audience by 'tuning in' to the 2nd XV, stationed conveniently off stage.

Yet such innocent exuberance was acted out against a backdrop of hatred and fear, which spawned events that were to disturb him for the rest of his life.

Radio broadcast, Northern Ireland Home Service, 20 December 1960

1920 to 1960

John E. Sayers gives his memories of the
changing social scene in Northern Ireland

Sometimes I call myself a child of the revolution. Not in any romantic sense, for sudden revolution, or revolution by violence, does not excite me. But I was born in 1911, and that was a time when Ireland was beginning to experience not only a revolution in its form of government, but an upheaval that led to a rebellion. And in 1920, when the Government of Ireland Act gave Ulster the Home Rule it never wanted, I was nine. Old enough to go daily by myself from Knock to the Methodist College on the Malone Road; old enough to see, through childish but impressionable eyes, the near-anarchy in which Northern Ireland was born.

So it is as a boy and as a man that I have grown up with the province; seen it establish itself and its security, and develop in a way that has proved, and quite remarkably, the effectiveness of a system of administration for which, at the start, few were prepared to predict success.

For me a symbol of 1920 was the tram, clanking over the square setts of the Newtownards Road and across the Queen's Bridge. We must have been a hardy race in those days, for the ends of the tram, top and bottom, were open to the wind and the rain. The drivers, winding at their brass handles, had no protection at all: in winter they were wrapped up like Sam Weller's father on the coach-boxes of seventy years before. But those things were not questioned, any more than I questioned many of the sounds and scenes of Ballymacarrett – the women in their head-shawls hurrying into the ropeworks like mourners to a wake; the scent of poverty and dirt that came from the tram's lower compartment with its shiny lengthwise cane seats. When the black, tasselled shawl was everyday wear, it was common to see mothers suckling their babies as the tram swayed along. Whatever would we think of such naturalism today? The Newtownards Road was lined with its public houses, spirit grocers and pawnshops. The three brass balls over windows that displayed the most intimate and pitiable of private possessions—blankets, boots, even the medals of the war that ended such a short time before— were the heraldry of hard times. But if I cannot say that at the age of nine I was conscious of such social conditions, there were other things to tell me that Belfast was a distressed and distressing city.

2

September 1920 was just about the start of the Troubles, and in those [years] I was to see sights that I have never been able to forget. Even today I cannot drive along the Newtownards Road without seeing in my mind the high wooden barricade that stood at the end of Seaforde Street to cut off a field of fire. Beside it a police cage car, a square armoured Crossley covered with a triangle of thick wire netting. Inside the men of the RIC hunched by their rifles. Farther along, charred and looted shops; the Roman Catholic Chapel at Bryson Street with bullet holes in its windows. It was there that I ran into my first riot. The tram was city-bound in the usual rush of traffic; I was, I suppose, no more awake than any schoolboy is at 8.30 in the morning; and a bullet gives no warning. Looking down from the top deck, I saw a carter suddenly double up and fall limply to the ground. Then the sharp crack of the firing, the splintering of glass, and the shout from the conductor: 'Lie down, lie down.' And lay we did, in the dust and cigarette butts on the rough, ribbed floor, squinting through the slit at the bottom and waiting, ears cocked for the shooting to stop. Thinking back, I cannot say that I was afraid; but that incident brought to a tight, nervous pitch the tension that people lived in in those days. School to me is a happy memory, but it is against a background of disorder, nights when the Belfast sky was red with scattered fires, Lewis guns rattled in the distance, and even in the quiet suburbs the loud 'Who goes there?' of the police patrol challenged anyone incautious enough to break the curfew. And my father being a journalist, the telephone would waken us night after night, and we would creep down stairs from bed to ask, a bit fearfully: 'What's happened?'

Along the Upper Newtownards Road I used to see the man who was to ride the storm, Sir James Craig, monolithic, grimly unsmiling, being driven to the Prime Minister's home at Cabin Hill, his car closely followed by a Ford flivver packed with detectives. Even my recollection of a great day in Northern Ireland's history, 22 June 1921, the opening of the first parliament, is coloured by a gun. To see King George and Queen Mary borne in their carriage to the City Hall we sat jammed on a bench in the window of an auctioneer's shop in High Street. It was next to Hoffman's, the barber's, and opposite a cinema called, I think, the Panopticon. Both have long since closed. The scenes of that day have become cloudy, but distinct in every detail is a meeting at that auctioneer's shop with a friend of the family, a young man not more than twenty. He was in the dark uniform of a Special, and as he moved among the crowd after the procession had passed, his revolver fell from his coat and dangled at the end of its lanyard. I watched it fascinated— but not, as I remember, with any thought to have one of my own. Life at that moment was a very strange mixture of thrill—and disquiet.

For the rest of the twenties my memories are largely those of home and school. So far as I could see, Northern Ireland was peaceful enough – and there was nothing about its problems in the curriculum at the Methodist College. In the early thirties, as a young apprentice journalist, I seem to have been only dimly aware of the hardships of the depression and the effect on Belfast of two empty shipyards. Until, about 1935, I found myself again in a riot. . . .

At that time unemployment was still severe; among working people suffering was widespread, and for those who were without unemployment benefit there was only outdoor relief and private charity. The bitterness of those days I got to know as a reporter at the meetings of the Board of Guardians in the workhouse. Finally, as the government's measures failed to remedy the situation, unrest broke out, there were hunger marches and demonstrations, and in some unhappy, uncontrollable way Protestant and Catholic were again in conflict. So that once more my memory is of violence and the forces of the law in action: troops from the barracks at Holywood wearing their steel helmets in a state of emergency in York Street. The riot was a glimpse of the mob, and an appalling thing it was. In the shooting people had been killed, and the funeral of one was passing my office into Lower Donegall Street. For no good reason that was ever discovered, men who had been walking with it, and others watching, ran wild; again shots were fired, and even passers-by who had done nothing and said nothing were cruelly attacked in an outburst of senseless sectarian passion. . . .

Yet such experiences failed to dim the enormous pride Sayers felt for his native province or his fascination with its history. From his own planter roots at Carnlough to childhood memories of a grim Sir James Craig being driven home to nearby Cabin Hill, he was always profoundly conscious of the thrill of the past and its life in the present. Equally vigorous was his admiration for Belfast as a capital and a great industrial city. For him the heroes were the original entrepreneurs who with their shipyards, linen factories and engineering works lifted the city out of its provincialism and gave Belfast its bleak vibrancy. At the same time, he was never impervious to the sway of its landed aristocrats. The Sayers family were the bedrock of any establishment: respectable, suburban, middle-class and 'financially constrained'. But they were not poor; unlike most of their local congregation at Mountpottinger, some of whose children, Sayers noticed, came to Sunday school on alternate weeks because there were not enough shoes to go round. But neither were they, in their own terms, particularly privileged, as Sayers was to discover on leaving school. His headmaster had encouraged dreams of Oxford, and there were more prosaic ambitions of careers in the army or the RUC as district inspector. More prosaic still was Thomas Moles, the editor of the *Belfast Telegraph*, who damped such hopes by bluntly pointing out that Sayers lacked the funds and the necessary English public school education. Tellingly, these rejections only served to foster a fascination with, and a desire to be a part of, the province's elite. To him its institutions seemed almost sacred, and fewer things gave him greater pleasure than his membership of the prestigious Eldon Lodge or of the Ulster Club. Temperamentally, however critical he became, Sayers was not born to rebel.

Thus it was that Sayers ended up a journalist on the *Belfast Telegraph* somewhat through default. Nevertheless, in so doing, he sustained this family's remarkable connection with the *Telegraph*. Both his father and his uncle were in time to be editors of the paper, and right from an early age Sayers was hooked on the gossip of great events, the 'being in the know' that is the hallmark of the instinctive journalist. At this time Sir Robert Baird, owner of the *Telegraph* and one of Ulster's first press barons, had a strict policy of never appointing the sons of employees. But with Moles combining the editorship with membership of both the Stormont and Westminster Houses of Commons and moreover being Deputy Speaker of the former, John Sayers, Jack's father, effectively ran the paper. This was a frustrating position for any ambitious deputy. However, in 1930 the *Northern Whig* was looking for an editor and offered to double Sayers's salary. Baird responded in turn by asking him to name his price, and thus at his father's request John E. ('Jack') joined the paper as a cub reporter on leaving school. Over the next few years he covered anything and everything from meetings of Belfast's Harbour Board to Collegians' rugby matches in which he was playing (signing himself 'J. S. Edwards').

On his father's accession to the editorship in 1937, he became the parliamentary correspondent at Stormont. There he had his first glimpse of the Unionist establishment from the inside—an establishment in which the *Telegraph* was more than prominent. After all, it did sell more than twice as many papers as its rivals, the *Northern Whig* and the *Belfast Newsletter*. With its former editor holding a powerful parliamentary office and its owner being Deputy Grand Master of Ireland in the Orange Order as well as founder of the Masonic Press Lodge, the *Belfast Telegraph* played its part unashamedly for the Unionist cause. Not surprisingly, Sayers's early parliamentary sketches were studiously loyal. If this seems rather complacent for an ambitious journalist, it was because complacency seemed perhaps the order of the day. Only occasional hints survive of any dissatisfaction with the tight, self-satisfied province.

Regular summer holidays spent on the great liners traversing the Atlantic may simply reflect his love of ships and a fascination for young, rich American girls breezily *en route* for European culture and an education. Maybe he signed up for the Royal Naval Volunteer Reserve only out of a sense of duty. What is certain is that unwittingly he had embarked on a course that would radically transform his outlook.

In May 1937 he was called up on a three-week exercise on board HMS *Courageous*. She was a relic from the First World War, which had been converted into an aircraft carrier. In her heyday she had broken the Atlantic crossing record, but she was now in 'a perilous condition'. Nevertheless, Sayers found much to fire the imagination.

Letter to his mother, 29 May 1937

> HMS Courageous
> Somewhere off the Humber

Dearest Mother,
... The landing-on of the machines was undoubtedly a thrill. Some of the planes had not been brought on board before and most people were in search of excitement; but they all came down safely and, I must add, rather miraculously ... Crashes are the most hearty anecdotes of everyone on board. ...

Along with the thrills came some challenges too, including his first experience of English Anglicanism.

Letter to his mother, no date

> Sunday
> due to arrive at Invergordon at 4.30

... Church this morning – a very admirable potted sermon by Padre on 'Ye are the salt of the earth'. He is extraordinarily good at finding human and understandable metaphors. We had a new tune to Wesley's 'Love Divine', but I picked it up better than the switchbacks of *Venite* and *Benedictus*. They may be the thing for choirs, but for congregational singing it is a series of races from beginning of a line to the end. I'm afraid there are Romanish tendencies on board – Sunday appears to end at midday. At all events there is a rugger match with *Furious* later this afternoon. ...

At Invergordon Sayers continued to act out his fantasy of imperial Britain in a bizarre scene that, no doubt intentionally, could have come straight out of *England Their England*.

Letter to his mother, 6 June 1937

> Invergordon

Dearest Mother,
... Our opponents were styled Ross County, and didn't we feel like first-class cricketers until the village blacksmith and a couple of boys turned up

6

and presented themselves as our opponents! However their whole XI was not too crude, and the match began. We were . . . woefully out of practice . . . and got to 20 for 5 wickets. I was third wicket down and had scored two runs from balls I knew very little about when one of the locals threw me out from 40 yards! . . . We ended up with 113. Their batting was funny enough, but no funnier than our bowling. If they had had two batsmen of ordinary skill, we would have been fielding still. A Chief Petty Officer eventually went on and so frightened the County that he took 8 for 36 and had them out for a 100. Another great victory for the British Navy. . . .

The summer of 1939 saw him once again on naval duty. Officially it was just a training exercise, but training exercises lasting three months were rare for volunteers. So was leave—with the consequence that Sayers found himself having to deal with stokers drinking disinfectant. But more worrying was the state of *Courageous* herself. As the crisis in Europe deepened, the fact that at top speed the *Courageous* still needed a five-knot wind for the planes to take off now seemed less a cause for mirth and left Sayers 'mouthing [like] a galley slave' in his letters home.

Letter to his mother, no date [6 August 1939]

Portland
Sunday

Dearest Mother,
[We are] miraculously . . . ready . . . for sea. . . . That is to say that the engines went round, the anchor people walloped through and watches stood by. But as a fighting ship we are still a negative quantity! [Lest] I have sounded Bolshevik, [as they sailed out of Devonport] for the first time the old navy glamour came into play. . . . It was a beautiful pearly 'Glorious Devon' morning. . . . The [Plymouth] Hoe was quite a stirring sight, and passing Drake's Island with the band playing – well that was the navy getting back to its winning ways! . . . It was a thrill to watch the cruisers (most of them obsolete to be sure) forming in line astern and steaming into the bay in position. . . .

Morale quickly picked up, inspired in part by a balmy English summer. But on 20 August plans for an exercise off Scotland were abandoned and all leave cancelled. Three days later an inspection by the King, resplendent in medal ribbons, provided some relief. When he left, however, they spent the afternoon putting the fuses in the heavy artillery shells. Inevitably, rumour was rampant, and Sayers hated not being on 'the inside of things'—for which daily copies of the *Belfast*

Telegraph were poor recompense. But the drift of events seemed un-mistakable.

Letter to his mother, 25 August 1939

Portsmouth

Dearest Mother,

It is all too plain that the high-ups believe war to be upon us. . . . Last night we were on a high degree of readiness for an air-raid. The ship was darkened [and] I was on watch from four in the morning. It was all quite tense in the darkness.

Last night as I waited at the telephone box, I had a very striking impression of how near to war we are. All lights were out, ARP people were on the move, thousands of reservists were going to barracks, and troops were marching by in hundreds.

We are still at peace and even yet we can remain so. The idea of war leaves me utterly cold but at least I fall back on the fact that we have done everything to maintain peace.

I shall send the Income Tax people a cheque. . . . When I think of the expense of today and the fact that the aeroplane we lost on Wednesday cost £8,000 I feel I should be a Briton and pay up! . . .

A week later Hitler's armies invaded Poland, and Britain stood on the precipice of war.

Letter to his mother, 1 September 1939

Friday

Dearest Mother,

It will be a long time before either of us forgets the date I have just written. It seems tonight that the hour has come, making all our hopes and instincts worthless. I can't help thinking now that it was all a brave disregard of the facts. Looking back on it, this was bound to come, and there is nothing now but to see it through. . . .

It was while in the Channel this morning in the midst of a fog that seemed to isolate us from all except the radio that we heard how events had moved. The news of the evacuation last night was ominous, but I wasn't prepared for the German onslaught [against Poland]. On board every precaution was taken, but, as the news bulletin came through, there was a crowd of officers to listen, calmly and resignedly. It means something to know it is just a war and that until the last moment we clung to peace. . . . You mustn't picture me in the midst of perpetual combat – we shall be spending many, many days doing a simple job of work. Even tonight, in the tradition of nonchalance, the whole mess sat down to dinner as usual in stiff shirts and with music playing! . . .

Although the Prime Minister, Neville Chamberlain, hesitated for two days before declaring war, all knew that Britain could not wait for long in the wings.

Letter to his mother, 3 September 1939

Plymouth

. . . We heard the Prime Minister on the radio at eleven this morning, and that put an end to all our doubts. Now we are ready and determined! Somehow I feel we have been insulated on board. I have missed the scenes in the streets; the reactions of the public. . . . I should have liked to see Belfast when war was declared! I shall look forward to reading how the *BT* announced it. . . .

I am not excited, only despairing a little for humanity and hoping that I shall do my duty in my own place. Believe me, beyond all else I think of home. . . .

As fate would have it, Sayers was not to enjoy a 'phoney war'.

Letter to his mother, 12 September 1939

Tuesday. 'At Sea' since
Saturday 9th

Dearest Mother,
At sea, of course, we are on the lookout for submarines and ready for action every moment of the day and night. The strain is in peering all the time into the distance. We steam along without lights [and] screened by destroyers and one never knows when we will meet something else with the same ideas of secrecy. . . . You wouldn't say now that I don't get enough fresh air! Every watch it swirls round the bridge in great Atlantic gusts. . . . I am thankful for my greatcoat. No longer is it part of my dress clothes. . . .

Talking of Ulster. I found . . . a Comber man with an accent sticking out a mile. Strange fellow, he was a farmer until one day—inspired, perhaps, by the creek up from Strangford—he joined the navy. And now he talks in the same rough Co. Down accent of Mexico and Montevideo and all points south! . . . I should say that no amount of foreign contrast would ever change him an iota. He told me of a shipmate who had 'a lovely funeral'. Who else but an Ulsterman would say that? . . . As [for] this Éire neutrality, in service lan-

9

guage it is 'a bad show', especially when one thinks of what Queenstown was last time.

It is a fresh sailing day now, and it is a grand sight to see the destroyers slashing through the sea. . . . I had my first thrill yesterday when a yell attracted my attention to a wash in the water quite near the ship. It looked startlingly like a torpedo, but, after all, it was only a school of fish disporting themselves on the surface. Some people claim to have seen a submarine at one time or other, but I haven't, although it happens time out of number that for an instant I think I have. . . .

On 16 September *Courageous* left on her first convoy across the Atlantic. In the rush Sayers dashed off a note to his mother, promising that 'next time, of course, I'll spread myself'. On the following night, 250 miles south-west of Ireland, the convoy came under attack. The *Courageous* was struck by a torpedo and almost immediately listed to port. Within five minutes came the order to abandon ship, and with her bows submerged and her stern cocked high up into the air, she floundered for only a further ten minutes. Because she had heeled over so quickly, the port-side lifeboats were inoperable. Later press reports made much of the heroism of the crew and praised their calm fortitude. But mixed with the tales of courage were unmistakable traces of horror, frenzy, even the bizarre. For those that died against the side of the ship as they jumped overboard, there were others who took time to secure their money in a safe pocket and discard their 'heavy coppers'. One man reported seeing 'a poor, frightened, little fifteen-year-old sticks [drummer boy] standing on the deck evidently not knowing what to do. Then I saw two men lash him to a raft and throw him overboard. I hope the poor little devil has come through.' Many didn't. Even those who made it to the water included stokers too badly burnt to be able to swim and older volunteers who lacked the strength to survive. For the rest they had to struggle in the dark and the cold for up to two hours, frightened and sick with the taste of oil. All in all, out of a crew of 1260, 518 drowned, including the captain. In naval tradition, he strode the sloping deck, urging his crew: 'Take your time, boys. There is plenty of time.' Then, as the *Courageous* slid under, he was seen to turn and salute the flag. Perhaps it is not surprising that this is how Sayers chose to remember many years later the night of 17 September.

The Sinking of HMS Courageous (Northern Ireland Home Service, 26 February 1962)

I was in my cabin getting ready to go on watch when the two torpedoes struck. In a minute we had begun to list and it was obvious that the ship was in a bad way. I went forward to my emergency station, the starboard seaboat, and ordered it to be lowered to take some of the people who couldn't swim. But on its way down the ship's side it was holed and, I fear, didn't stay afloat. By now the ship's company were diving into the water one after another all along the deck. I took off my uniform and waited until the carrier was almost along her side. Then a group of us walked down towards the keel and just stepped in to the water. I started swimming. A long, steady breast-stroke to conserve my strength. I covered perhaps a hundred yards, when I turned round *Courageous* had gone. All around me were hundreds of heads bobbing in the Atlantic swell. Presently I found myself with six or seven others clinging to a Carley float. It was rapidly getting dark, and the few ships that were picking up survivors were miles away. It must have been an hour later when we were getting worried at the prospect of a very long night that a passing American merchantman picked us up. A happy end for my small group, but about 700 of my shipmates had been lost. Many of them were reservists too old to survive in the water. For *Courageous* had a very scratch complement—a fair example of Britain's unpreparedness for war. They told me later that when the torpedo hit us, the Captain, who was drowned, said: 'That was a damned fine shot.' I thought that very British too.

That night Admiral Donitz wrote in his diary of the 'glorious success' of U-29, commanded by Lieutenant Schuhart. Back in Britain Winston Churchill tried to raise spirits by reminding his staff of similar disasters at the outset of the First World War. However, for the Sayers family waiting in Belfast for news, this would only have been a small comfort. Because Sayers's neutral rescuers wished to maintain radio silence, his name did not appear in the official list of survivors published in the *Belfast Telegraph* on the evening of 18 September. It was not until the next afternoon, as the paper steeled itself to produce its first leader on the catastrophe, that the news came through. Such were the *Telegraph*'s relations with Stormont that a debate was actually interrupted to announce his safety. However, to his father, already badly shaken by the episode, it proved too much, and he died soon afterwards of a massive heart attack; for this his son never forgave himself. Six weeks later, when he reported back to the Admiralty for duty, the boyish enthusiasm had gone.

Letter to his mother, no date [23 October 1939]

Dearest Mother,
The train ran an hour late, and London was at its most dismal, the rain pouring on deserted streets and sodden sandbags. . . . I went for a walk (in plain clothes) down Shaftesbury Avenue and across the Mall to make sure of my ground at the Admiralty tomorrow.

London, for all the fact that it was Sunday was strangely drab and sober. It seems to live under a cloud. Everybody carries their little square gas-mask case. In a Lyons [teahouse], however, everything was much as usual, and if I was a Boy Scout, I should have had great fun tracking all the people with foreign accents. London was ever thus! . . .

Believe me, I was never sorrier to leave. Perhaps at one time I had an adventurous attitude to the war, but now it is completely anathema.

Pater would have liked the service in the Baptist Church. It was in a basement lecture hall, and there was a good congregation. . . . I liked the preacher. . . . Like all good preachers he was simple and conversational. His sermon helped me [and showed that] life can be bright even in our trouble. . . .

In the Admiralty he was to meet Richard Pim. Pim was an Ulsterman, educated at Lancing and Trinity College, Dublin, who in the 1920s was not only private secretary to Dawson Bates, the Northern Ireland Home Secretary, but had also helped to establish the RUC and the Ulster division of the Royal Naval Volunteer Reserve. Through the latter, he and Sayers became firm friends and on hearing that Sayers had been saved, Pim rang offering him a post in a department concerned with the docking of ships. This was certainly congenial after the rigours of the Atlantic. But, as Sayers discovered, Pim had other ideas. The docking department turned out to be a 'cover' for the creation under Pim of a private 'Map Room' for Winston Churchill, then First Sea Lord. It was an opportunity that was to prove the most formative experience of Sayers's life. Many years later, on the day Churchill died, the 'Chichester' column of the *Belfast Telegraph* carried an anonymous tribute to those days.

Belfast Telegraph, 24 January 1965

AN ULSTERMAN REMEMBERS

Three officers of the Ulster Division, RNVR had the honour of serving on Sir Winston Churchill's personal staff during the Second World War. They were Captain R. P. Pim, Lt-Commander H. W. McMullan and Lt-Commander J. E. Sayers. Today Sir Richard Pim (his knighthood was for his war services) is the retired Inspector-General of the RUC, Mr McMullan is the BBC's head of programmes in Northern Ireland, and Mr Sayers is editor-in-chief of the *Belfast Telegraph*.

The Map Room was formed in Admiralty House the day after Churchill was appointed First Lord, and for the next six years he was never without it. When he became Prime Minister, it was transferred to the Downing Street annexe, a fortified building near Birdcage Walk, where the Cabinet had its offices, and Sir Winston and Lady Churchill a flat. Far below ground were the air-raid shelters they disdained to use.

The brightly lit Map Room—the artist in its owner insisted on pastel shades—gave the operational picture of the war at a glance. In it were shown all the far-flung naval and military theatres; civil defence and the air war in Europe were plotted too. The wall also bore graphs telling the state of the Battle of the Atlantic in tonnages for imports of food, war materials and oil; aerial reconnaissance photographs of enemy territory; and war effort statistics of all kinds.

Such an information centre came to have many uses. Night after night it was the scene of meetings of the Chiefs of Staffs and the Defence Committee that often went on till well after midnight. At other times it was a reception room where one by one the great figures of war came to see the Prime Minister. [Here he] had *tête-à-têtes* with the generals, Alanbrooke, Wavell, Alexander, Montgomery, Eisenhower, Marshall; or visitors like Smuts, Menzies, Wynant, Hopkins, de Gaulle and other Allied leaders. Most of all, it was where Sir Winston, siren-suited, cigar in hand, thought out strategy. Alone he would ponder the global situation, deeply absorbed for long intervals of time. When this happened, no one on duty dared break the silence.

In the following year the Map Room reached the White House in Washington, and the President was so impressed that he ordered one of his own. As Anglo-American co-operation flowered the Map Room was constantly on the move. It was at the conferences at Quebec, Casablanca, Cairo, Yalta and Potsdam; and it basked in the sunshine of Marrakesh when Sir Winston was recuperating from one of his illnesses. Surrounded by his maps in an exotic villa near the pyramids, the Prime Minister had his only meeting with Chiang-Kai-shek.

At home the Map Room was an essential part of the No. 10 routine. Every morning when Sir Winston was still in bed the duty officer gave him a report of the night's signals and telegrams. Once Captain Pim woke him at 4 a.m. with the news of the German invasion of Greece and received the peremptory order 'I am not to be awakened unless England is invaded.' After that he never was. Always his staff knew they were in the presence of an incalculable genius, whose heroic cast of mind, faith in the British race, deep humanity and impish humour were an unfailing inspiration to everyone in his circle. Sir Winston was never down, even when ill, and he was at his greatest when the news was bad. The miracle was that he could remain buoyant and ready to meet every new situation produced by the surges of war. Part of the secret of this energy was his afternoon sleep. He rarely missed this 'recharging of the vital forces' that enabled him to work far into the night.

Chichester

With his new posting went privileges, including honorary membership of the RAC. This may have left him feeling anything but 'like an honest citizen'; yet it appealed to a side of him that was real enough.

Crying in the wilderness

Letter to his mother, 12 November 1939

Sunday evening

Dearest Mother,
I walked down to the club and once more was glad of its quietness, comfort and exclusiveness. Where else would I get tea and toast and cake for eight pence without tipping and paying rent for my hat and coat? From there I went to hear Dr Soper in Kingsway Hall, and I was very much moved to think of how Pater was there when last we went. Do you know I have found myself wonderfully soothed at the services I've been to here. They mean more than they used to, especially because of the humanity of the speakers. Dr Soper was touching on Pacifism once more, and indeed so much do I regret this war I felt for his point of view. However, there is more in it than any mere dread of mine. . . .

An IRA bombing campaign in Britain broke the reverie.

Letter to his mother, 6 February 1940

Dearest Mother,
Did you see that the IRA have been at their misdeeds again because there has been no reprieve for men convicted at Birmingham? I hope trouble does not break out in Ireland. I cannot understand the mentality of people in the South who wrote appealing for the men to be let off. These anarchists deserve all they get. . . .

Soon the pace of events in Europe intensified. On 4 April he received £109 19s 1d in compensation for his experience on the *Courageous*. The next day the Germans attacked Denmark and Norway. Over the next two months the Map Room team could only look on helplessly as they marked out the stunning advance of the Nazi Blitzkrieg through Holland and Belgium and on to France. Churchill, now Prime Minister, paced the Map Room, a slightly absurd figure in his dressing-gown of many colours. Fiercely egotistical, often explosive, his bullishness and idiosyncrasies lightened the gloom and endeared him to his staff. For the rest of their lives Sayers, Pim and McMullan dined out on stories of their chief. Throughout the campaign Churchill would always refer to France as 'my patient' or 'my aunt' and on arriving in the map room would inquire: 'And how is my patient this morning? Am I correct in saying that the upper wound is healing but suppuration cannot be stopped from the other wound? Too bad.' Offhand instructions to ring M. Reynaud (the French Prime Minister) or

Marshal Pétain would have the Ulstermen pitting their French accents against a disintegrating system and bemused telephonists. On 20 May 1940 Sayers was deputed to wake Churchill with the news that Amiens had fallen, unfortunately pronouncing it 'Aim-y-ens' in the colloquial style used for the Dublin railway station of that name. 'Amiens!' bawled Churchill, using the correct French pronunciation, leaving Sayers to joke in the company of his chums: 'How was I to know, being only a poor wee chap from Belfast?' Churchill himself was renowned less for his pronunciation than for the strength of his views. It was never 'Iran' but always 'Persia'. Any attempt at linguistic precision over a foreign place-name drew a withering 'Don't be so damned BBC'. Once Pim, on bringing what he felt could only be good news— the sinking of two U-boats—was met with a flat denial. Flustered, he produced the naval signal. Churchill paid no attention to it, but repeated: 'You are incorrect.' Then, after an eternity and very calmly, he decreed: 'Our submarines are, unfortunately, sometimes sunk, but please remember that U-boats are DESTROYED.' It was the sheer unpredictability of it all that made it such fun, and they indulged his whims like schoolboys with a volatile, irreverent and much-loved schoolmaster. There was never any doubt who was to be centre-stage, and Sayers only dared to steal the floor once with the quip that 'in Ulster the L[ocal] D[efence] V[olunteers] were known as the Look, Duck, and Vanish boys'. The tyrant was amused, and Sayers escaped with all limbs intact; not all were so lucky. But it was not all laughs. By 10 June, with France on the verge of collapse, Churchill was dangerous company. His secretary John Colville recorded that the Prime Minister was 'in a bad temper, snapped everybody's head off, wrote angry minutes to the First Sea Lord and refused to pay any attention to messages given to him orally'. Three ships had been lost, and Italy had declared war on the allies. Strangely, the fall of France eight days later afforded some relief, and, writing to his mother on his twenty-ninth birthday, Sayers could only ponder on more parochial issues.

Letter to his mother, 13 July 1940

5.30 a.m.

Dearest Mother,
... Yesterday ... [was] none other than the Twelfth of July. But, do you know, nobody seemed to take any notice! There wasn't a lily to be seen or a drum to be heard. However, I was able to satisfy my musical instincts, if not my Protestant ones. I went to the National Gallery concert—my first for weeks— and heard a Mozart programme. ...

15

By September the Battle of Britain was at its height and the first bombs were falling on London. Although the Germans soon abandoned their half-hearted assault, the British war effort continually suffered reverses in North Africa, the Mediterranean and the Atlantic. For once Sayers let a despondent tone creep into his correspondence.

Letter to his mother, 27 February 1941

Dearest Mother,
I find myself these days with my mind rather a prey to the desperate problems of the war as we see them. Up to a point bad news has no effect, but it grows, and the strain on the faces of those who carry the responsibility serves to add to it. We must endure more of it as the year goes on. . . . My watch last night had its share of that bad news. . . .

There was to be no let-up. Yugoslavia fell, and British troops had to evacuate Greece. Prestige ships were sunk including the *Ark Royal* and *HMS Hood*, then one of Britain's fastest warships; of her crew of 1,500, all but three drowned, including Admiral Holland, whom Pim recalled as 'a charming and even-tempered man who was prepared to argue at 4 a.m. whether a preposition should or should not be placed at the end of a sentence'. After Pearl Harbor they found themselves mapping the relentless Japanese march on Hong Kong and Singapore. Back at home the blitz continued with massive air-raids. In March 1941 Sayers and Pim travelled to Birkenhead to launch a new destroyer, only to discover that German bombers had laid waste much of the town the night before. The next month Sayers, on duty, could only watch as Belfast was bombed, with 745 killed in one night; the next day 100,000 evacuated the city in some disarray. Then at the end of May he heard that his brother-in-law was missing in action, and it was nearly two months before the family heard that he was in a German prisoner-of-war camp, OflagVB, 'which', as Sayers informed his mother, 'stands for something much longer'. But it was not all gloom. News that the Italian fleet had left port 'always brought joy to the Prime Minister's heart' (Pim), and he followed avidly the manoeuvrings of the two fleets before the navy's comprehensive victory at the Battle of Cape Matapan. But the greatest pleasure came with the sinking of the *Bismarck*. For seven days the navy, led by the *Hood*, shadowed the German battleship through the North Sea and out into the Atlantic. Hour by hour the Map Room staff plotted the course of the battle. On the long blue-clothed table lay the maps, brilliantly lit and surrounded with dividers, parallel rulers, speed and endurance tables. Silently the positions were adjusted with each new signal that reached the Admiralty, while in the darkness Churchill in his siren suit and the admirals watched, transfixed by the chase. Then on 24 May they heard that the *Hood* had been lost off Greenland. Spirits only revived with the news that torpedo aircraft from *Ark Royal* had crippled the *Bismarck*. 'Hit him hard; he ain't got no friends' growled the Prime Minister; and on 27 May the *Hood* was avenged. There were few memories of the *Courageous* as Sayers found himself caught up in the jubilation that followed. But then there were other reasons too for his exhilaration. He had been promoted to Lieutenant-Commander and second-in-command of the Map Room, reporting regularly to Churchill. Such elevation was barely marred by his appearance during October 1941 in the West London police court and a fine of £2 for having lights on in the blackout! Even the war in Europe was looking up. With the German invasion of Russia and her declaration, along with the Japanese, of war against the USA, Britain stood no longer alone. However, such events had unexpected Irish consequences, with Churchill's dramatic telegram on 8 December 1941 offering de Valera a united Ireland if he would agree to join with the allies. There is no evidence to suggest that Sayers knew of the offer at the time, although his disappointment at the British government's reluctance to introduce conscription in Ulster suggests perhaps a degree of anxiety. In the end, and not for the first time, Ulster Unionism was saved by the Irish leader. Some months later Pim found himself at lunch in Downing Street with Churchill, Lloyd George and J. M. Andrews, the Prime Minister of Northern Ireland.

Sir Richard Pim's Memoirs, 21 July 1942

The three Prime Ministers proceeded, with the assistance of wine glasses, salt and pepperpots, to discuss in detail the Irish question since 1900. The discussion lasted over an hour, and needless to say it was superbly interesting. Both Mr Lloyd George and Mr Churchill made it clear that they regretted no step which they had ever taken on the Irish Question, neither under any circumstances would they permit the coercion of Ulster in the future. At the same time, both made it very clear that they still entertained the hope that in the future some statesman would rise in Ulster who would feel justified in making a move towards closer harmony with the South. Similarly, it was their hope that Éire would produce a statesman who would make a reciprocal move towards closer harmony with Northern Ireland. They believed that if such a change of heart was to be found in the North and in the South, then the North, because of the history of its ancestors, would automatically become the real controller of the new Ireland, which she would bring again fully within the folds of the British Empire.

Churchill always insisted that his Map Room should accompany him on his conferences abroad, if only to show it off to other leaders. Thus it was that early in 1943 Sayers found himself in Casablanca. Here he and Pim saw Churchill confer with Roosevelt over the future of the war. Also there was Harold Macmillan, engaged in tortuous negotiations to persuade the French generals de Gaulle and Giraud that they were on the same side; while late into the night Field-Marshal Dill and Generals Alexander and Brooke poured over the maps of Libya planning the next step of the Eighth Army under Montgomery—all four were Ulstermen, a matter of no small pride to the Ulstermen in the Map Room. On his return, Sayers went to Belfast for a week's leave, during which Jack Beattie of the Northern Ireland Labour Party—whose calls for a coalition he had derided at the outbreak of the war—won the West Belfast seat from the Unionists. Back in Downing Street, Sayers found Churchill more appreciative of the Unionists' plight.

Sayers's diary, 15 February 1943

Saw PM: 'Ulster's strength is in unity. They are very foolish if they allow [the] vote to be split. It means they will lose their coherent identity, and that is very dangerous.'

Maybe he was just becoming more sensitive to the Ulstermen around him. When he wrote on the occasion of Andrew's resignation (29 April 1943) a letter full of praise for Ulster's war effort, he gave it to Pim to vet.

After Sayers had accompanied Churchill to conferences in Washington and Cairo, the Map Room was reorganised, with the three services retaining their individual map rooms and Churchill establishing his own, the Defence Map Room, in No. 10 Annexe in Storey's Gate. It would co-ordinate all the information and was manned by only four officers, including Sayers and Pim. It was to here after his heart-attack that a frail Churchill returned to meet daily with Eisenhower and Montgomery to plan the invasion of France. Churchill soon recovered his old verve and impatience, and on the occasion of the fall of Cairo he could not resist seizing the brush from the duty officer to draw the positions himself.

For all the frenzied activity in the build-up to Operation Overlord, Sayers found some moments for relaxation. At the end of June he saw Australia beat England by one wicket at Lords, and there was always time to hear Myra Hess at the National Gallery and for a new interest in opera and ballet. In October 1944 he heard Menuhin play in the Albert Hall, and the following month saw Gielgud's Hamlet at the Haymarket and Fonteyn dance Giselle. Then in the new year he went with Tyrone Guthrie to a performance of *Uncle Vanya*. During this period many important people passed through the Defence Map Room to savour the anticipation of final victory, the mood only soured by photographs sent by Eisenhower on 6 March 1945 of the first concentration camps. With Hitler dead, the Map Room closed for the first time in six years, and 'Winnie's little band' assembled in the Trocadero restaurant to celebrate with speeches, toasts and doggerel verse 'the Brotherhood of the DMR'. On the following day Sayers successfully proposed to Miss Daphne Godby.

Old habits, however, died hard and Churchill retained the Defence Map Room, as he determined to settle peace. In July he called a general election and then set off for Potsdam on the ironically entitled Operation Terminal. For Sayers and Pim the sight of a Germany literally reduced to rubble made a profound impression.

Sir Richard Pim's Memoirs, 16 July 1945

In the afternoon I motored with Jack Sayers and Diana Lyttelton into Berlin, in company with the British and United States Chiefs of Staff. The route lay through the Grunewald Forest, and here and, in fact, all afternoon, we saw families moving their belongings in hand-carts, wheelbarrows or prams out of the city.

First we visited the Tiergarten—that wooded park where stand, though now in many cases badly damaged, the statues of the German kings and heroes of the past. On to the Unter den Linden and through the Brandenburg gate to the Reichstag. The bare walls stood, but the building was damaged beyond repair. Indeed, Berlin was a terrible sight.

Next we went to Hitler's Chancellery. This had been bombarded by the Russians at short range and was in an awful mess. We went into Hitler's study—a very long and imposing room, and then below ground to his Bunker, the equivalent of the Map Room. His famous marble-topped desk was still there, but smashed.

Three days later they flew back in order to convert the Map Room for the general election due on 26 July. Here Sayers came into his own. 'The Ulsterman with the card index memory', as Churchill dubbed him, quickly replaced all the maps of battlefields with electoral charts showing the state of the parties in each constituency. On the walls he erected an elaborate score-board, recording gains and losses and the fluctuations of the vote. Pim may have disparaged this contraption as 'rather on the lines of an American tennis tournament court', but Churchill was thrilled. With anticipation he awaited the result. Yet within an hour of the first declarations he found himself facing a humiliation at the polls. With considerable equanimity, he sat in the Map Room while Sayers and his team coloured Britain red. Only once, when his wife suggested that it might be a blessing in disguise, did he let his feelings show: 'At the moment', he snapped, 'it seems quite effectively disguised.'

Appreciating the significance of the occasion, and with the imminence of civvy street reawakening his journalistic instincts, Sayers made his notes.

Sayers's Notes on Election Day, 26 July 1945

'I never thought such a thing could happen.'—Beaverbrook.

'They are voting against all the discomforts they have had.'—W.S.C.

'It is determined voting.'—Beaverbrook.

'It is a terrific landslide.'—W.S.C.

'It is a great event in English history. They have never had a majority like this before. Their people will expect them to act. They may be forced to do something violent!'—W.S.C.

'Do you think they will crow.'—Mrs Sandys.

'Crow? If they stop at crowing, there will be nothing to worry about.'—W.S.C.

'Now we will see the New World.'—W.S.C.

General election results, Defence Map Room, 26 July 1945. Present—W.S.C., Beaverbrook, Bracken, Sandys, Margesson. Sir J. Anderson.

Two days later Churchill bade farewell to the Defence Map Room. Suddenly a way of life in which Sayers had been immersed for six years was folding up all around him. There would be no more late-night 'jawing' or impossible demands; no more glamorous conferences or walking in the trail of heroes. Sayers was not blind to Churchill's faults, but nor did he ever forget the debt he owed to this experience. For all revelations of later historians, Sayers never wavered in his admiration of the man, whose signed photograph was always prominently displayed on the piano in the drawing-room. When Churchill died, he delegated the obituary for the *Telegraph* to a young reporter, as he felt 'too close' to his former chief. Yet in his papers are some draft notes attempting to encapsulate what to the last had been a powerful fascination.

Draft Notes, No Date [c. January 1965]

Churchill is endowed by nature with the most rhetorical mind that I have ever known in a public man. Other men have been as good or better rhetoricians with their tongues, but none of them thought or lived rhetoric as he did. To discuss a question with Churchill was to see him dramatise it in successive scenes with effective lights and colours and then at the end choose the scene which was best dramatised and most effectively lit. It was fascinating to watch him at work painting scenery and building up wings, but at times one had an uneasy feeling that truth and practicality and even common sense were left behind in this breathless chase after the picturesque. Nothing seemed to appeal to him unless it could be presented in this form, and he appeared to be capable of leaping from one side of an argument without the slightest sense of incongruity if opposite lent itself to a more effective [tone. I have heard . . .] Churchill called unprincipled by people who were angry with him, but that is to do him an injustice. His mind did honestly work in this way, and his real inclination was to conclude that a thing was right and true if it could be stated in a rhetorically effective manner. . . . Years may have changed him, but at the time when I knew him best and when he was making his reputation, no man seemed to live in such a perpetual state of mental excitement or be able to entertain so many vivid and jostling ideas at the same time or to be so honest and brilliant about them all [as Churchill].

As with many of Sayers's generation, the experience of the war years had proved the most formative of his life. It was then that he developed and consolidated the ideals that were to dominate his later career: patriotism and the values of empire; duty in the service of the community; and the moral responsibility of those in authority to pursue the cause of justice. At the same time, his secondment to Churchill's private Map Room had exposed him to the exotic world of the 'high-ups'. Here, amid the despair of 1940, he had observed his mercurial leader plot the downfall of the Third Reich. Here also he met the famous and powerful, from Churchillian cronies such as Beaverbrook and Bracken to world leaders such as Roosevelt, Eisenhower (who he once tried to lock out of the Map Room on grounds of security), de Gaulle and even Chiang-Kai-shek. His years in wartime London consequently served to challenge what had been a rather parochial Ulster background and encouraged a lasting affection for English manners, efficiency and culture. Moreover, it opened his eyes to international politics and the issues that would dominate the postwar world (communism, refugees and the establishment of European stability). It also left him with a genuine sympathy for the problems of leadership, and in later life he was instinctively (perhaps too much so) understanding of government. But this did not mean adulation. In a daily life peopled by heroic figures, Churchill's emotional, bullying manner and the politics of squabbling generals and admirals revealed that these champions of empire could be very human indeed. But their company did undoubtedly fire his imagination and ambition. Having lived in the heady atmosphere of achievement, of executive power, of borders being redrawn and societies transformed, he came to believe that governments could be an instrument of reform and social renewal; and in his 'beloved Ulster' he had just the opportunity he needed.

2 The Return of the Honest Ulsterman

With the end of the war, Sayers's thoughts inevitably turned to the future. In October he was married in Holy Trinity, Brompton (later confused with Brompton Oratory by some in Ulster who then, assuming his wife to be Roman Catholic, viewed his liberalism in this light). A month later he had resumed at the *Belfast Telegraph* and soon found himself back at Stormont, listening to a budget debate. To many this would have seemed quite a let-down and a rather parochial fate for a man who could have had the pick of Fleet Street. Indeed, right from his release from the navy, he had been writing regularly for an array of national papers: *Daily Telegraph*, *Observer*, *Daily Sketch*, and for Reuter's. Nor did anyone doubt that he was ambitious. But his ambition had always been to follow his father. Moreover, as John Cole remembered, 'he conceived it to be his duty to stay in Belfast and to fight for what he believed in'. This was not simply a question of family loyalties or the role of journalism, but reflected a deep-rooted concern for the future political development of the province. During the long night watches in the Map Room conversation had often drifted onto the subject of post-war Ulster, only for Pim and McMullan to be startled by the passionate irreverence of Sayers's Unionism. It was to witness and encourage the realisation of these dreams that Sayers returned to Ulster.

That Ulster was ripe for modernisation was beyond question, but cannot of itself explain Sayers's return. Rather, for all his progressivism, the answer lies in his conservatism and in his image of Ulster. For a start, the move to Belfast did not represent a major upheaval, because Sayers's Ulster was in every sense British. When he scripted for the Northern Ireland Home Service a retrospective on Ulster in 1950, the highlights he chose were (1) General Sir Gerald Templar dedicating the Regimental Chapel of the Royal Irish Fusiliers in Armagh Cathedral; (2) Wales seizing the Triple Crown from Ireland at Ravenhill; (3) Sir Basil Brooke's being made a freeman of Belfast; (4) the Queen, in the pouring rain, presenting colours to the Royal Inniskilling Fusiliers; (5) the visit of Sir Adrian Boult and the BBC Symphony Orchestra; and lastly (6) a Campbellian winning the British Boys' Golf competition. With its acceptance of 'British' standards of public life and its contribution to the defence of the Empire, Ulster's Britishness was for the Unionist elite an unquestioned assumption—a faith neatly symbolised in Churchill's Map Room, where the future heads of the RUC and BBC, Dick Pim and Harry McMullan, together with Sayers had fraternised with Generals Montgomery and Alanbrooke recounting childhood holidays spent in Donegal. However, Sayers's admiration for all things British was never slavish. Five years in cosmopolitan London, for all its thrills, had left him yearning for the moral redoubt of planter values. Here we enter into an imaginary world of the 'Honest Ulsterman', as popularised before the war by the prolific novelist, George A. Birmingham. This held that the 'inherent' characteristics of the Ulster race were industry, decency and loyalty. Not given to many words, these were a people whose plain common sense was laced by a fierce independence of mind: men and women whose ancestors had defiantly resisted autocratic powers in defence of freedom for three hundred years. Sayers undoubtedly preferred to dwell on the Presbyterian Volunteers of 1798 rather than on events of 1690 or even 1912, but there was no escaping that his 'Ulster' in 1945 was wholeheartedly Protestant. For him, the 'prime specimens' of the 'Ulster stock' were the Ulster Scots in America, whose 'frontier spirit' and modesty reassured him that the boastful rowdiness he occasionally witnessed in Ulster was only 'superimposed'. What is striking about such views is that five years after the Holocaust they did not attract ridicule, but instead struck deep chords with his audience. Indeed, fifteen years later Terence O'Neill was to take up the same cause of the Ulster-Scots, using much the same language.

Ulster at the same time offered Sayers a spiritual haven. Not only did the war revive 'community spirit' through greater awareness of the slums, but in the vigour of the Protestant faith there was also a barrier against materialism and secularism. As for sectarianism, he felt that 'the Ulsterman remains well balanced . . . and never likely to be stampeded or led astray' (8 June 1949). Choosing to take the Orange Order's commitment to 'civil and religious liberty' at face value, he took comfort in what he called the 'classlessness' of the Order and the Unionist Party. Of course, most of this is sheer myth, but to dismiss it as wilful nostalgia is to miss the point. For it was perfectly possible for intelligent observers to perceive Ulster in these terms, unchallenged as they were while both Catholicism and Protestant fundamentalism lacked effective political expression. Equally, such ideas are crucial to an understanding of Sayers, not only to demonstrate how far he was to move intellectually, but also to explain why he did not move faster and farther.

Finally, there was in his return to Belfast the irresistible lure of a challenge. Post-war Ulster was confronting severe threats from the irredentist South, a socialist government in Westminster, and an economy that had failed since its inception to match British standards of living and now faced greater world competition. To Sayers the attraction was not simply whether Ulster could survive, but whether the 'unique experiment' of devolution within the United Kingdom could be made into a success. Intriguingly, he even felt able to argue in 1948 that Stormont *might* indeed become the model of a stable Christian state for a continent torn asunder by war and communism.

To his fellow-journalists it soon became apparent that he was a cut above the rest.

John Cole, 'Proud His Name', Northern Ireland Home Service (Radio 4), 30 August 1970

What I remember particularly about him was what a superb craftsman he was as a journalist. I remember him particularly taking a shorthand note of Lord Brookeborough, who was then Prime Minister and, to put it kindly, wasn't one of the most organised of public speakers. Jack took this impeccable shorthand with the back of a fountain pen, which is a pretty odd way to do it. You would see the odd irritable flick as he cut out a bit of verbiage that he'd taken down, because he cared greatly about words, about the English language. And then he'd be off into the phone box with the material beautifully organised and ready to pour it down the line to the office.

He had a great sense of humour. I remember on one occasion at Stormont when a very eminent politician fell asleep on one of the benches. Jack drew my attention to this, and we sat and watched him for a while. He was very still indeed, and finally Jack said with a twinkle: 'Do you realise, John, that if he were dead we wouldn't know in time for the Sixth Edition?' And he paused for no more than a moment, and then he said: 'Tell you what, I'll go downstairs and get them to have a vote, and we'll see if the division bells rouse him.'

Others too were quick to recognise his talents, and early in January 1946 McMullan—now at the BBC in Belfast—invited Sayers to work on radio as a freelance commentator. One of his first contributions was a monthly newsletter for 'Ulster's Half Hour' on the BBC's overseas service.

However, it was in a series of fortnightly talks on Ulster politics, 'Ulster Commentary', that Sayers began to establish his name. As the sole political commentator on local radio, he now quickly came to occupy a position of some influence. Admittedly, as the BBC strove for political 'neutrality' he had to operate under a house policy which forbade any discussion of the central political issue in Ulster, the border, and looked askance at any hint of controversy. Instead Sayers concentrated, as a true servant of Reith, on an educational role, tackling the complex issues of welfare reform, health, housing, transport and unemployment with striking clarity in 'sermons' of just over ten minutes. Not a 'natural' on the air, he relied heavily on scripts that seem rather ornate and formal in style. Nevertheless, his seriousness commanded respect, and with his modest manner in what was still a deferential age, he created a degree of intimacy that soon won him a large following in the province. If he eschewed judgement in favour of fact, he did nevertheless aspire to stir up political consciousness and expand horizons, especially in the artistic field. But in politics there was no escaping the Unionist and governmental line. Not that Sayers particularly minded. While he resented accusations of 'whitewashing' the government (26 June 1947), on at least one occasion, in October 1949, he sent his script 'to the Government Press Officer for scrutiny'. Sayers openly admitted that he only included in his 'Ulster Commentaries' 'what one *feels* to be right and in the best interests of the country'. For to him the BBC was but one institution, along with the government and the churches, which co-operated as in the war to provide leadership against the unseen (economic) enemies of the peace. In this battle Sayers saw the need for bolstering morale in a society suffering from the deprivations of rationing, inflation and renewed unemployment. Up to 1949 Sayers was always ready to wax lyrical on the growth of new industry and the achievements of agriculture. Such was his ability to talk up the resilience of Ulster's staple industries that, as one civil servant reminisced, 'the *Belfast Telegraph* built more ships than Harland & Wolff'. This was not simply a cynical exercise in propaganda. The concept of 'plucky Ulster' and the strength of a uniquely Ulster character was something that Sayers wholeheartedly believed in.

'Ulster Commentary', Northern Ireland Home Service, 29 May 1947

The fact is, of course, that nearly all of us in Belfast have our roots firmly planted in the country. You'd have to search for a long time to find someone whose great-grandfather was actually born and bred in the city. My grandfather came from a Co. Antrim farm that still belongs to the family, and I'm sure that that is true of a great many others. For at least two hundred years men have been leaving the country to go into business in Belfast and our larger towns, and the result is very clearly that we are all of the same stock and essentially of the same character. . . .

The Ulsterman has been described in good terms and bad terms, but whether he lacks vision or imagination, there are few more sterling, moral, dependable and industrious types of men on the face of the earth. Is that too bold a claim? I don't think it is. We have only to look at what Ulstermen have done at home and overseas and the extraordinary number of great men to whom it has given birth to see that it has been one of the cradles of the English-speaking world. . . .

Sayers's unabashed pride in what he called 'my own country' sprang in part from sheer optimism in the early years. In the immediate aftermath of war Ulster seemed to be more than holding her own economically, and Sayers was not the only one to take pride in a healthy Imperial Contribution from the province. Moreover, by accepting the system of parity of services throughout the United Kingdom, the Brookeborough government displayed hints of the legislative dynamism that Sayers believed necessary. Between 1946 and 1948 acts passed through Stormont providing for national insurance, pensions, a health service, housing, education and roads. For Sayers this represented a social revolution that would in time create a society in which justice and humanity would prevail. Indeed, in a talk on New Year's Eve in 1947 he claimed already to see signs of new liberalism. By this he meant 'a sense of community spirit and social betterment'. Yet he was not uncritical and in the same talk recognised that as a 'political community' Northern Ireland lacked 'complete maturity'. Behind such euphemisms was much that had disturbed Sayers on his return: the Election and Franchise Act (1946), which rejected the British move to 'one man, one vote' in local government elections; the strength of Protestant opposition at Stormont to an education act that proposed 'conscience' clauses for religious teachers and increased grants to the mainly Catholic voluntary sector in parallel with the transformation of the (Protestant) state schools; and the Safeguarding of Employment Act which sought to prevent a deluge of Southern (predominantly Catholic) labour. BBC restrictions ensured that Sayers could only raise the subject of sectarianism by treating it as a moral rather than political question. By raising it for the first time on radio, he displayed not only his integrity but also his fervent desire that Ulster too should witness the New Jerusalem.

'Ulster Commentary', Northern Ireland Home Service, 26 June 1947

I confess that when I look around . . . I'm always conscious that this is a country of deep divisions. In that way, if in no other, I do not forget the minorities. There are some people who would shut their eyes to such discordant facts, but I submit that no one who takes a broad view *can* do that, and that few can live their lives in Northern Ireland without regretting that between all the people there is not at least some friendlier feeling and even a limited unity of purpose.

What troubles me is the fact that certain quarrels have been going on so long that each side has practically given up the thought of making an appeal to the other. They have drawn apart so much that hardly at any point do they meet at all. I wonder is it wrong or hopeless to speak of that and to look forward to something better; or if it's impolitic to ask whether either side has not some capacity left to make a gesture, to cut a trace and to find some common ground?

I know so well the reactions that many of you are having to that, the scorn and cynicism of some, the grimness of others, and, I believe, the genuine despair of quite a large number. . . .

Whether it's been tried before and failed or not doesn't altogether matter; the important thing is surely whether good will and good feeling aren't objects worthy of attainment at all times. On them the door should never be shut, and the voice of moderation should never be altogether silent. . . .

That such animosities survived was for Sayers the consequence of weak leadership and complacent provincialism, the roots of which he explored in a broadcast in April 1948.

'Ulster Commentary', Northern Ireland Home Service, 7 April 1948

It was the night of the big fight. I was listening in, and with me was a friend of mine who happens to be English. How it ended most of you will remember—the Scotsman was knocked into insensibility, and the Belfastman was duly declared the winner. And with rather more than a hint of his Irish background, the commentator launched into quite a build-up of what a great sporting year it has been for Ireland—we were the holders of the Triple Crown at rugby, we produced the British open golf champion, and we had topped it all by winning the world's flyweight title.

My friend took all this in and then, very dryly, said to me: 'Well, anyway, you can't win the Boat Race.' (*Pause*) I must say that I couldn't forbear to reply that the stroke of the Cambridge crew (who as it turned out were the winners) was also an Irishman, but the remark did bring it home to me that we are *so very* apt to make a song about our own people and their achievements. In this part of the world we are always on the lookout for an Ulsterman who is making some kind of name for himself, and if we can't find an Ulsterman, we usually contrive to find an Irishman. . . .

But it is *so* true that with Ulstermen in particular, whether they are field-marshals or pugilists, we are constantly seizing the chance to tell everybody at large just from what spot on mother earth they come from; just what relationship, close or distant, that they bear to our native stock. And that, I believe, is a very interesting phenomenon. Because when you come to think of it, the ordinary Ulsterman, as an individual, is a comparatively modest person. He has a certain self-confidence, but no one could say that it runs to boastfulness about himself—you must know Ulstermen, as I do, from whom you could hardly drag a word about themselves. Yet these same men have such a pride of race, call it what you will, that inspires them to speak of the more illustrious of their fellows as though they had been made purposely to hold civilisation together.

Of course, I must confess that we newspapermen do a lot to keep this legend alive. It's the job of a local newspaper to give the local news, and if a man who wins a battle or cures a Maharajah or just falls off the end of a pier into the Zambesi can be connected with Ulster, then it's right that he should be. . . . If nothing else, it is a reflection, and I should say a faithful one, of what *is* a strong characteristic.

The question is why that characteristic should be. Is it pride of race, as I have suggested; is it because we are a small compact people who happen to have given many men and women to the world? Is it that there's been so much that is defensive in the history of this part of the world that people are stirred to keep the flag flying? Is it possibly that deep down there's something of an inferiority complex? And apart from *all* the reasons why we acclaim and parade our own, are they, are we, as good as we think we are? . . .

The extent of this insecurity was sharply revealed by the frenzied response to de Valera, now out of office, as he indulged in republican rhetoric on a tour of the USA in April 1948. With Labour in power in Westminster, some Unionists began to fear another British offer of a united Ireland. However, Sayers, now writing regularly for the London-based and influential Commonwealth journal, *The Round Table*, viewed such anxieties as of little consequence. Given the impracticality of the British government acting without the consent of the Belfast parliament, he argued that 'It matters little that Mr de Valera should stump America and that the Unionist Party too should be seeking to rally overseas support. These manoeuvres can have no more direct influence on the outcome than the cheers of rival crowds on the result of a football match.' (*The Round Table*, May 1948)

To Sayers, so recently at the hub of world affairs, the cold war, and in particular the communist blockade of Berlin, offered far more cause for anxiety. Yet here again the local response disappointed.

'Ulster Commentary', Northern Ireland Home Service, 29 September 1948

A few months ago I was at a luncheon in Belfast, one of those luncheons that always end up by someone giving a talk. Often they are quite informative, although one has the feeling that the audience is usually too busy digesting to do a lot in the way of concentration. Anyhow, on this occasion the speaker was a journalist who had just returned from a tour of West Germany, including Berlin, and in his case there was no excuse for inattention. I say that because it was not only a first-hand account of social and political conditions but a challenging reminder of this country's responsibility towards the defeated and towards Western Europe as a whole. The conclusion it came to was more than that Germany should be defended against communism; it was that for the sake of civilisation we should aim to restore the life of the German people, making sure, of course, that they are powerless to rearm.

Now, for myself, I thought it was a thoroughly sound and well-argued address from a man who had been *there* and who had seen the dangerous void that is left by a long and disastrous war. It wasn't based on sentiment, nor was it just the 'moderation in victory' counselled by Nelson. It was the realistic view of a man trained to look beyond his own shores. That, at all events, was how it struck me, and it left me somewhat disconcerted when someone else, in moving the vote of thanks, expressed a downright opposite and isolationist opinion. What it amounted to was that we should look after ourselves and let Germany go on paying the price of her aggression.

And yet, you know, that kind of thought comes naturally enough. Twice in this century the Germans have played havoc with our lives, and few of us can be so saintly that we've forgiven them. . . . The only question is whether we can secure peace by ourselves or whether we must go further and remove the causes and the breeding-grounds of war.

Now, the luncheon I've been talking about took place before Berlin began to be blockaded, and what sticks in my mind in looking back on it today is the way that foreign policy since then, and especially our policy towards Europe, has been forced into our consciousness. I daresay that then a lot of people agreed with the man who moved our vote of thanks. . . . But what, I wonder, are they thinking now? . . . Even if at that time they weren't bothered about the state of Europe, they must have become dreadfully aware of the perils that exist today. . . .

In fact, it's come to the point when we all, some of us in spite of ourselves, are obliged to ask what is our outlook, what do we believe in, and what we must do in the way of foreign policy. And for Northern Ireland that's something rather new and rather strange. . . .

Yet if we should be tempted to feel that all the strife is remote from us, then, no matter how well-meaning and virtuous we may be at heart, we shall not have behaved as citizens of the world who have the liberty—the liberty—to stand up for what we know to be right and good.

Right and good, or nearly so, we may be in our own Ulster affairs, living quietly and attending to our own business—estimable and worthy qualities, to be sure, the way of life that so many countries want: but is it enough even for six small counties 500 miles from the continent and under the protection of British arms. I wonder?

However, when the Irish Taoiseach (Prime Minister), John A. Costello,

sought to head off de Valera's challenge to his government by an-
nouncing Éire's intention to leave the Commonwealth the following
Easter, it was inevitable that Irish questions would predominate. Even
the BBC, under its new controller, Andrew Stewart, could no longer
ignore the border, and Sayers was sent off into the minefield.

'Ulster Commentary', Northern Ireland Home Service, 13 October 1948

. . . Partition never happened without reason. Before it became a fact there
was an historic struggle of wills and there was considerable civil disturbance,
all arising from a cleavage which politicians of that day weren't able to resolve *in any other way*. The same circumstances have been at work in India,
and partition has been the result, and it looks as if it may be in Palestine. But
does anyone think that in twenty-five years time those borders could be wiped
out and that India and Pakistan would reunite? . . .

And surely you have here the kernel of what I don't hesitate to call the unhappy state of Ireland. The border was created not merely by act of parliament
but by certain essential differences between two lots of people. The act of parliament was a recognition of their differences, and to remove the border it's not
enough to have a repeal. You must go further and try if you can to resolve the
differences. But what strikes many about the policy that is now being followed
by Éire is how much they rely on either Great Britain or the Western Union
stepping in to do it in some authoritative but altogether unspecified way. . . .

When anyone possesses something that you may want to acquire, you don't
usually get it on demand, or by talking about how much you want it to someone else—you have to set about making a bargain. And it's fair to say from
the Northern Ireland point of view that the offer has not been made either
with the diplomacy or with any inducement that would smooth the path towards agreement.

Of course, it's equally fair to say that those in Éire are practising no deception. . . .

Now, I realise that some of you will feel that I have leaned too far towards
the need for unity, but I make no excuse for that. At the beginning the Northern majority did not want a border either between the British Isles or between the two parts of Ireland; and as for me, while I know the whole range
of the antipathies, I think I may say so without offence to those who want to
remain as we are that it is still a civilised ideal, not only for the sake of peace
and amity but of national prosperity.

And I should like to add, and with all respect to those of nationalist spirit,
that there will yet be a realisation that the destiny of Ireland is bound up
with that of Great Britain in the same way that the destiny of Northern Ireland may be bound up with that of Éire. I find it difficult to think otherwise
of two small islands lying so close together off the shores of Europe. Believing that to be so, I, for one, don't share the very general reaction that the
North has nothing to say to the rest of Ireland. . . .

Sayers's plea for a reunion of the British Isles reflected the richly nostalgic, imperialist strain in constructive Unionism. For all Sayers's competence, noted the *Irish Times* critic, he was 'a little dazzled by the glories of Empire; a little overawed by the wonders of the centre of Empire; a little over-conscious of the bonds linking his own region to the Empire' (31 Oct. 1946). This was undeniable. But it was not fair to accuse him of turning 'a blind eye' to the South. Sayers had many social and family links with the South (including J. J. Horgan, one of the last surviving Redmondites) and regularly made the trip to Dublin for rugby and cricket internationals; visits, moreover, where a selective eye could still pick out 'the relics of ould decency'. Thus on 11 July 1947 he travelled down to watch Ireland lose by 57 runs to the South Africans, and after dinner at the Gresham returned north for the 'Twelfth'. Intriguingly, when recording in his diary the significant anniversaries for 1946, he included Parnell's centenary and Grattan's bicentenary as well as the twenty-fifth anniversary of the establishment of Northern Ireland's parliament.

It may have been a civilised ideal, but it was not what Ulster expected. Inevitably, Sayers's quaintly Anglo-Irish view provoked fierce criticism in some quarters, and the visit in November of the BBC's Director of the Spoken Word, George Barnes, led to the decision to break Sayers's monopoly on 'Ulster Commentary'. Nevertheless, on the radio that night Sayers returned to a favourite theme and spoke of another border—that of the mind—between Ulster and the British mainland. Fears of a British sell-out over the border and detestation of socialist legislation from Westminster led to frequent calls (1945, 1947–8) for greater independence for Ulster within the Empire.

'Ulster Commentary', Northern Ireland Home Service, 13 November 1948

. . . When the Irish problem is brought up, as it is today, many attempts are made to show that Northern Ireland is an anachronism or a monstrosity or a political blunder, whereas, if one can only disassociate it from the nationalist aspect of things, it has proved to be a profoundly interesting essay in the delegation of government. And yet . . . it seems to me we have the very debatable question of whether self-government has dignified or enhanced our essentially regional background or whether it has only served to intensify our provincialism? . . .

The Dominion conception sounds spacious enough, but look at it closely and you can see that it was rather retrograde, a retreat into ourselves. Those who are allergic, shall I say, to socialism have shown something of the same tendency, or readiness to cut themselves off and live like Diogenes in a tub. More than once in the past few years we've seen an attitude of mind that is the antithesis of Unionism, a forgetfulness of the fact that Northern Ireland is part of the United Kingdom and has national obligations no matter what the complexion of the government in London.

The need is to ally the best of our provincial qualities, integrity, shrewdness and industry, with what we know at bottom to be the broad stream of international progress. By doing that we were less prone to be satisfied with our own efforts and our own standards and the scope of our own back yard.
. . .

To Sayers the Union was Ulster's political, economic and cultural lifeline, 'a bond of affection', as Churchill had written in 1943, that had been 'tempered by fire' and was 'now . . . unbreakable'. Indeed, the war years and their aftermath had seen, through military service, marriage and the job opportunities provided by government expansion, an intensification of what has been called the 'Ulster-British' perspective, primarily among the professional classes. On his return after the war, Sayers was regularly critical of what he saw as the growth of an Ulster nationalism, which was not only hostile to the South but also aspired to self-reliance within the United Kingdom. Sayers disliked the Safeguarding of Employment Act precisely because it excluded British workers as well. Few Unionists genuinely wanted Dominion Home Rule, but Sayers was horrified that it was seriously considered at all. Yet such sentiments had deep historical roots in the Ulster psyche, and these had been greatly reinforced by partition and the emergence of two hostile sectarian states. The Second World War and Churchill's rhetoric in praise of loyal Ulster further intensified the North–South divide and, significantly, Ulster's sense of self-importance. However, for those Ulster-British Unionists like Sayers with an all-Ireland perspective, it was the declaration by the Southern government of a republic in 1949 that came as the real shock. For the first time they perceived the border as permanent. It was in the light of this that Sayers wrote his elegiac 'Ulster Commentary' of 27 April 1949.

'Ulster Commentary', Northern Ireland Home Service, 27 April 1949

The other day I happened to be climbing the steep hill that runs through Hillsborough. Halfway up it, partly concealed between the houses, is an old milestone. Mile*stone* probably isn't the right word, for this one is made of iron, but I judged it to be old if only because it said, 'Dublin 70 miles, Dromore 4 miles, Lisburn 3 miles', all in Irish measure. Of course, the Dublin road is through Hillsborough and it's not surprising that the milestone should say how far it is away, but it struck me very forcibly as a *link with the past*. Not on account of its age, but by the fact that it was put there in the days when Dublin was the capital and the centre of things. It was the road to Belfast too, yet Belfast didn't even get a mention. Everywhere was measured by its distance from Dublin.

And, you know, when you think about it, that wasn't so very long ago, a matter of less than thirty years. What a change of outlook, in its literal sense, there has been in that comparatively short space of time. From being part of a country run from Dublin for centuries, the North of Ireland no longer looks southwards for its administration. Instead of the old milestone we have yellow motorists' signposts that say how far they are from Belfast.

I felt it was a coincidence too that I should have noticed that milestone not only in Hillsborough, where Government House itself is a sign of the times, but in the same week that Éire had re-emphasised the division of the country. It was indeed a moment to recall the days when 'Dublin, so many miles' was the way to express location, and a moment to wonder how many more are the changes that lie before us.

Politically, perhaps, the change is as complete as it can be—but this isn't a matter of politics alone. If differences created the border, the same is true the other way round and that the border itself has created new differences altogether. . . .

But there must be lots of you who remember when the Lord Lieutenant lived in Viceregal Lodge in the Phoenix Park and the Chief Secretary ruled from Dublin Castle, when the law came from the Four Courts, and much of our learning from Trinity. Why, Belfast, for all its industry and commerce, must have been a provincial place in those days. . . .

To what extent people in the North looked to Dublin, apart from the seat of government, I don't know. Even before the Great War division was in the air but I suppose that it was still the capital of the country and acknowledged as such. Certainly I can't imagine that anyone who went to Dublin at that time can have had quite the same sense of being in another country that some people confess now. It's just an example of the way new differences have added themselves to the old. And it's more than the Irish street names, and the green pillar-boxes and the tall helmets of the metropolitan police. It is, I suppose, the natural drawing apart of two sections of a country that have become free to go as they please without reference to each other.

But it does seem that this drawing apart has gone a *long* way. Intercourse of all kinds has diminished, and gone is nearly all that distributive trade that places in the North like Belfast and Londonderry and Newry once had with the South and West. There are nationally-minded people, of course, who come and go as before – although I think the Ulster people as a whole are inclined to keep to themselves – but for the rest, the closeness of their contacts with the South has been getting less and less, and with it their acquaintance with the rest of the country and its growth.

For the majority in Northern Ireland the causes are not hard to find. The old Anglo-Irish population with whom they had a more intimate link has been decreasing, the kinship has become less marked, and marriage doesn't seem to carry on, as it did, the chain of family relationships. My own grandmother came from Co. Cork, but I doubt if there will be as many after me who will be able to say the same thing. . . .

Look back too, and you will see that one of the things that has been lost is personal contact even between Irishmen of differing opinions. If you read the biographies of the leaders in the Home Rule days, you'll see that they encountered each other not only at Westminster but in their own country, and that in many cases they still had time for friendliness and to band together as Irishmen when the need arose. How little of that there is now. . . .

There are, of course, some spheres in which both parts of the country still meet together: sport for a large part is still universal, and there are still some countrywide institutions like churches; but there is always the possibility, much as it is to be deplored, that events may prove too strong even for some of these. . . .

Once the newspapers in Belfast reported events over a good half of the country, but now they look over the border only when there is something special in the news. What happens in Dublin Castle or the Four Courts is of common interest no longer—although more can be said about what happens at Leopardstown or Baldoyle.

But don't take it that all this is merely because a majority of the people in Northern Ireland prefer to associate themselves with the rest of the United Kingdom. The same process is going on in the Republic—part consciously and part unconsciously, just as it is here. For that matter, there's reason to think although the will for a united Ireland is greater in the South, there isn't that knowledge and understanding of the North that would be most likely to achieve it. . . . What has happened is that some differences have been accentuated, but others have sprung up that can hardly have been thought of when partition was first put forward as a remedy. And taking them all in all, I fear that by now they amount to a formidable total. The question is whether since last week they may not become larger still.

And so to the thought that's really behind this talk. What has been the effect of these past twenty-eight years of separation and self-government on people in Northern Ireland? Granted that Ulstermen as a whole are independent and that throughout Irish history they have usually stood by themselves, where is this influence leading? For those who have not ceased to look to Dublin as the capital *I* can't speak. . . . Faced with the business of making a living . . . the contrast in some of the conditions on the two sides of the border must be as apparent to one man as it is to another. Yet no one would suggest that time and circumstance have made them any less Irish.

But is it true of the other body of Ulstermen and women? I have an idea it is not, and if that *is* the case, I suggest that it may be one of the most significant facts of our recent history. And today the thought crosses the mind that the appearance of an Irish republic may possibly carry on that whittling down of nationality that has really little to do with politics as we know them. . . . The countryside may still be Irish, and lots of country people, close to the soil, will not cease to be indigenous, but often I wonder whether those who are more exposed to mass influences aren't becoming more 'Ulster' and less 'Irish' and whether that subtle change isn't still going on. . . .

The trouble, I think, is that the number of those who are equally at home in the North or South and who best combine the two in themselves is declining. It's almost inevitable that a man from the North, without that sense of contact with the rest of the country, cannot be as complete an Irishman as his father was in his day. Before 1886 the term Ulsterman was probably far less in use than it is in 1949.

Don't let me underestimate what Northern Ireland has done on its own. As I have often said, our system of delegated government has a great responsibility. Already it has brought development on regional lines that might not have been possible if we had been ruled direct from London or from Dublin. As supporters of the link with the United Kingdom claim, it is responsible for much social and economic progress, and what is of equal, if not larger importance, it has kept us in touch with the world. . . .

But there's something rather nearer the surface that's worth a thought in conclusion. It's that if the social revolution goes on apace in Great Britain and should threaten to leave the more independent, and slower-moving, people of Northern Ireland behind . . . then Northern Ireland might be forced, from yet another direction, back into itself, and the question, I think, would be whether it is big enough, or mature enough, to be able to find and follow a way of its own. It just might turn out that many of its people weren't quite Irish on the one hand, and not quite British on the other, and that they would form a kind of enclave, a little state existing on its own and with a minimum of friendly contact with its neighbours.

That may be a bit fanciful and exaggerated . . . but it's an impression of the future that comes to anyone who is in the mood to regret that Ireland should ever have had to be divided and, so recently, should have become more divided still. One of our own cabinet ministers was bold enough to say the other day that no one would welcome a united Ireland more than he, and he must have been wishing, as others do, that it was possible to belong to a Northern Ireland, to an Ireland and to a United Kingdom in one and the same mind.

With Southern irredentism and the Ulster Unionists playing the border card for all it was worth in the general elections of 1949 and 1950, Sayers's Irish hopes had to be satisfied with cross-border economic co-operation on the Erne drainage schemes. In any case, he soon found himself involved in the propaganda war between Dublin and Belfast. On 22 March 1950 he recorded an 'Ulster Commentary' bemoaning the 'frozen nature' of Ulster politics. That night he caught the boat-train to London, making his connection the next morning via Waterloo with the *S. S. America*. For Sayers was bound for the USA as Brookeborough's press officer on a campaign to defend Northern Ireland's reputation in a society where Irish nationalism had a powerful hold. After the narrow politics of Ulster, Sayers was to find meetings at the Pentagon, visits to the United Nations, wreath-laying at Arlington Cemetery and press conferences at the British Embassy utterly exhilarating. It brought back memories of Churchill's press conferences, and Sayers relished his battles with the New York press. Brookeborough too revelled in the fray, and Sayers was won over by the famous charm of Ulster's Prime Minister. 'We loved having him with us,' wrote Brookeborough to Jack's uncle, R. M. Sayers; 'your nephew . . . was a tower of strength to me.' All in all, the trip proved a great success.

America also provided Sayers with the chance to catch up with old friends. However, it was new friends met at Scots-Irish societies that were to make the greatest impact and led to an extraordinary panegyric on the Ulster race. Here in America he had found all he admired in his native Ulstermen.

'Ulster Commentary', Northern Ireland Home Service, 19 May 1950

As Damon Runyan might put it, I am standing in the middle of Pennsylvania Station checking my traps and thinking more than somewhat. Because the baffling thing about railway stations in New York is where to find the trains. The buildings are vast, airy palaces of glass and marble as unlike our sooty grottoes as you can possibly imagine. But Penn. Station has one thing in common with Euston, some statues of railroad kings, and as I stood there one of them particularly caught my eye. For boldly inscribed on the base was the name Samuel Rea.

Samuel Rea, a plain name, a solid name, a name, I said to myself, that must surely have come from Ulster. I couldn't be certain, of course, but as I went in search on my train I was betting heavily that my instinct was right. And in an odd way I found that it was. A few days later I was at a dinner given by the Pennsylvania Scots-Irish Society in Philadelphia. On the programme was the list of its former presidents – among them was the name Samuel Rea. Was he, I asked, the man who was connected with Pennsylvania Railroad and whose statue stood in the station in New York? The answer was 'the same'.

Well, there I was 3,000 miles from home, in a country of 150,000,000 people, a country that even now suggests a new world, and yet I knew in my bones that that man, long dead and gone, and whom I'd never heard of before, was 'of the rock whence I was hewn'. . . .

My mind saw the Scots who three hundred years ago planted the North of Ireland, who became a new race of Ulstermen, who went in their thousands to America, and whose descendants even today can be identified almost at a glance as belonging to the same stock as you or me.

I wonder if you get this pleasure, this quiet sense of pride, at discovering such links. . . .

The Pennsylvanian Scots-Irish Society, of which I've spoken, is composed largely of people who trace their American ancestry back for two hundred years, and yet it wasn't so hard to imagine that they were fellow-countrymen of my own. Certainly *their* names also, McCrackens, Galbraiths, Vances, Crawfords, told me what they were and where they came from. Probably they are the oldest Ulster stock overseas drawn together not only in honour of their founder forebears but of the land that gave them and *their* fathers birth.

When such men still have such pride of ancestry, it's not surprising that people of our blood wherever they are should still look back to Ulster as their native place.... Once I was travelling across Canada with a party whose names had been in the newspapers. When the train stopped at a place called Moosejaw, someone came on board and asked to see me. I found that he had been born in Moneymore and that he had travelled for miles, just to speak to an Ulsterman. The late Robert Lynd was with me, and I remember him saying: 'Can you see an Englishman doing that?' Well, as the story goes, not without a proper introduction. . . .

Could there be just a suspicion that the Ulsterman abroad, be he American, Canadian, New Zealander or Australian, is slightly nearer the true character of our race even than we are? For the events of fifty or sixty years here on our own heath seem to have altered not our determination—we've always been a stubborn lot—but our temper. There's a well-known appreciation of the Ulster-Scot by Professor Heron that refers to his dislike of making a display of the deeper and more tender feelings of his nature, and to his quiet and undemonstrative deportment. But since that was written some at least have changed, and there are Ulstermen today who make parades of feelings, who shout in slogans and use language that for all its defiance is inclined to be unnaturally boastful as well.

But that, perhaps, is only superimposed. What I really have in mind tonight, having just come back from the United States, is the thought that there is a fibre, a reserve of strength, in the Ulster character that lives on. Mr Hugh Shearman has said that Ulster always has been one of the salty, stinging, and unexpected elements in the life and flavour of this planet. That is certainly one aspect, but mine is the more conventional one of a people who at home and abroad down the years have displayed side by side the same vigour, the same solidity, the same application to business, the same tenacity and the same blend of the radical and the conservative that makes citizens of the highest worth. . . .

It's the destiny of this province, itself largely peopled through migration, that it should be like a tree, perennially bearing fruit for others to pick. . . .

When you realise how these nations cry out for more people and how overcrowded is Britain with 50,000,000 struggling for economic survival, it comes right home to you that if we could redistribute the British race, the world could take a new lease of security and begin a new age of plenty. . . .

As a traveller returned, my tribute is to those Ulstermen and women of every period, and of high and low degree, who in saying farewell to home have brought honour to themselves and to us, and, unconsciously perhaps, have a stake in the saving of the world. . . .

The 'Honest Ulsterman' tradition in Ulster literature was at least as old as Ulster Unionism itself. But the significance of having to go abroad to have one's faith renewed seems to have escaped Sayers. This was a distinctive Protestant culture that Sayers was mythologising as characteristic of an Ulster race. It was not that he did not recognise Ulster's divisions. Rather it was because in the early years after the war such cultural alternatives were not pushed to the fore, and so Sayers was free to indulge in an assumption. The next ten years would not prove so accomodating.

3   The Spectre of Sectarianism

With his regular appearances on radio Sayers became something of an establishment figure. By the early 1950s he found himself a member of the Ulster Club and of the Eldon Lodge, the most socially prestigious lodge of the Orange Order. At the same time, under the guidance of his uncle, R. M. Sayers, he began to work his way up through the ranks of the Press Masonic Lodge. A shade more glamorous perhaps were the invitations to garden parties at Government House and even on one occasion Sunday lunch at Mount Stewart. Politically he moved now in the higher echelons of Ulster Unionism, with regular access to the Prime Minister and the party authorities in Glengall Street. On top of this, he remained the pre-eminent political journalist in the province. When Brookeborough was interviewed in the first live television broadcast from Northern Ireland (17 Nov 1955), it was only to be expected that the one local representative among the panel of interviewers on that historic night was Jack Sayers. At the *Belfast Telegraph* his uncle came more and more to take the advice of his nephew—so much so that when W. R. Baird died in a motor racing accident, to be succeeded as chairman by 'R. M.', it was almost inevitable that 'John E' would in turn succeed him as editor. That he had to share the position with a long-standing servant of the *Telegraph* merely reflected his youth, rather than any sensitivities over nepotism.

Sayers had been born into a *Telegraph* dynasty, and his promotion to joint editor in 1953 had something about it of the inheritance of a sacred trust. However, he also brought to the post a vigorous interest in the wider concerns of journalism and the defence of free speech in a democratic society. Above all, he brought an ambition for quality. A master craftsman in his own right, he ruthlessly demanded the highest standards of professionalism necessary for the *Telegraph* to retain its reputation as a paper of worth. But he also sought to broaden the range of issues in a series of feature articles that could give a provincial evening paper more of the character of a national daily. In the 1950s this meant giving great prominence to the Suez crisis and the Hungarian uprising, while at home there were searching articles on unemployment, industrial development and social progress. Many of these written by academics, where the policy was to talk up rather than down, aiming to win over 'opinion'. At the same time, none of this was at the cost of the paper's local coverage, and Sayers never lost sight of the importance of the *Telegraph*'s ability to 'feel the pulse of the province'. He had tremendous confidence in the power of the written word and consciously sought to provoke debate and persuade minds. Hence the importance he attached to the leader. Editorials were given a prime slot in the paper, top left on the front page next to the headline story, and offered an instant interpretation. To write them was 'an honour' requiring not additional pay but integrity, courage to raise the unacceptable, and above all the ability to be radical from within the establishment. Under Sayers a paper had to have a purpose, a policy. It could not simply be detached, reacting to events. It had also to be involved and committed. The paper he inherited was respectable and respectful, largely uncritical and even genteel in its Unionism. With the largest circulation by far and read by both communities, the *Telegraph* held a unique position within Ulster. Under Sayers it would be no less Unionist, but it would be much more demanding of its creed and seek to reactivate its liberal traditions. Nor was the perspective narrowly party political, for he was concerned with the development of Ulster as a whole. What emerged was a concept of the *Telegraph* in which 'the politics cannot be segregated. The whole paper has to be a setting for our policy'(Sayers to Conolly Gage 21 June 1969). Thus, in his campaigns against architectural eyesores, pylons, and the 'creeping disease of breeze blocks and asbestos roofs' in the countryside, and in his support for civic weeks, the Methodists' 'meet the teenager' drive of October 1965, and even the restoration of St Anne's Cathedral in Belfast, the vision that he was promulgating was of a modern, progressive society.

He also found himself developing quite a reputation as an after-dinner speaker.

Sayers Speaking at Collegians' Rugby Dinner [c. March 1951]

. . . I wonder if you know a famous Ulster story about a good Republican who was talking to his priest about the day of judgement, and was perturbed to find that on that day there would be gathered together King James and King Billy, Lord Carson and Michael Collins, Lord Craigavon and Mr de Valera and all the Orangemen that ever were beside as many Fenians. And the good Republican pondered this for a few minutes and then he said: 'Father,' says he, 'I'll be telling you something. I'm thinking there'll be no judging done the first day!'

Some months later, however, he faced a considerable setback. On undergoing a routine medical examination on the eve of his fortieth birthday, it was discovered that his blood pressure was dangerously volatile. An emergency operation in July was but the first step, and for the rest of his life Sayers was bedevilled by frequent headaches, occasional blackouts and the depressing after-effects of drugs. As a consequence, he had to cut back on the more stressful aspects of his work, particularly on radio, but after a holiday in north Donegal he was soon back to work at the *Telegraph*. He was by nature a workaholic, and in any case there was much to excite him as he witnessed the apparent revitalisation of Ulster. In an atmosphere of political and financial stability, the province had seen places in secondary education doubled, a rapid acceleration in the housing programme, the elimination of tuberculosis, and the quadrupling of the number of cars. Yet it was the opportunity that this material progress offered for a reassessment of traditional loyalties that most aroused Sayers's imagination.

The Round Table, February 1951

A recent speech by the Minister of Home Affairs, Mr Brian Maginess, KC, was a timely relief from the acerbity which characterises so much political utterance in Northern Ireland. In it he spoke of the development among the Nationalist minority of a new consciousness of their place in the community and of pride in the achievements of the province as an area of self-government. He suggested at the same time that the violent antagonism of the past has been lessened, except among a decreasing number of irreconcilables, and this happier condition he attributed to the impartiality of the administration, the recognition of the special position of Roman Catholics, particularly in relation to education, and a state of material prosperity based on thriving agriculture and the benefits of the social services. . . . Yet, as Mr Maginess has himself acknowledged, much of the change is below the surface. When instinctive loyalties and sentiments have been so long and so sharply in conflict, signs of better feeling are slow to find positive form; at best they appear in the lower note of controversy, and in the relative lack of cohesion and enthusiasm among the anti-partition parties. . . .

It can hardly be said, however, that Unionists as a body have responded so fully as they might have done to the portents of a truce. Many of them have been brought up in a rigidly defensive attitude of mind which allows no concessions to be made to their traditional opponents. They are slow to perceive that a progressive domestic policy is capable of working a change of heart towards the regime, and their vision is prone not to extend beyond local politics, in which friction and exclusiveness are most prevalent. Nevertheless, the soberer elements on the side of the government, among whom Mr Maginess is taking a lead, would seem to be pondering the advantages of a more liberal outlook. As yet the party organisation has not given much expression to this tendency: it aims to retain the support of extreme sections more than to attract votes from elsewhere. But it may well prove that the example of the cabinet, which is more moderate in its make-up than much of its following, will bring about a deviation in a party line which runs too close to the demarcation between Protestant and Roman Catholic. Already a fall in the Unionist vote in the West Belfast by-election for the British Commons, though admittedly this is a cockpit, has been blamed on a distaste for the sectarian character of the campaign at the hustings.

If the sectarianism of West Belfast depressed him, there was little politically to raise his spirits thereafter. The assumption in the face of public 'acerbity' that beneath the surface (and out of sight) private attitudes were changing was a traditional characteristic of constructive Unionists. So too was the faith in the continuing deference of the rank-and-file and the capacity of leaders to lead. But matters were not helped, as Sayers readily acknowledged, by Southern politicians determined to reopen the partition issue, continually forcing Sir Basil Brooke (soon to be elevated to the peerage as Lord Brookeborough) 'to make retort when otherwise he might be engaged in cultivating a friendlier atmosphere at home'. Moreover the rejection of Noel Browne's Mother and Child Scheme at the behest of the Catholic hierarchy (4 April 1951) served to 'provide material for many speeches from Unionist platforms for years to come'. To Sayers and his friends sectarianism was not only distasteful but actually harmful to Unionism. However, the plea for British standards cut little ice amidst a very Irish quarrel. Leading moderates such as Colonel Hall-Thompson and Dame Dehra Parker seemed to be falling by the wayside and the drowning of John Maynard Sinclair [Minister for Finance] in the *Princess Victoria* disaster (31 Jan 1953) robbed them of their only alternative to Brookeborough. When the Unionists lost votes to Labour in the 1953 Stormont election—for once preoccupied by unemployment in the staple industries and not by the border—the party retaliated in characteristic fashion with the Flags and Emblems Act. The banning of the tricolour resulted from disturbances provoked by Orange bands attempting to celebrate the coronation of Elizabeth II by marching through strongly nationalist villages. To Sayers the new act seemed 'somewhat minatory' and in its turn provocative. Writing for *The Round Table* (Feb 1954), he reported a little anxiously on 'the sudden revival of what is not far removed from fanaticism [which] has disturbed all who remember the past and would keep it buried'.

To Sayers these events threatened to leave Ulster a provincial backwater, and he deplored the easy acquiescence in this of so many fellow-Unionists as the province diverged further and further from the experience of the rest of the United Kingdom. The Safeguarding of Employment Act, the exclusion from National Service, and the abandonment of the principle of equality of taxation raised for Sayers issues that were as much constitutional and moral as economic. To him nothing symbolised this more than the Northern Ireland government's chosen route in the rapid pursuit of equality of living standards with the rest of the United Kingdom which threatened paradoxically to corrode 'the Ulster character' and the bond of Union.

'Ulster Commentary', Northern Ireland Home Service, 9 July 1954

'My son, fear thou the Lord, and the King, and meddle not with them that are given to change.' If you walk down May Street in Belfast, you can see those words graven in stone on a building known as the Victoria Memorial Hall. They're something more than a text—they've served as an Ulster motto, to express the attitude of a great many North of Ireland people. What I ask myself tonight is whether the injunction is still being observed.

Now I don't mean particularly the first part of the quotation—this isn't a talk about religious faith. . . . Instead I'm concerned with the changes that are taking place in our outlook as a people . . . changes in relation to our customary standards of thought about business, and virtues of independence and self-help. And, perhaps an even larger thing, changes in the way we look upon ourselves and towards the rest of the United Kingdom. . . .

Today we see the government spending millions, not as loans, not in the creation of assets which remain public property, but in outright gifts – remissions of tax if you like – to companies and individuals. If it's unpopular to use the term subsidy – why, that in itself is one of the very changes I'm talking about. I don't think that a quarter of a century ago we could possibly have called it anything else. . . .

It's been noticeable that most of this has happened since the textile slump of 1951, when unemployment here soared and we were faced with the same depressed conditions we had before the war. I think it was realised then that the pace of our expansion was too slow, that we hadn't gained as much as we might have done from the boom times, that we are still vulnerable and, with the rising population, far short of full employment.

Indeed, the conclusion that must be drawn is that the revolution in our ideas and rules and methods has been brought about only by the gravity of the economic problem. There's no contesting that far-reaching steps are necessary; that the government feels compelled to prime the pump more than it has ever done before. It remains to be seen whether its actions will be effective, whether we *can* become viable, or whether we are just *buying* employment; or shall I say, keeping the patient alive with blood transfusions. . . . For the kind of policy we're now committed to can hardly be more than a desperate short-term remedy. No industry can for ever rely on subsidy for survival, nor can we in Northern Ireland count on receiving endless privileges and preferential treatment. What a challenge it is to a province so full of pride as ours, so self-made, and so keen on twenty shillings in the pound. Little wonder that every time public assistance is given out it is accompanied by the call to industry to get back to self-support and use its own initiative.

. . . For be sure that business cannot be divorced from our character and that these changes can soon effect the whole of our provincial life. I hear it said that there is forming an Ulster consciousness. I suppose there always was one, but the present-day opinion is that self-government has given us a new pride; pride of possession, pride in paddling our own canoe, pride in our achievements. The more we look to our own parliament the more we mature and the more we become an entity like Scotland or Wales – that's how the argument runs at any rate. And no doubt this is all very worthy. But for my part I begin to question whether we are not tending towards a kind of provincial nationalism that's really foreign to most of our cherished ideals. The test is whether we are strengthening our place in the United Kingdom or weakening it. . . .

We claim much from Great Britain; do we accept all the obligations of citizenship that go with it? . . . For the present at any rate I believe that our purpose *is* to be a full-subscribing part of the United Kingdom. But we must recognise that in the lengths we go to seek economic stability we're running risks. We are in danger of finding that we want tax concessions all the time; we are in danger of becoming addicted to subsidies as people are addicted to drugs, and of never becoming fully competitive, fully abreast of the times. If these injections of public money aren't successful, we may end up with an artificial economy, for grants and gifts and aid are no substitute for the enterprise and hard work that made us what we are. You know, the extraordinary paradox is that the more we strain to bridge the Irish Sea for trade, the more we threaten to widen it in modes of thinking and in affinity. It's broad enough and deep enough, goodness knows, without being made more so by possibly self-centred, self-sufficient, even self-indulgent, policies.

Nothing I've said reflects on loyalty. There's no reason to think that that has changed. But loyalty to the Crown and loyalty to the Union are rather different. When I read of times before 1921, I get the impression that there was rather more common feeling with the people of Britain than there is today. That without radio or television or aircraft, people here lived and moved and had their being more nearly with the rest of the British people. Nowadays great national issues can be raised, international issues too, and they are apt to leave us unmoved. That Irish Sea is an insulator, that consciousness a bit parochial.

Where are we heading? . . . I don't think now of constitutions or forms of government, but of the chance that we may end up as a little favoured enclave, neither of Ireland nor of Great Britain. Living unto ourselves, hoping to get the best of all worlds, taking much and giving little. The Ulster *I* know is too good for that, and the Union too noble a conception to be reduced to a loose and do-as-you-please connection—and us to a state of what I've called provincial nationalism. 'Meddle not with them that are given to change.' It's not to be taken too literally, I know, but if it applies to anything, it applies to those things that to us in Ulster are all-important.

This could, of course, work both ways. Significantly, the Brookeborough interview—the first programme broadcast live on national television—opened with something of a geography lesson for its 'mainland' audience. To the backdrop of Belfast's City Hall, the voice-over intoned: 'By the Union Jack which flies in the front of the flood-lit dome you can see that Northern Ireland is part of Great Britain.'

Nevertheless, such was the evidence of social progress in post-war Ulster that it won a sympathetic report in Thomas Wilson's *Ulster Under Home Rule* (1955). Sayers, a close friend, contributed a chapter to this volume on the political parties, and in so doing revealed many of the assumptions behind his political thought at this time. He rejected forcefully the argument that the Unionist Party's prolonged electoral dominance demonstrated that Ulster was ruled by 'a reactionary semi-dictatorship'. Instead he chose to emphasise in Ulster Unionism an unideological classlessness, powerful loyalties to religion and crown, and the fierce defence of liberty, so important to an individualistic Scottish 'dominant strain'. Historically he traced this trend back to the aftermath of the 1798 rebellion, which, he held, saw so many Ulster Presbyterians eventually support the Union as the only realistic guarantor of their liberties. Such an analysis enabled him to conclude that Unionism was fundamentally an extension of the eighteenth-century Protestant liberal tradition. However, much as he indulged in historical fantasy, he did recognise that sectarianism was the 'fundamental issue [that] dominates politics'. Indeed, he went so far as to claim that 'the divisions today are deep, deeper even than in the last century'. Yet for him the solution lay in economics and a faith in the healing virtues of lasting prosperity, so reminiscent of nineteenth-century advocates of the policy of 'killing Home Rule by kindness'. Despite all the nationalist frustration, he felt that 'they have been recompensed by prosperous conditions and by peace'. As for the border, by 1952, in a conversation with Andrew Stewart, Sayers was content to rely on the emerging (European) Common Market to undermine this traditional obsession. Interestingly, in Anglo-Irish relations he was more worried that Ulster's exclusion from National Service had left it 'in a position of being in but not of the United Kingdom'. Within Ulster he deplored the lack of real political debate, especially among those 'who are more Orangemen than political theorists'. If this made 'strong leadership essential', he remained highly sympathetic to the Orange Order as the guardian of Ulster's values whose dynamism was under-used. 'The Orange Order', he argued, 'though it embraces thousands of working men and is a democratic movement of formidable power, confines its pronouncements to the defence of Protestantism; whereas, if so minded, it could effectively balance the upper- and middle-class element that more often provide the voice of Unionist doctrine.' He continued to argue that Unionism was an inclusive creed. But in this he clearly displayed a complacency towards the minority similar to that shown by his friend and fellow-moderate, Brian Maginess, when he set up the Ulster Folk and Transport Museum. This was to represent all rural traditions in the province, but the prevailing assumption that there was a cohesive Ulster tradition was very much a Unionist one. Thus, to some extent, Ulster Catholics were alienated by well-meaning as well as by reactionary Unionism. The 1955 general election, clearly demonstrated with Sinn Féin polling 152,000 votes, what little progress had been made in improving relations between the two communities and what danger lay in Ulster succumbing to what Sayers in the anonymity of *The Round Table* now called an 'apartheid' state.

The Round Table, November 1955

... In Northern Ireland the barrier between the two communities remains solid and forbidding: such quietude as the area has known in post-war years has come more from acquiescence in the division than from efforts by either side to establish co-operation. In this situation it is difficult to avoid the conclusion that the initiative rests with the party in power. The Unionists have had thirty-five years of self-government; they have built up Ulster socially and economically and have proved the usefulness of devolution and the lasting nature of the Irish settlement. But in domestic politics the experiment has not been so successful. As Ireland is divided, so is Northern Ireland, and the possibilities of even a working measure of conciliation receive little attention. The neglect is all the more conspicuous having regard to the favourable state of mind induced by impressive improvements in public welfare. The raising of the standard of living of the minority would seem to be incidental, for no direct attempt has been made to use it as a basis for a conversion to a British system on which it rests. Nor has any identifiable section of Unionists given support to the positive political creed which Mr W. B. Maginess, the Minister of Finance, addresses to the Nationalist middle classes. To the great body of Protestants, Roman Catholics are disloyal and untrustworthy and bent on the destruction of the constitution. It is a defensive, almost atavistic, attitude of mind and, at times, an inglorious demonstration of the virtue of civil and religious liberty. . . .

However, Sayers's plea for the party to cultivate the middle-class Catholic vote was overtaken by events. A renewed IRA campaign that flared up in 1956 inevitably saw border issues predominate, and Sayers fully backed the government's resort to the Special Powers Act. Such an atmosphere also encouraged among some Unionists greater vindictiveness towards the minority, to which the government pandered with a bill to restrict child benefit for large (mainly Catholic) families. Nor could the moderates look to Britain for support. Not only did the Suez crisis tarnish the imperial ideal, but in the affairs of Northern Ireland British governments displayed a sublime complacency. When a group of Ulster's Westminster MPs met Harold Macmillan at No. 10 Downing Street to protest at the lapse in security when the IRA raided the Gough Military Barracks, the Prime Minister retorted: 'But aren't IRA raids good for loyalty?' Yet by the following year things were looking up. Not only had the Southern government co-operated by interning IRA activists, but it was also becoming apparent that the campaign was floundering through lack of support from within the Catholic minority in the North. At the same time, with the rise of Morris May and Brian Maginess, the moderates had greater influence in the cabinet. And this at a time when the old guard were on the defensive after the publication of the Cuthbert and Isles Report (1957), which in its review of the Northern Ireland economy castigated the lethargy of the government and concluded that 'provincial autonomy had been a doubtful privilege economically'. By 1958 Sayers was in buoyant mood, full of anticipation of a reformist programme (including local government) and seeing, in the election of four Labour MPs, signs that at last Ulster politics was assuming the British mould.

Belfast Telegraph, 1 April 1958

UNIONISM'S WAY AHEAD

... In such a lightening atmosphere the Unionist Party is called on to do much rethinking. The loss of seats to Labour is only a symptom. The problem for the party is how it can retain the allegiance not only of people of individual mind—an Ulster characteristic too long in subjection—but of the rising generation as well, and by so doing prove that it is not suffering from hardening of its arteries.

It has to accept that in Belfast, and possibly in Antrim and Down, it no longer has the exclusive right to speak for pro-British sentiment, and that it must take its stand less on loyalty and self-preservation as on the evolution of a political philosophy that can also attract and enthuse.

It cannot do so, we suggest, without appealing to the widest section of people. No narrow, blind, partisan or arrogant approach will answer the case. Unionism must have room for all men of tolerance and goodwill, who recognise the benefits of British citizenship and who dispute the claims of socialism in the belief that organic and enlightened Unionism offers something better. . . .

We advance another reason why the Unionist Party must re-emphasise that it is a party of the centre. There is being created a body of moderates. Catholics among them, whose votes are being mobilised and will go, outside the most industrial constituencies, to the party that offers reasonable discussion and impartial dealing, true civil and religious liberty and equality of citizenship.

It will be said that this would endanger the support of the true-blue incorruptibles. The answer is that this is not 1690, nor 1912 nor 1921. It is the opening of an era in which Northern Ireland is secure, free, maturing and in search of a fresher mental sustenance.

This Unionism can most satisfyingly provide by being true to itself and what is best in its unique political synthesis of Tory and radical, master and man, town and country, the zealots and those who wish only to live in unity with their neighbours.

The Unionist Party did not see matters in quite the same light. To them the emergence of Labour was entirely the fault of a *Telegraph* leader suggesting that the world would not end if there were a few Labour representatives at Stormont. Sayers's uncle, a member of the Ulster Unionist Council, was highly upset at being hauled over the coals by the party and had to make strenuous efforts to ensure that the *Belfast Telegraph* was not mentioned by name in the party's official *post mortem* into the loss of these seats. His nephew had promoted Labour's cause not because he was socialist—far from it: for Sayers, the political bible was not *Das Kapital* but Quintin Hogg's, *The Case for Conservatism* (1947). However, Sayers was sympathetic towards the social radicalism so prevalent in Methodism and embodied in the Northern Ireland Labour Party by Vivian Simpson and Billy Boyd. Nevertheless, the real motive in pressing the case of Labour's respectability was that it could provide an official opposition that would broaden the political debate. This in turn would improve the quality of government and thus the legitimacy of Stormont and devolution as a whole. Up until then the *Belfast Telegraph* had found itself having to fulfil the role of effective opposition, as in 1956 when it successfully condemned the attempt to restrict child benefit. None of this, as he admitted to Conolly Gage, added to his popularity in Glengall Street. But in his comments to Gage, Sayers, as he knew full well, was preaching to the converted. The former Westminster MP for South Belfast, who had left politics in 1952 to pursue a legal career in England, had been one of the more liberal Unionists, as perhaps one would expect from a nephew of Sir Denis Henry, the Catholic first Lord Chief Justice of Northern Ireland.

Letter to Conolly Gage, 30 July 1958

Dear Mr Gage,
I should like you to know how very grateful I am to you for having written us so splendid an article. I am delighted to be able to show that you so much appreciate the policy we followed at the general election. It has brought us a certain amount of opprobrium, but we have been well supported by Unionists of broader mind, and especially by the MPs at Westminster who, like yourself, can view Northern Ireland in a larger perspective. . . .

With best wishes,
Yours sincerely,
John E. Sayers

Detecting in the 1958 election results 'an *ennui* [among Catholics] with party politics in their old and clamant form', Sayers pondered in the August edition of the *The Round Table* on the challenge that this posed to Unionism. In particular he was struck by the 'inarticulate' stand of those in the cabinet who sought a more progressive policy towards the minority. As a result of their preferring to end conflict 'by silence rather than public counsel', Unionism had 'yet to produce a wing or a movement readily identifiable as liberal. . . . One must, therefore, seek to interpret atmosphere.' This he did largely as he wished to. Thus he placed less significance on the fact that Brian Maginess was hounded by a violent loyalist mob as he canvassed the Iveagh constituency in Co. Down, and rather more on the evidence that Maginess had sustained his majority by winning Catholic votes for Unionism. He was also greatly encouraged by a conference held the next month by an essentially middle-class Catholic social study group at Garron Tower. For a week they debated the potential role of 'the Catholic in the Community' with leading lights such as G. B. Newe arguing that Catholics could only hope to win greater social justice for the minority if they were prepared to involve themselves in the workings of that community. For Sayers the conference represented a 'public examination of the Catholic conscience in relation to life in Northern Ireland, the community in Northern Ireland'. As such, it seemed to him a watershed which augured the beginning of the end of sectarianism.

Letter to Conolly Gage, 6 August 1958

Dear Mr Gage,

. . . From my observation and many contacts I believe that there is a notable broadening of opinion here. The best proof I think is the steadiness of the whole population in the face of the IRA attacks, but I am also satisfied of the existence of a new desire on the part of a good many Roman Catholics to take stronger interest in affairs. . . .

It is fair to say, however, that all this puts the Unionist Party in something of a dilemma. It can either modulate its tone to appeal to the most broad-minded of Protestants and Roman Catholics, or put its main emphasis on the more extreme view. The two sides are represented I should say by Brian Maginess on the one hand and Ken Topping [Minister for Home Affairs] and Brian Faulkner [N.I. Government Chief Whip] on the other.

It is a pity that Maginess has not an identifiable group of support within the party. As you appreciate, much will turn on the succession to Brookeborough as Prime Minister, but God willing that will not be for some time. . . .

Will you let me know when you are next visiting Belfast? I should like very much to have you come to lunch.

> With best wishes,
> Yours sincerely,
> John E. Sayers

Disappointed by the official response, Sayers once again turned to the influential *Round Table* (Nov. 1958) and the freedom that anonymity gave him to keep the pressure on Brookeborough. With the premier now over seventy and in hospital suffering from a duodenal ulcer, Sayers 'inevitably' raised the question of the succession and called for a statesmanlike approach towards the minority.

What was more likely was that such 'stirrings in the minds of thoughtful Unionists' would not go unchallenged. Extremist factions such as Ulster Protestant Action, which in 1959 had provoked a major riot on the Shankill Road and later humiliated the radical Methodist, Dr Soper (whom Sayers had so admired during the war), were vigilant in the hunt for 'Lundies'. In September Sayers found himself writing for the first time on a young Free Presbyterian minister who had risen to prominence in the UPA. But Ian Paisley and his friends were never regarded as in any way representative of the Unionist rank-and-file. Indeed, it was a fundamental assumption of Sayers's thinking that his values prevailed in the privacy of ministerial hearts and that 'thoughtful Unionists' would eventually triumph over a noisy right-wing rump. Consequently, the controversy that racked the Unionist Party in the winter of 1959 came as a rude shock. On 2 November Sir Clarence Graham, chairman of the standing committee of the Unionist Council, acknowledged that there was nothing to stop Catholics joining the party or becoming the party's candidates. This was admittedly an off-the-cuff response to a conference of Young Unionists at Portstewart. But taken in conjunction with the impassioned plea that followed by the Attorney-General, Brian Maginess, for 'greater toleration and co-operation between all sections of the community', it seemed to many Unionists to undermine the exclusively Protestant nature of their creed. The counter-attack was not long in coming. The ruling executive committee (of which Graham was an *ex-officio* member) reaffirmed on 7 November the party's attachment to the Unionism of Carson and Craig and, in the phrase 'civil and religious liberty', to the Protestant faith. Three days later the Grand Master of the Orange Order had no truck with coded niceties and bluntly declared Catholic membership unacceptable. Even co-operation with Catholics was derided by Brian Faulkner as 'co-operation to achieve a united Ireland'. For Sayers such intolerance was abhorrent, and he determined to enter the fray. Yet within the *Telegraph* hierarchy many found distasteful the prospect of being once again the target of Unionist hostility. On the night of Graham's speech the *Telegraph* had enthused over the Unionists becoming a party of the centre, but now it took Sayers three days before he could win acceptance for even the most tentative leader.

Belfast Telegraph, 10 November 1959

UNIONIST DEBATE

In the past ten days the Unionist Party has given public expression to the thoughts on the future that many must have been pondering in private, and they have now become the subject of popular debate. . . .

At this significant point it is unfortunate that the issues before the country are being reduced to nothing more than whether the Unionist Party can receive as members any Roman Catholics who may cease to be Nationalists. . . .

The larger problem, however, is whether more people whose sentiments may formerly have been Nationalist can be encouraged to support the constitution and so add to Northern Ireland's security.

That was clearly Sir Clarence's purpose. . . . The same view was inherent in Sir George Clark's speech last night, although he pronounced the Orange Order as being against Roman Catholics as party members.

Here one is brought up against another divided aspect of Unionist policy, that while the government strives constantly to increase the prosperity, health and well-being of the whole population, the party in general could do more to use these immense achievements to convince its opponents of the value of the British connection and the British way of life.

There is also Unionism's more domestic need, the reattraction on an active basis of all the most responsible elements in our society; to uphold the party – and we quote Sir Clarence Graham again – 'as a coalition of all those democratic people of the centre whose belief is in freedom, progress and plenty'. . . .

Simply, the issue is one of tolerance. . . . tolerance that will ensure that Northern Ireland becomes the larger unity without which peace and full employment are more difficult to realise. . . .

To suggest that such views were 'inherent' in Clark's speech, save at the level of rhetoric, was generous indeed and perhaps reflected the restraining hand of his uncle and chairman, R. M. Sayers. Thus it was only in private that he could give full vent to his anger and then only to an outsider.

Letter to Conolly Gage, 11 November 1959

My dear Judge,
Your letter came as a solitary gleam in a darkening sky.

Those of us who have been trying to get the Unionist Party out of extremist hands have had a disastrous setback. Since you wrote you will have seen that Sir George Clark, as Grand Master of the Orange Order, has declared that no Catholic can be a member of the Party.

You will be interested to know the background of all this.

For a long time Glengall Street, which appears to be entirely beyond the control of the Prime Minister, has been determined to extinguish Brian Maginess and the 'liberals'. The chance came when poor Clarence Graham, himself a good Headquarters man, made the comment which you quoted. The tragedy was that this was not in his prepared speech, but was said in answer to a question which he could well have parried by saying that it was a matter for the future.

At the Unionist executive last Friday he was pressed to recant, but he stood by Maginess, and the result was the fairly safe statement on policy.

I was afraid, however, that there was a subtle meaning in 'civil and religious liberty', and that is what Clark has now exploited. I suspect he was put up to this, as his speech was circulated to the press on the Glengall Street typewriter.

You will be aware of the appalling effects of all this. The party has been hopelessly compromised, and there is not a moderate left who dares to resist.

It was only after a struggle that I was able to get a leader through last night, and it did not say all that I should have liked.

I blame the PM for having been so slack—he has never had a Chief Whip who worked as Herbert Dixon worked with Craigavon. The whole cry now is that action has been taken to reunite the party, but it is all being done at the expense of the best people here, and more and more are shunning politics like the plague.

It is becoming extremely difficult to get anyone to stand up to Glengall Street, and yet so many, most of the Ulster MPs at Westminster among them, know that the party is going to the bad.

I fully realise that you cannot write for publication, more's the pity. It was most heartening for me to have your letter and to know that you side with us.

With your permission I will show it to my chairman, who is sympathetic but, naturally, anxious about the position of the paper.

I really mourn the fact that you are no longer in South Belfast, for I believe that you could have saved the day.

> With best wishes,
> Yours sincerely,
> John E. Sayers

At the height of this row Sayers went to Colebrooke, Co. Fermanagh to interview Brookeborough for local television. As the publicity for the programme made clear, this was to be a profile of 'the person rather than the politician. . . . Viewers will be meeting the country gentleman, the family man, the up-to-date farmer who has a large estate in Co. Fermanagh.' The interview that followed was so deferential that it serves to illustrate just why Sayers's occasional and always mild critique of established beliefs and figures could cause such offence. It could only have been a rather frustrating affair were it not for the fact that Sayers was very fond of Brookeborough. Since the trip to the USA they had often met for interviews, during which the Prime Minister would let drop flattering references to his happy 'memories of 1950'. In any case, Sayers was invariably susceptible to the allure of the 'Big House'; and for all his democratic principles, he retained a firm belief in the benefits of paternalist leadership, however complacent.

Interview with Lord Brookeborough by Sayers and Robert Coulter,
Northern Ireland Television (BBC), 18 November 1959

Sayers: I am very interested, sir, how you find yourself in politics when you didn't really want to be there. If you haven't political ambition, that was a sense of duty was it?

Brookeborough: Well, if I said yes, it would sound rather smug, wouldn't it? No, I think that if you are trained as a soldier, there are certain jobs that you are told to do, and you do not ask the reason why. You do them. I was asked by Lord Craigavon . . . and I said that, if you ask me, I'll do it.

Sayers: Would you ever like to have been in the House of Commons at Westminster?

Brookeborough: Yes, I think for a short time . . . for the experience of the mother of parliaments. But I think I should have missed my contacts with the Ulster folk, and the Fermanagh folk in particular. . . .

Well, we are short of leaders, there is no doubt about it, in this country. If you take the Boy Scouts, these sorts of organisations, the Territorials, RNR, the difficulty is to get the officer type to come in.

Sayers: There seems to be a problem, sir, here. Your family were devoted to public service, you are a landed family, you had time on hand, and, since there are not so many families in that fortunate position, where are the new leaders to come from? How are they to spare the time for parliament?

Brookeborough: You've spoken about a very real difficulty, because the young men nowadays have got to earn money, especially if they're married. . . . But I think we will always get people saying there is nobody here, nobody there. Generally, there is good fish in the sea as there is out, and generally it will work out in the end.

Sayers: You've accomplished so much, sir. Is there any unfilled ambition that you have got?

Brookeborough: Solve the unemployment.

Sayers: You would put that above all else?

Brookeborough: Yes. If I could see the unemployment problem completely solved, I should be a very happy man.

Sayers: At what point, sir, did you ever feel that you were going to be the next PM. Sometimes we hear it said that Lord Craigavon groomed you to be one of his successors.

Brookeborough: Well, I have never noticed the grooming (*laughter*).

Sayers: As PM, what do you feel was your greatest achievement?

Brookeborough: That is rather a difficult one, isn't it.

Sayers: Could I suggest one?

Brookeborough: Yes.

Sayers: I am not sure that history wouldn't say that in getting self-determination under the Ireland Act you brought off a great thing for Northern Ireland.

Brookeborough: Yes, that's quite flattering. . . . but it probably is true. It does not rest with Westminster, it rests with us now. . . .

Coulter: During your trips to America you were renowned for the way you handled these picket men.

Brookeborough: Well, they only caught me once, coming out, you may remember, at Philadelphia.

Sayers: Very well, sir.

Brookeborough: One dear lady smiled at me as I blew her a kiss and she did the same to me. She had a nasty, rude remark on her banner, but still it didn't seem to affect her. It was a very futile thing: they generally gave the job to the unemployed.

Sayers: What would you hope to see in the next twenty-five years in Northern Ireland, apart from solving unemployment?

Brookeborough: I'd hope to see greater industrial expansion, and I'd hope to see, when I go round the country, prosperity on every farm.

Sayers: And the growth, I suppose, of what has been called this Ulster consciousness?

Brookeborough: Yes.

Sayers: Pride in country?

Brookeborough: Which I think exists now.

The air of genuflection in the presence of blue blood and the inability to conceive of leaders coming from other than the exclusive circle of Ulster's few 'landed families' should not disguise the fact that Sayers had in the course of a non-political interview pushed beyond his brief. Twice he offered the Prime Minister the opportunity to declare himself on the Catholic question, but in both instances Brookeborough restricted his stated ambition to the solution of the unemployment problem.

Yet significantly it was to Brookeborough that Sayers looked to reassert decency and tolerance in the face of rowdy reaction. But this Unionism of the quality, whose 'British values' he propagated in the *Telegraph*, had never been as established as he thought. Its proponents had been lulled into a false sense of security, in part because they were too snugly cocooned in what to them were the key citadels—the cabinet, the upper civil service, Westminster, and exclusive, highly pleasurable retreats such as the Regional Committee of the National Trust. Intellectual condescension and occasionally sheer snobbery ensured that none of them were closely affected by the appeal of the 'Border Unionism' that was so strongly represented on the back benches at Stormont and at the party's headquarters at Glengall Street.

Brookeborough had no such illusions, and on 21 November in his Fermanagh heartland he reassured his following that 'our principles are not elastic' and that 'there is no use blinking [at] the fact that political differences in Northern Ireland closely follow religious differences'. It was with some desperation that Sayers chose to interpret this declaration as equivocal. In his leader of 23 November he attempted to shore up the moderates' position without alienating Brookeborough. Yet, for all the coded language and the use of Carson as a legitimising icon, in a manner typical of a one-party state, he did not pull any punches. If the piece demonstrated anything, it was his growing ascendancy within the *Belfast Telegraph*.

Belfast Telegraph, 23 November 1959

TIME FOR REFLECTION

The unity and strength of the Ulster Unionist Party is one of the most remarkable political phenomena of the century. Over a span of more than fifty years no other party in the English-speaking world has had such unwavering popular support.

The secret of this success is not alone that Northern Ireland looks to Unionism as its means of self-preservation. In itself the party represents an almost unique fusion of people and interests which has enabled it to form an undivided and invincible front.

There are in the wide embrace of Unionism men and women of Conservative, Liberal, and even Labour opinions, employers and workers, rich and poor, townsmen and countrymen, Orangemen and non-Orangemen.

The essence of all this is more than common purpose. It is balance, the same quality that has been struck between the fervour of patriotic emotion and the deliberate good sense that is a native characteristic.

In the past few weeks something of this equilibrium has tended to be lost.
. . .
Many will agree with Lord Brookeborough that speculation about former Nationalists becoming members of the Unionist Party is academic and a remote contingency. Yet the raising of this question, untimely as it may have been, has provoked the more urgent one of whether the party is to declare itself wholly sectarian in character. . . .

For it must be recognised that by such an action it would become the only party of its kind in the Commonwealth, and one divorced from the whole of British political tradition. The consequences would inevitably be highly injurious to Northern Ireland and its reputation in the eyes of the world.

Nor has such exclusiveness ever been an inviolable tenet of Unionist faith. Circumstances of time and place and society may have suggested it, but it was not so before 1920 when people of every creed could be found among those who resisted Home Rule.

The executive committee of the Unionist Party, in its carefully worded statement of policy and aims, has said that these are as laid down by Carson and Craig. It is well to remember that it was Carson who said in his farewell to the Council on 4 February 1921: 'From the outset let us see that the Catholic minority have nothing to fear from the Protestant majority. Let us take care to win all that is best among those who have been opposed to us in the past.'

Carson was the last man to have been blind to the grave perils of Roman authoritarianism, against which Northern Ireland must be constantly watchful and forearmed. But it is clear that he could acknowledge individual Catholics in Ireland as being as loyal to the Crown and constitution as their co-religionists in England.

His call to the Unionists of his time was therefore one of statesmanship, and if the party should be forced by current events to impose a new and formal bar to its enlistment, that statesmanship will have been abdicated.

With it could go much of the balance and the cohesion that experience has shown to be vital to the party's well-being and progress. . . .

However veiled the threat, Sayers's assertion that a return to official sectarianism—so often a rallying-cry in the past—would now isolate Northern Ireland, within the United Kingdom, as well as undermining the pan-class alliance upon which the Unionist supremacy depended, represented the opening salvo in the coming struggle. That within fifteen years Sayers's dire predictions were to have been proved correct was, on the other hand, far from obvious at the time. In 1959 few of the moderates had ever intended that this affair should end in a challenge to the Prime Minister, and, with Terence O'Neill, then Minister of Finance, calling for party unity, the protest caved in. Reporting back to Conolly Gage after his regular lunch with Maginess in the Midland Hotel, Sayers put a brave face on events.

Letter to Conolly Gage, 2 December 1959

My dear Judge,
I have delayed replying to your letter of 23 November, which again fortified me very much, so that I could bring you up to date with events.

I had lunch yesterday with Brian Maginess, and his account of the meeting of the standing committee on Friday was encouraging. Clarence Graham made a bold statement, and in Brian's opinion ninety per cent of the meeting was with him.

Towards the end, however, Faulkner intervened to say that if a resolution was passed, it would tend to drive a wedge between the party and the Orange Order—as if the wedge was not there already! Accordingly, no vote was taken, and no statement was issued to the press, and I am sorry to say that the political correspondents in their reports did not quite show the strength of the feeling against declaring the party doors closed to Roman Catholics. Maginess and, I think, Graham are regretting that something was not done officially to make this clear.

By now there is certainly a fairly general desire to allow the controversy to cool off. But it is liable to come into the open again when the Grand Lodge meets next week and must endorse the statement of the Grand Master, although it is just possible that someone (which should be the PM) will intervene to see that a loophole is left, if only for individual Orangemen like myself, who will insist on the right of private judgement.

Maginess and I agreed, however, that it will not be easy to reactivate the moderate policy we have been advancing. We shall have to be quiet for a little and look out for an opportunity to get things moving again.

I should have said that David Campbell [MP for S Belfast] and the Ulster members at Westminster were at the meeting, and that Campbell would have spoken if the tide had not been running so favourably. But I confess that I am a little tired of hearing all the people who would speak if . . . Even so, I feel vindicated to the extent that the party at large is really sensible, and that these dangers would not arise if there was better management at Glengall Street. The party will not be on a right footing until the offices there and the functions of the Chief Whip are reformed—and the 'Boss', William Douglas [Secretary to the Unionist Council], passes from the scene! . . .

If well-drafted euphemisms could keep Sayers's party loyalties intact, those to the Orange Order would prove more difficult to save. Sir George Clark's stark rejection placed Sayers in an acute dilemma. Again he looked to the Prime Minister to moderate the official line – and again he looked in vain.

Letter to Conolly Gage, no date [c. 9 December 1959]

. . . You will have seen last night's *Telegraph*, and I am sending you also a copy of today's *Newsletter* to bring you up to date with the situation.

I am very much afraid that the Prime Minister failed to rise to the occasion at the Grand Lodge. His speech seems to me to have been a repudiation of those who are trying to think intelligently about the future of the party, and so long as he will not give a lead it is harder than ever for others to speak freely.

To write now is to challenge the Prime Minister himself, and that makes reasonable discussion more than ever difficult.

The Grand Lodge meeting seems to have been quiet enough, and the only point of interest is that the resolution did not repeat exactly Tony Clark's words about Roman Catholics. To that extent it has been realised that he went too far. But what are we to do when some of the people who supported Clarence Graham at the standing committee also supported Clark at the Grand Lodge.

Thank you for showing me Campbell's letter, which I have destroyed. He, of all people, should be able to put over to the PM what reasonable people are thinking, for I am sure that Basil simply doesn't understand what is going on.

I notice you are going to write to Burdge [a leading Orangeman and Secretary of the Grand Lodge of Ireland]. The rumour is that he drafted Clark's speech, which was afterwards reinforced by Douglas at Glengall Street. Certainly I hardly think Burdge is on the side of the angels!

Where we go from here I don't know, and it would be good to have your advice.

With best wishes,
Yours sincerely,
John E. Sayers

Undoubtedly Sayers had misjudged the mood of the party. It was typical of him that he should attach so much weight to the support of the Westminster MPs and their friends for Sir Clarence Graham's stand. They may have been congenial company, but they could never have moved a Prime Minister in thrall as much to Fermanagh as to Glengall Street. Nor had they the resolve for revolt, although (to be fair) they were wholly unprepared for the hostility that overwhelmed what they had held to be orthodoxy. Sayers's resignation from the Orange Order was the gesture of a man of principle, but it didn't hide the fact that, with the Prime Minister siding with reaction, the moderates could only beat a tactical retreat.

Letter to Conolly Gage, 29 December 1959

My dear Conolly,

I am so sorry not to have written this before. Christmas was a crescendo of events, and I could not get down to writing a considered letter.

I value very much what you have said, and agree wholehcartedly on your long-term proposals. Throughout the campaign we have been conducting in the *Telegraph* it has been our desire to strengthen the party and its good name in the interests of good government, and that still comes before our naturally liberal ideas on reaching out to the minority.

My great fear, intensified by the partisanship of the past month, is that the best people in Northern Ireland are going to shun politics, and that the Unionist Party will be reduced to a Tammany Hall. Already parliament is very poorly representative of Ulster abilities, and, as you know, we are not sure where to look for another Prime Minister. In a few years' time we may even be casting about for a reputable cabinet.

I had a visit from Phelim O'Neill [N.I. MP for N. Antrim] last Thursday, and as you might expect he is terribly exercised. He is highly intelligent and takes an antiseptic view, and to hear him speak I thought that the party was sick indeed! Unfortunately he has not the common touch and, I am afraid, will not be very influential. He agreed with me that the first thing to be done is to mobilise as much backing as possible for Clarence Graham at the Unionist Council meeting in March. There is some talk about him being removed – what a blot on us this would be! – but even if that is not done, it would be well to produce a strong show of support.

I have also been talking again to Brian Maginess, who is worried about his personal position. I have urged on him not to think of resigning, but it is highly likely that he will be offered a county court judgeship, and in his own interests I think he must take it. He cannot hope to become a High Court judge, and in a new administration might well find himself without a job. His problem and mine is how to show that the issue has not been resolved, and it is doubly difficult because anything we say now can be construed as an attack on the Prime Minister. However, I am planning a New Year leader in which to make the point. 1960 is the fortieth anniversary of the Government of Ireland Act, and a good opportunity to inspect the course.

Brian and I also discussed how to bring home to the Prime Minister that he must give greater heed to some of the moderates in the party, and pay less deference to the extremists. But David Campbell has failed to do it, and one or two others I have heard of have attempted it without much success.

The Prime Minister, I fear, either cannot see what is involved or, as you suggest, is now reluctant to face the music. We thought of [Sir Anthony] Babington [formerly Lord Justice of Appeal for N.I.], and even the Lord Chief Justice [Lord Macdermott], and I felt that a letter from you might have carried weight. What do you think?

Incidentally, I wonder if I might have your permission to let Brian Maginess read your letter to me.

Don't think that I am not without hope of better days. William Douglas cannot last long at Unionist headquarters, and once he has gone it may be possible to create a better spirit.

As you will have seen, Faulkner has been hoisted to Home Affairs, and Topping has left politics altogether, and these are the two who have been the most long-tongued of the Unionist policy-makers.

Which I think rather goes to prove the point that the heart of the party is sound, and that we are in our present condition only because of the demagogic weaknesses of the few. . . .

I agree that Cyril Nicholson should never have been passed over. This again was due to the Prime Minister taking flight from the proposition that two of the High Court judges should be Catholics. It was a sad blow to Cyril, who is a very good friend of mine. . . .

The acerbic reference to Brian Faulkner illustrated that Sayers's stand was beginning to cost friends. He had always been a great enthusiast for Faulkner's campaign to develop Ulster's industries, and from time to time both families met socially. But the 1958 election and then this dispute soured the relationship, and although a reconciliation was quickly effected over the dinner-table, there was never again to be the same trust. The affair also revealed Sayers's reluctance to break with the party. To do so would, of course, have hurt his uncle and also ended treasured hopes of continuing the family tradition in the editorial chair. In any case he was never an instinctive rebel. However, to choose to stay within the fold and seek progressive reforms through the party left Sayers with few opportunities in the short term. A lengthy analysis from Conolly Gage only confirmed that the moderates could for the meantime only concentrate on survival.

Conolly Gage to Sayers, 20 January 1960

My dear John,
Thank you for your letter. . . . I entirely agree with you that the heart of the party is sound. Indeed, I would go so far as to say that the great majority of responsible people in Ulster are alarmed at the thought of an RC being excluded from the party simply because they are RC; and that, if they were made to think about it, the majority of the humbler party members would take the same view. It is only a vociferous minority who take the opposite view.

The difficulty, as I see it, is that the PM, so far as he can be understood, has come down on their side. That creates the situation that anyone who persists in Portstewart views too openly is liable to be labelled a rebel. While sometimes this is no harm, generally speaking in politics a person labelled as an open rebel – no matter how good his cause – does not get far. . . .

Apart from this, the crux of the matter is the PM. If he can be got to support BM and CG, everything would be well. But here I am frankly despondent. I don't think the L[ord] C[hief] J[ustice] would or could in his position take any part in the matter. Even if he did, I doubt if he could persuade the PM to do anything else. Tony Babington would, I am sure, try, and I shall write to him if you wish, but I doubt if he will be able to influence the PM. Your mention of Phelim O'N[eill] made me wonder if his father [Lord Rathcaven] might not have more influence. . . . BB had a very high regard for him. . . .

Finally, may I say that I found your leader excellent, and I think you are right to keep the matter alive in this way until the moment presents itself.

The portrayal of Brookeborough almost in terms of an absolute monarch who merely had to issue the word and the unthinking masses would follow was of a piece with the belief that the voices of Protestant 'reaction' must be a minority simply because they lacked coherence and respectability. But then the alternative – that Sayers and his friends had merely been fellow travellers in a sectarian party – was too awful to contemplate. To Sayers, the whole episode had proved a salutary experience and it led him to reconsider his political objectives. Now the priority lay in reshaping the Unionist movement through the revitalisation of its creed. The next decade would see if ideas (or even newspapers) had the power to break the political mould of Ulster.

4   From Tactical Retreat to Terence O'Neill

If the débâcle of November 1959 had found Sayers guilty to some degree of taking too metropolitan a view of provincial politics, it was not from want of exposure to the Ulster beyond the capital. As early as 1954 Sayers had become involved with the highly popular radio programme, 'Your Questions', on which he joined a panel that toured the province answering questions from local audiences. Since his colleagues included Charles Brett [prominent solicitor and NILP supporter], Jim Beckett [Professor of Irish History at Queen's] and J. J. Campbell [lecturer at St Mary's] , this was an attempt by the producer, John Boyd, to create a civilised framework in which politics could be debated in Northern Ireland without descending into ritual abuse. For all the intention that Sayers, Brett and Campbell would represent the three main parties, there could be no denying that this was company more reflective of dinner parties in South Belfast. Nevertheless, Sayers found it a liberating experience to escape the chores of the office and exchange ideas with like-minded souls on the long car journeys to country towns in the west. Invariably such occasions encouraged comforting impressions of prevailing reasonableness, which now with hindsight may appear hopelessly misleading. Yet there is a vigour and a lack of complacency about the debate that suggest that liberal ideals had some appeal outside Queen's University.

'Your Questions', 100th Edition, Northern Ireland Home Service, 9 May 1960

JJ Campbell: The majority of us here do not want sectarian bitterness. . . . I think that the press should cease to take note and publish accounts of bitterness in speeches whether they come from politicians or anyone else. I think, for example, that a man of God, a clergyman of the Christian church . . . who contributes to bitterness in our midst, is a man who should not be noticed by any newspaper . . . and then we will cut out sectarianism. (*Applause*)

Sayers: Well really, this is the first time that I have known my friend, Campbell, to be so facile. Let me answer first for newspapers. Our duty is to report what exists, and I don't think that any good is done for Ireland by suppressing people who express themselves in a bitter way. I think that is merely disguising the situation. But to look at this thing more broadly, I think he is also facile in saying that sectarianism has merely to be cut out. I can only quote the example of the Republic of Ireland, which represents the ideal of the Nationalist Party in Northern Ireland, and it professedly lays down that it is a Catholic Ireland. Now there's sectarianism for you. And my answer to this question before I heard Campbell speak was to say that the English constitution names no religion but produces a society and an ideal in society of social and economic betterment, and that, I think, is all that you need!

Campbell: But I think that this question refers to Northern Ireland and what can be done in Northern Ireland.

The historian JC Beckett then intervened to win loud applause for his suggestion that sectarianism would only disappear when all political parties tried to recruit from all denominations.

Campbell: I would like to come back for a moment to the press's responsibility in this matter—and Sayers seems to disclaim responsibility. But when you get people whose only aim in making bitter and sectarian speeches is to get into the press in order to get themselves noticed, then I think that those people should not be noticed. . . . By the way I am not in any way casting any reflection on Sayers in this matter. (*Laughter*)

Sayers: Well, I am very glad to hear that, and perhaps I may reassure Campbell if I tell him that we know a man who is interested in self-advertisement as much as he does. But that is not to say that it isn't our duty still to show that in Northern Ireland there is a range of opinion that goes all the way from black to white.

Campbell: He means from Orange to Green, of course.

In answer to a question on the Sharpville massacre and the conflicting press reports on the number killed, Sayers stressed first the twin problems of government repression and journalistic bias – a problem not unknown in Ireland.

Sayers: This is a story we journalists tell about the three papers in Dublin. *The Irish Times* reported on a girl that was killed in an accident on a railway in England, and the heading in the *Irish Times* said: 'Train kills girl'. And the *Irish Independent* said: 'Irish girl killed by train'. And the *Irish Press* said: 'English train kills Irish girl'. (*Loud laughter*)

And then more seriously,

. . . It is suggested in some quarters that to write about the level of unemployment [in Northern Ireland] or about the fact that incomes are lower is disloyalty, that this . . . is letting Northern Ireland . . . and the government down. I would never accept that. We must be frank, we must always be asking ourselves can we do more. . . . But side by side with that, it is right to say that we must always make known that there are people in Northern Ireland ready to work.

As this suggests, if Sayers represented anybody, it was the world of newspapers. At his office in the *Belfast Telegraph* overlooking Royal Avenue he sat where his father and uncle had sat before him, very much in his element. Beneath him in a warren of nooks and crannies all was frenzied activity in the daily battle against deadlines. Despite years in the profession, Sayers never lost that sense of excitement (mingled with some relief) on hearing the presses rumble as the first edition went into print. He may have been the last of the writing editors, but there was nothing old-fashioned in his fascination with journalism. If his conversation was peppered with anecdotes from the past, in his determined efforts to improve the training of journalists he had his eye firmly on the future. Consequently, among the young reporters of talent, whose careers he promoted, there was universal respect for the relentlessly high standards he demanded of himself. And also of them. Nothing caused greater anxiety than finding on their desk a note simply saying: 'Please see me—J.E.S.'. Such brusque missives were typical of a regime that, however paternal in spirit, was decidedly formal, even austere in reality. As with many autocrats, Sayers had very little in the way of small talk and, sailing preoccupied along the corridors with arms full of papers, he not infrequently cut colleagues dead. Not surprisingly, many saw this along with his anglicised accent, as pure snobbery, and perhaps it may have been, but it also reflected that he was from a generation that expected chiefs to command. He was as much disturbed by their modish disrespect towards the establishment as they were by his references to 'lesser gentry'—a distinction that meant little to them. When a reporter filed a story on a car crash in which the injured included some 'soldiers' out with the daughters of one of Ulster's leading families, Sayers exploded: 'Good God! Those girls would not go out with soldiers'; and with a flick of his pen he substituted 'escorted by officers'.

And yet, for all these differences of taste, he encouraged at the level of ideas an independence of mind among his journalists that was certainly rare in Ulster. Not that he ever abdicated his editorial responsibility, and *any* restraints, of course, irked ambitious reporters. Nevertheless, believing that if Ulster had a future it lay with the young, Sayers was determined to give these journalists their head. Consequently, many new recruits would find themselves drafted in as leaderwriters. Arriving at around ten in the morning in dire need of caffeine, they would stare weakly at the national headlines until Sayers appeared at the door. 'I think that we can take Terence up on his speech,' he would say, and with that the editorial conference was over. O'Neill's oration would usually have been delivered the night before somewhere in the furthest reaches of the province, and it could be safely assumed that the apprentice journalist would know absolutely nothing about it. There then ensued a frantic scramble of research and writing, with copy-boys for ever at one's elbow waiting for the next paragraph. After this there would in time come the summons to Sayers's office. There they would find him leaning back in his chair, peering at the proofs before swooping to correct grammatical errors with an elegant flourish of the pen and much headmasterly tut-tutting: 'Oh no, John [Fairleigh]. Dear me, John'.

'There are no sacred cows at the *Telegraph*,' he would proudly proclaim, although all knew that, as David Gilliland put it, 'any word of criticism of Harland & Wolff . . . would lead to the rack and thumbscrew, operated personally by John E'. Equally, insiders would chuckle quietly over the Batemanesque possibilities on the day that there was no reference to Professor Charles Carter in the 'Chichester' social column. But such trivialities aside, none doubted that the editor was committed to a radical critique of Unionism. Sayers saw his mission as one of revitalising a ruling creed through the encouragement of economic initiative, the spread of education and a far greater emphasis on the winning over of the minority to the state. None of this, however, would lessen the need for the traditional moral values that to Sayers were so characteristic of Ulster; values for which, as this leader suggested, the Orange Order could still serve as a guardian.

Belfast Telegraph, 12 July 1960

1690 AND 1960

On another Twelfth of July the similarity of these dates gives food for thought. If 1690 symbolises the day, what has 1960 to say to Northern Ireland and to the Orange Order that is so tightly woven into its fabric.

The change of which we must be most conscious is surely social. Ulster today has a large measure of prosperity, and the evidences are more than ever seen when the people are celebrating the summer holiday.

It speaks for the strength of Orangeism that softer living has done little to reduce its appeal, and that it remains undrugged by what has been dubbed the 'phenobarbitone politics' of the times. We can be sure that the Order will continue to be one of the pillars of our society. In this island there cannot but be a vital place for a well-organised defence of Protestantism. . . .

Despite all that may be said on today's platforms of the merits of Protes-tantism, there are few who will not know that religious conviction, even in Northern Ireland, is losing ground.

We have the word of the clergy of all denominations that many Orangemen, faithful enough to their lodges, have ceased to go to church. In that they are no more than representative of a broad section of the British people.

To this challenge of materialism and false values we believe the Orange Order could provide a more effective answer than it does. Through it true religion could have an added means of expression; by it could be given that united Christian witness which the churches are seeking and without which all of them may fail.

Who can deny that in 1960 the most crying of all our needs is a spiritual reawakening? And if the Orange Order was to share in that revival by putting first the religious fruits of the Reformation, who could measure the real and uplifting power of its political influence?

At a more practical level, it was the need for an economic reawakening that was more pressing. Although there had been some improvement in unemployment and output, the shipbuilding and linen industries on which Ulster had relied for so long now seemed in terminal decline. Reluctant to take tough decisions on businesses whose workforce tra-ditionally formed the backbone of working-class Unionism in Belfast, the government resolved to be irresolute. Whereas Sayers had previ-ously been among the first to defend Ulster to the hilt, by July 1960 the *Telegraph* was running a leader entitled 'Can nothing be done?', scath-ing in its criticism of government inertia; and with the USA on the verge of electing John F. Kennedy the Unionist old guard seemed very old indeed. Speaking on 'Ulster Commentary' (1 Nov. 1960), Sayers took a broader perspective and chose to attribute the leadership's paralysis to its preoccupation with political strife. A consequence of this was the stifling of debate where 'too often criticism is confused with heresy: the party line is a strict one and there is not over and above it any high criterion of public conscience or touchstone of wisdom and folly'. Significantly, now he linked economic progress and the transfor-mation of Northern Ireland into 'all we want it to be' to the 'harnessing of all sections of the community to the task'.

In such a situation, the role of education became paramount, and Sayers dedicated a talk in celebration of the state's fortieth anniver-sary to this theme.

'1920 to 1960', Northern Ireland Home Service, 20 December 1960

. . . What have we to show for the millions and millions of pounds that Northern Ireland has given to education over forty years? Not in turning out people for the labour market, to earn their livelihood, but in training them to take their rightful place in society, better to live with their neighbours, to behave as responsible, co-operative citizens?

That we *have* learned there is no doubt. The war has taught its own lessons; Northern Ireland, for all that politicians, north and south of the border, may say to the contrary, is in no imminent danger of being overthrown; the opportunity to work has proved the best outlet for human energies. There is more wisdom too: a livelier knowledge that violence is no solution to Irish quarrels. If that were not so, the IRA might in the last few years have plunged us back into civil strife. All this we have to be gratified by and proud of.

But I wonder still what true education—and I mean not only from the schools and the university, but from the churches and the press and the radio—is being accomplished, and particularly what fruits we are reaping from the great educational plan of 1947. . . . What more we can see in leadership, in the formation of public opinion, and in the working out of some common purpose among a people so much divided and separate from one another in character, belief and outlook?

I judge that, while we can feel a lightening of a once oppressive and dangerously explosive atmosphere, there is not yet that complete tolerance, that self-examination, that freedom of expression and of intercourse on which we must surely base the next forty years. . . .

But . . . I do not despair. The truth, you know, is that in our individual lives forty years is a long time, but in the history of a country it is no more than the span of a hand. I prefer to think that in the fifteen years since the war we have begun an advance on a broad front, and that that advance will increase in momentum. So that perhaps I, as a so-called child of the revolution of 1920, will, before *my* life ends, know Northern Ireland less for its division and its tensions than for its pursuit of happiness and the art of living.

Hindsight has proved cruel to such hopes and brought into doubt the prevailing belief in the power of education single-handedly to mould opinion. But such thoughts also demonstrated Sayers's fond admiration for educational institutions, especially Queen's University. He was highly sensitive over his own lack of a university training, and undoubtedly this explained in part his deference to academics and his policy of appointing graduates. But Queen's also was a source of hope where the young of both communities mingled and the fount of new ideas. Like the *Telegraph*, it was engaged, he felt, in the historic mission to guide the Ulster people out of the seventeenth century. Spreading this gospel lead him to address the Irish Association—a body founded in the late thirties to foster better relations between north and south. Calling for 'a bolder effort by the Unionist Party to attract an even wider support for the British connection', he declared that 'there could be no moral justification for any policy which discouraged Catholics from taking a fuller part in the public life of the province. . . . The political and social challenge of the 1960s for Northern Ireland . . . [is] . . . to take account of the great influences for peace and co-operation, which are sweeping through the world and make sure that we are not left behind.' (*BT*, 26 Jan. 1961)

As an indication of Sayers's growing appreciation of Catholic issues, he commissioned Dennis Kennedy to write two articles highlighting housing discrimination in Fermanagh. However, there was little prospect of improving community relations while the border remained the staple diet of political rhetoric both within Ulster and in its dialogue with the South. A spat between Lemass and Brookeborough over the Taoiseach's proposal for an all-Ireland free trade zone led Sayers to reiterate the cost of partition.

'Ulster Commentary', Northern Ireland Home Service, 21 March 1961

. . . There is a sense in which our politicians say: 'There is no Irish problem. It was all settled in 1921.' I do not see it in that way. To most people relations between North and South and relations between Protestant and Roman Catholic are just problems to live with; very few have reached the point of seeing them as problems to be solved.

For even if Ireland should be used to lagging behind the rest of the world, we cannot deny that this is an age when racial and international barriers are one by one being broken down. It is an age of common markets, of countries forming themselves into communities, even those who have long been enemies, and communities in which national sovereignties are being submerged. In the same way neighbourliness has become the bond between white and black, and Britain is engaged in the most widespread integration and exchange of people and ideas and teaching and knowledge that the Commonwealth has ever seen.

And let it be said also that the Irish Republic, at UNO and in the Congo, has emerged from the past and is playing its part on the world stage. All this—and yet between two governments less than a hundred miles apart there is contact of only the most intermittent kind.

I present these as the facts: I do not say that they can easily be altered. They rest on political foundations that I know, and you know, go very deep down. . . .

All that I will say is this. Men who have always stood for a united Ireland cannot well be expected suddenly to renounce their instinctive beliefs. But the time could come when that instinctive aspiration could be reconciled with a more normal association between North and South as neighbours, and a greater acknowledgement of essential differences—and essential needs—than we have yet seen. Yet true recognition will not come until the forty-year-old process by which people North and South knew less and less about each other is reversed. The state of Ireland 1,500 years after the death of St Patrick is that while religions and loyalties are still profoundly dividing, the deepest division is created by ignorance and the absence of practically all contact between ordinary people. Until that meeting is established not even all the trade of Araby will bring about the constitutional détente that we would hold to be the key to a future in keeping with contemporary world opinion.

A friend of mine in Cork said to me the other day: 'There is only one way to deal with the border – forget about it.' The tragedy is that the border cannot be forgotten so long as in Tyrone and Fermanagh one explosion follows another, and this bridge and that customs post is added to the ruins of the fondest hopes....

Sayers, however, had his own distractions. By 1960 it was apparent that death duties were compelling the Baird family to consider selling the *Telegraph*. After early meetings in August, negotiations began in earnest in November at the Donaghadee home of the entrepreneur Cyril Lord. The prospective buyer was the Canadian press magnate Roy Thomson. Such was his reputation that many feared for the paper's local identity, high standards, and especially for the 'quiet, liberalising revolution' (*Irish Times*, 18 May 1961) that Sayers had wrought. Throughout the spring of 1961 there were regular threats of industrial action, and on top of this the Bairds and the Thomson organisation were feuding in the High Court. Sayers's days were spent oscillating between meetings to pacify the NUJ and flying off to London for pow-wows at Thomson House with Denis Hamilton. Small wonder that it took Yuri Gagarin's expedition into space to remind him that there was a world outside. The Twelfth, however, brought him back to Earth.

Letter to Conolly Gage, 12 July 1961

My dear Conolly,
It takes the Twelfth to remind me of my duty—and my manners. I am sorry indeed to have been so long in replying to your letter. For part of the time since May I have been away from the office, and for the rest have been very preoccupied with our future.

At the moment, at long last, there are attempts at a settlement. In fact, if the parties could get over the always difficult hurdle of costs, it might be all over and we could be making our new start under the Thomson banner. I must say all my contacts with him and his people have been agreeable enough. I don't think the character of the paper will undergo any radical change, and we shall certainly benefit from more expert management....

Not being a complete believer in government remedies, I am not over-hopeful for the future, more especially as we are running into another economic headwind.

I do think that we should be given the final benefit of some kind of tax relief—for new industries, anyhow—but we will never solve the problem until there is a renewal of local enterprise.

The great failures of Brookeborough's regime have been that he has not brought better men into politics, and that his government has not succeeded in making people do more for themselves. I don't mean by exhortation, but by fostering or sponsoring a growth of local financial institutions.

And now, of course, we have the Common Market! You will see from tonight's paper how, like the clouds, it overhung 'the day'. I doubt our people are less concerned about Europe—and Australia—as about an Éire that would be more or less a partner. But these are changes that we shall have to face, and I am just sorry that people here have not had their minds better prepared. There are going to be some shocks and cause for sensible readjustment. If we don't have that, the results could be some outbursts of feeling. I just hope that Lemass will not start crowing, for that would be most injurious to the whole country.

I have always been able to feel that I could put our affairs in a historical perspective. For instance, economically I think we are seeing the gap between the end of the dominance of the linen industry, and even of ship-building, and the beginning of a new era already being founded by our new industries and due to be reinforced by a rebirth of commercial adventure at home. But this Common Market is so vast a project and has so many implications that I find it almost impossible to put it into place.

Tomorrow I am fifty and I suppose the truth of the matter is that I am not as good as I was at keeping an open mind! However, I sense from some of the speeches a little spread of the spirit we have tried to create and encourage in the last few years, and that makes me feel that the job has been worth doing. . . .

Yours ever,
John

Rising to the daunting challenge of the EEC (on the day the Irish Republic applied for membership), Sayers tried in *The Round Table* to spread some more of the spirit of political imagination.

The Round Table, August 1961

. . . Northern Ireland, as much as the countries of the Commonwealth, is not a little afraid of where the British government may be leading it. On trade and industry it is half prepared to have to take the rough with the smooth; on the political implications of joining in the European Economic Community it is unready to face contact with a wider world in which British loyalties seem in a strangely disturbing process of change. When the Prime Minister of the Irish

Republic, Mr Lemass, can say—with something less than the true spirit of co-operation—that within the Common Market partition will be a patent absurdity, the majority of Ulstermen hear a call to the ramparts. . . .

In this debate Ulster has been made uncomfortably aware that it is a small place, and that the Irish problem is one of the least of those that the Common Market will either raise or settle. . . . The qualms that are now felt spring from the knowledge that great international forces are at work, and that even the United Kingdom cannot be certain of its future relationships. It may be a hard judgement that Lord Brookeborough and his colleagues have not educated their people in this new conception of world affairs, for Northern Ireland would not have preserved its integrity without constantly looking to its moat. But it may be pondered whether in the post-war era a broadening policy at home would not have produced greater strength and confidence of mind to enable Ulster to face as candidly as Mr Macmillan the choice of European integration and the prospect of an historic readjustment. A country that remains as divided against itself as Northern Ireland after forty years of self-government is hardly prepared to face co-operation with others. Allowing for the political necessity of moving slowly and of avoiding the kind of split that extreme Unionists never fail to threaten, the party has made no conscious effort to project its appeal to the whole population on the basis of the still growing evidence of the advantages of the British connection. Possibly it may now be realised that this is the time when every Catholic vote in favour of the constitution will count. The Minister of Education, Mr May, in his 'Twelfth' oration, made Protestant flesh creep with the statistic that nearly half the children in primary schools are Catholic. But it was hardly a cure for him to say that the Protestant birth rate must be raised. Ideas as much as numbers must guide the politics of the rest of the twentieth century, and Northern Ireland is clearly faced with a challenge to its inveterate mode of thinking. . . .

'We are grateful to anyone of any country who will come and start a new industry here,' the Minister [of Finance, Terence O'Neill] said, 'but unless local initiative takes more advantage of the facilities offered, then the Ulster people themselves will have to take a back seat and allow our province to be developed by the English, the Americans, the Germans, the Dutch, and possibly the Japanese.' With this threat of conquest, and the Common Market besides, Northern Ireland may indeed begin to wonder exactly where it stands.

As it was, at de Gaulle's insistence, the United Kingdom's application to join the Common Market came to nothing. Nevertheless, foreign development was providing quite a few shocks nearer to home.

Letter to Conolly Gage, 7 February 1962

My dear Conolly,
I am the most ungrateful of editors not to have replied to your last letters. Your card, for which also many thanks, has pricked my conscience.

I can only plead that we have been much buffeted by the wind of change. The Thomson management is in full control, and it has taken a great deal of getting used to. R. M. Sayers is retiring next month, and in anticipation we have a new general manager from Cardiff, David Thomas. I have become editor-in-chief, and on R.M.S.'s departure am to be a director, and will represent the paper out of doors. Not that the board ever meets or ranks a fee.

I cannot think what all this is doing to the spirit of Sir Robert Baird, but I have had to tell myself that change is inevitable, and that for the sake of the paper we must make the best of it. I cannot say that there has been interference with editorial policy, but the other influences are severe.

For instance, there is a great economy in newsprint, of which this week's adoption of a nine-column format is a reflection, and we are faced daily with the problem of getting into the paper all that we think it should carry. This, of course, can be a discipline, for we have long been accustomed to make rather an extravagant use of words. I just hope that the effect of these changes will not be to take away from our standing and our leadership of opinion. I should be glad, indeed, if you would tell me frankly how the paper is shaping.

I find Thomas an agreeable fellow with editorial sympathies, but the fact is that business policy is dictated from London, as you might guess if you have been looking at Roy Thomson on television. My verdict on him is that all big men like him are humbugs, but that he is not as big a humbug as most. Nevertheless, I miss the sentiment and sense of public service which should be actuating a local newspaper like the *Telegraph*. I know you will agree with me in that.

I am so glad you liked our editorials. Sometimes I feel we are getting too far ahead of public opinion, but, as you will judge from the debate on capital punishment, it is necessary that at least one paper here should be reaching out towards the future.

I am disappointed that Faulkner should have been so utterly uncompromising. He and Teddy Jones [N.I. M.P. for Londonderry City] are out of the Old Testament.

You will have seen that there is a shindy about appointing an expensive public relations officer in London to procure a better Ulster image. I cannot make them see that it is the rigid refusal to move with the times which harms us most.

Now we look forward to the general election. The party is undoubtedly going to take it very seriously this time. The feeling is that the Labour Party will either be wiped out or come back with eight seats. But I should say that the position will be largely unchanged.

Economically, we are really making progress and the shipyard slump has been surprisingly contained, so that I would not say that Labour has made any strong advance. I just hope that the Prime Minister will not listen to Glengall Street and try to climb on the back of the Covenant celebrations in September. That would be anachronistic indeed.

I have a suspicion, in fact, that he will go in May before he is met with the added complication of the Common Market.

Thank God the border trouble looks to be over—why Lemass did not do it long ago will be a lasting regret for all who love the country.

I am being accused of starting the election campaign by publishing our series on the Prime Minister—in fact, for that reason we wrote Monday's leader just to show that we still have an independent cast of mind!

I hope you will like Flackes's account, which is a straight narrative and it is not at all intended to put the man on a pedestal.

When the election comes, we shall be trying again, while supporting the government as we gladly do, to hold the ring and to try to make Unionism in practice what I believe it to be in spirit. . . .

Thank you again for being so reliable a 'touchstone'. It means a great deal to me.

All good wishes,
Ever,
Jack

The reference to the Old Testament related to the cabinet's decision to execute a man who in a drunken fit had killed his wife. It was the first execution for eighteen years, but it served as another illustration to Sayers of how Ulster was diverging from opinion in the rest of the United Kingdom. Others were to follow, and particularly galling was Brian Faulkner's electoral law reform which, for fear of losing the 'Maiden City' of Derry, shied away from adopting the British franchise for local government. Nevertheless, if these seemed missed opportunities, there were for the moderate Unionists plenty of grounds for optimism. A Catholic lawyer found herself 'flabbergasted' to win the Queen's University seat for the Liberals. In Belfast the Lord Mayor broke tradition to pay a courtesy call on the new Roman Catholic Bishop of Down and Connor, Dr Philbin. And most extraordinary of all were the talks held later in the year between the Orange Order and nationalist groups to discuss their differences. Even in Brian Maginess's Iveagh constituency, which in the two previous elections had required Brookeborough's personal intervention to keep Protestant extremists in order, the mood seemed to have changed.

Letter from Brian Maginess, 23 May 1962

Royal Courts of Justice
Ulster, Belfast

Dear Jack,
Thanks very much for your letter and your congratulations.

I think that the organisation in Iveagh [electoral division in Co. Down] is very good and has been kept that way in recent years thanks largely to Clarence Graham and a number of other enthusiasts; and intending candidates from the opposition would be slow to tackle such a formidable proposition on that account.

Apart from that, such views as I express no longer meet the opposition they did at first. People, in my opinion, are coming round to our point of view, that in our community we should live in the present and for the future and that political animosities based purely on religious grounds have no place here.

There is a much better feeling among the different sections of the community, though it would be idle to pretend there was not still a considerable amount of distrust and suspicion remaining.

I think if we keep it up we can still do a lot to promote this feeling of goodwill and have all our people taking a pride in Ulster and working for the benefit of the whole community. You yourself, if I may say so, have made a very substantial contribution towards this end. . . .

Sincerely yours,
Brian

The election, when it came (31 May 1962), proved to be, in Brookeborough's glib phrase, 'a drawn match'. Notwithstanding this, the result was quite a rebuff to the Unionist establishment. Labour had retained its four seats and significantly increased its vote. In contrast, the Unionists had lost three seats since the previous election in 1958. It was perhaps a sign of the times when the Orange Order felt it necessary to declare that Orangemen were at perfect liberty to vote for Labour. Yet what most encouraged Sayers was the tone of a Unionist campaign in which 'its more demagogic voices [were] kept, like an awkward member of the family, in the kitchen'. But it all had too much the stamp of expediency to convince him that this was a change of heart.

Letter to Conolly Gage, 19 June 1962

Dear Conolly,
. . . I should have written before to thank you for your letter on the election. It was very good of you to remember that the *Telegraph* had an influence on the way in which the Unionist Party went into the campaign. I am told that Morris May was the strongest voice on the policy committee. What a great pity he isn't alive today.

I have tried to draw some conclusions in an article which you will see in the paper tonight, but I am not too confident that the party is really set on a new course. Possibly if Terence O'Neill was to take over, and Billy Douglas was to retire, we would see a real reorientation. . . .

Yours ever,
Jack

With the election of 1962 being fought on social and economic issues, and the defeat of the IRA through lack of minority support, Sayers saw glimpses of a new dawn. In this mood, it was inevitable that he should look favourably on the rise of Terence O'Neill. O'Neill symbolised planning, a youthful energy, an active executive, and above all a vision of a progressive and dynamic Ulster. Like Sayers, he stressed the importance of British standards and of Ulster's place in a wider world. Flattered by the regular consultations with O'Neill over lunch at the Ulster Club, Sayers took up the standard of Ulster's answer to John F. Kennedy.

Belfast Telegraph, 19 June 1962

IN SEARCH OF A NEW DYNAMIC

'We are strengthened and invigorated.' So Lord Brookeborough greeted the results of the general election. His feelings may also have been compounded by relief, but his government has undoubted reason to be fortified as it takes up a new mandate.

Yet the question over-hanging the parliament that is opened tomorrow is whether the Unionist Party as a whole has found the new dynamic it needs, and whether in 1967 it can contain another and possibly more critical Labour challenge.

Even now not all Unionists have realised the change in official attitudes which led the party to fight the election on its domestic record alone. More than half a century of exclusive claim to guardianship of the constitution ended when the Labour Party was given the tacit acknowledgement of equal democratic status. . . .

Certainly the Unionist Party has not been guilty of apostasy. In the past it was formed by Tories and Liberals in equal parts; for the future it has again to show that this union of the conservative and the radical can win the vote of the working man.

Not only the working man, but the young men and young women who know little of 1921, and who could be won by the Northern Ireland Labour Party's own brand of radicalism if they are not given an alternative.

What they must be offered—what they themselves must help to create—is a party concentrated not on loyalty or religion, but on making Northern Ireland a freer place to live in. . . .

The Minister of Finance said during the election that we should have the largest training scheme in Europe. But why 'should have'? For the government to say that this is its first priority in the new industries drive would be one of the strokes that Northern Ireland is waiting for.

With it—and possibly the Hall Committee will serve as midwife—could be a plan for management and the revival of private enterprise. What would serve Unionism better than the successful application of local capital to the provision of new employment and a wider extension of home ownership?

Even more embracing would be a reinvocation of Ulster pride on the lines eloquently drawn by Mr Brian Maginess. Not in the strength of its allegiance to the Crown, but in the further raising of the standard of living and the building up of a new society.

On the Minister of Health and Local Government especially is the onus of inspiring a new attack on the housing problem by slum clearance and redevelopment. Will he now bring in a planning bill that will convince young people that Ulster has a real design for the future? . . .

But not everyone will be convinced that a party so long set in its defensive ways has a genuine new faith. The conversion has to come from the top, and it will take time to reach the divisional associations and those on the touchline. . . .

Another leader now needs to be found, and in the new parliament, Common Market and all, nothing will be more important to Northern Ireland than the emergence of the man who will succeed Lord Brookeborough as Prime Minister.

Recently no one has shown more insight or looked further into the future than forty-seven year-old Captain Terence O'Neill. This parliament will show whether his is the age [with] the ability, and the persuasiveness to give Unionism the new purpose and expression called for by the nearness of a half-century of devolution and political experience.

This article was the opening shot in a campaign to promote O'Neill as Brookeborough's successor. Sayers had always praised O'Neill's 'buoyant budgets' and admired his international perspective gained through attendance at world conferences of the IMF. Like Sayers, O'Neill on visiting the United States had been very taken with the Scotch-Irish associations. Moreover, as a grandson of a Liberal viceroy of Ireland, and as a serving officer in the Irish Guards in the Second World War, O'Neill had just the Anglo-Irish credentials that appealed to Sayers. However, it took the Hall Report (23 Oct. 1962), with its damning condemnation of government timidity in the face of economic stagnation, and the publication two days later of Carter and Barritt's much-heralded (by the *Telegraph*) *The Northern Ireland Problem* to ensure that Brookeborough's days were numbered. In the following month O'Neill made his pitch for the leadership with his Pottinger speech, having already primed Sayers. For the latter, Pottinger was the yardstick or, as he rather tortuously insisted, the 'datum line' for moderate Unionism. To him, O'Neill now represented the philosophy and the style of the future, and he swung the *Telegraph* behind the 'new dynamic'. By 25 March 1963 illness had enabled the Prime Minister to retire with honour. While ministers spent the next twenty-four hours caballing over his successor, O'Neill was with the Governor accepting office. He then left for the privacy of his secretary's house to make his ministerial appointments. Only later—considerably later—was there time left to remember one of those who had prepared his way.

Letter from Terence O'Neill, Prime Minister of Northern Ireland, 13 April 1963

My Dear Jack,
I see with horror that your kind letter still remains unanswered. Please excuse scribble from home, where I am trying to catch up with my mail.

For the last twenty years Northern Ireland has been administered. I expect it will kick and scream before it will agree to be governed. Civil servants have been promoted either by age or because of their London connections— if the latter, they have tended to regard themselves as Whitehall officials temporarily resident in N[orthern] I[reland].

Lacking my predecessor's charm, and his ability to say with truth and sincerity that he hadn't the slightest idea what his backbenchers were talking about—I shall I am sure be in serious trouble before long!

With renewed thanks,
Terence

5   Struggling for the Soul of Ulster

O'Neill's arrival unleashed an expectation of change, which he did
little to defuse. Right from his earliest speeches outlining striking plans
for motorways, the busiest airport in the United Kingdom outside
London, and a new hospital at Londonderry—the most modern in
the British Isles—he heralded an age of triumphant progress in Ulster. It was also an age of 'planning' and Sayers was delighted to see
his friend Tom Wilson (Adam Smith Professor of Political Economy
at the University of Glasgow) commissioned to draw up an 'economic
plan' for the province. On top of this there were to be extensive slum
clearance schemes and the implementation of the Matthew Plan (including the creation of a new town in Co. Armagh). The intention was
not simply the modernisation of Ulster, for, as one senior civil servant reminisced, 'we did feel that we were changing the culture.' Talk
of new brooms also raised new possibilities in North–South relations.
After a cold war lasting forty years, such meetings were fraught with
danger. Robert Gransden, recently retired as Secretary to the Cabinet, pondered on some of the obstacles to an event whose symbolic
importance would stretch well beyond the province.

*Letter from Robert Gransden, formerly Secretary to the Cabinet, 18
September 1963*

My Dear Jack,
As you might expect I have followed with interest—and some trepidation—
the long-distance sparring between Lemass and O'Neill on the possibility of
co-operation between North and South.

It is time, in my view, that both sides stopped public utterances on the
subject. Each party knows where the other stands and should start from there.

You and your paper have with courage and wisdom spearheaded two
points: (1) the improvement internally of the attitudes of majority and minority groups; (2) the scope there could be for co-operation externally in
certain fields.

The second issue (with effect on the first) can only be tackled by people
who are prepared to examine problems realistically, which can be thwarted
and bedevilled by public statements attracting utterances from the diehards
on both sides. Hence my feeling of trepidation.

We now seem to have reached the point when some progress can be made. I am fully conscious of the difficulties, but I think it is necessary to proceed on the following basis:

(1) No question should be raised at this stage of a summit conference.
(2) S[outhern] I[reland] should not be singled out as the only party to make proposals—we should have our own to make.
(3) A private meeting—without prejudice or commitment—should take place between emissaries of both govts to consider whether there are *any* subjects of mutual interest which lend themselves for discussion— what are they and how would a co-operative effort on these matters improve relations between North and South and add to the well-being of the whole Irish community.
(4) Such a meeting should be promoted, without the searchlight of publicity on it, by 'diplomatic feelers' as to the acceptance of discussions.
(5) Our desire for improved relations should be made evident by making the approach diplomatically ourselves.
(6) If anything positive emerges from the meeting which I have suggested, ministerial talks would then follow, and a summit conference could take place for 'sealing' the agreements.
(7) A meeting between the two premiers, if it eventually took place even on a limited field of co-operative effort, would greatly enhance O'Neill's position externally (and I would hope internally as well) and would add enormously to N[orthern] I[reland]'s prestige.

As a postscript—there is no doubt of the feeling beyond our shores that we are inward-looking and that we should make an effort to 'shake hands' over some matters at any rate. The agreements which we have already reached (electricity, fisheries, transport, etc.) have never been highlighted, but if they were made today, they should be 'sealed' by inter-premier meetings.

This whole problem will be the touchstone of O'Neill's premiership, and N[orthern] I[reland] will be judged accordingly.

There are, of course, grave dangers if the process breaks down. What would be the effect internally, and would the result be a recrudescence of ill-feeling amongst our own people which would not be compensated by the goodwill we might have generated externally for making the attempt?

This emphasises my fear about publicity, and I'm sure Lemass would be realistic enough to accept the need for proceeding underground.

My apologies for inflicting all this on you, but I have admired the stand you have taken in leading our people into the sixties.

Warm regards,
Yours ever,
Rob Gransden

Such schemes were not utterly unrealistic. Indeed, at their first meeting (22 Nov. 1963) after his accession to Downing Street, Sir Alec

Douglas-Home suggested to O'Neill just such a meeting. If this was for the future, there were plenty of signs to encourage O'Neill to risk dialogue with Lemass. That summer had seen the flag flying at half-mast over Belfast City Hall on the death of Pope John XXIII. Sayers noticed a new mood too in the unprecedented response in Ulster to the assassination of John F. Kennedy, who as late as June had reaffirmed his Irish Catholic roots in his visit to Ireland and in his refusal of O'Neill's belated invitation to the North.

Letter to Conolly Gage, 30 November 1963

My dear Conolly,
In fact I did not write the leader you mention, but I appreciate your letter none the less. The author was our dear old senior leader-writer, Brownlow White, who is always at his best when looking at America. Alas, he is retiring in March, and I shall be left with no one with his vein of sentiment. The younger men do not have it, and I think we are the poorer for that reason. They also veer strongly to the left, which takes a bit of correcting sometimes.

I must say I have been struck by all the reaction here to the President's death. It was quite forgotten that he was a Catholic, so that tragedy as it was, his assassination would seem to have been another contribution to better feeling. It really is astonishing the way barriers are being broken down here. What disturbs me still is that more practical steps are not being taken to see how far people can be brought together in everyday affairs. I am planning an inquiry into this in the New Year. . . .

Best wishes,
Ever,
Jack

The first shot of this campaign appeared in his New Year's Day leader, 'Lift Up Our Eyes'. Typically, he highlighted the new premier's youthfulness and 'vigour' in order to emphasise the arrival of new order. Yet for all O'Neill's fine rhetoric, Sayers was disturbed lest 'the promise of material progress' prove the sum total of policy. 'A gesture to the Roman Catholic community would', he insisted, 'be in keeping with the growing understanding between the churches and towards the declaration that must come, that politics can no longer be subject to religious divisions.' Once again, the instrument of the required revolution in attitudes was to be education: 'not the avenue to careers, but education in the highest uses of intellect and emotion, in tolerance . . . and happier human relationships, in responsibility and service to others, pride of country, love of beauty.'

Sayers's concern for education gained an unexpected tribute with the award of an honorary D.Lit. from Queen's University. For him this was the supreme accolade. The night before it was announced he spent with friends at the theatre. During the interval he could not resist letting drop that he was expecting a pleasant surprise in the morning papers. When his guests assumed that this meant royal recognition, he retorted: 'Oh no ! Something far more important!' To one denied a university education it must have given particular pleasure—more so, as Sayers chose to interpret the honour as a public reassurance that he and his views were in the mainstream of the Unionist establishment.

Letter to Conolly Gage, 19 March 1964

My dear Conolly,
. . . Everyone has been extraordinarily kind about the honour, I am becoming reconciled to the assurances that Queen's has not after all gone overboard. But it is still a staggering surprise. . . .

The important thing is that it can be said to endorse our editorial policy, and I like to think what we try to do in maintaining a serious standard of journalism. I am just hoping that it will help some of the diehards to see that I am on the side of the angels!

I expect you will have read the leader I wrote on the eve of the Unionist Council. When I saw the serried ranks which never seem to change year after year, I felt it was a very pious exercise. Somebody must soon 'come out from among them'. But I fear it won't be Terence, who is fettered in many ways.

I was in Down Cathedral on Monday night to hear the Archbishop of Canterbury telling the congregation, among whom there must have been Orangemen, just how they ought to behave towards Roman Catholics. For the first time Ramsey really impressed me. On television he always strikes me as too churchy by half!

My remembrances to Mrs Gage.

Ever,
Jack

Soon after this the Prime Minister flew to the United States and secured interviews with Secretary of State, Dean Rusk, President Johnson, and the next best thing to J.F.K., his wife Jackie. On his arrival back in Belfast, he did little to hide his pride in his efforts to 'raise the level of appeal of Northern Ireland outside the province'. Later that night Sayers gave his assessment of O'Neill's first year in office. While his sympathies were obvious, he did use the broadcast to raise again his doubts over the substance of O'Neillism.

Crying in the wilderness

'The First Year'. Northern Ireland Home Service, 23 March 1964

... I don't think that enough attention has been paid to the quality of the new Prime Minister's speeches, apart from those in which he has announced new measures. These have been signpost speeches and often inspiring in their freshness. He has pictured Northern Ireland in a great age of reform; he has advocated a policy of scrap and build; he has made a call to youth, even at the risk of irreverence about the old men, one could say the time-servers, that he had met in his earlier days in politics. He has, if you like, rejected much of what was common currency in Northern Ireland for the past forty years. Yet it remains the case that no one can be entirely sure what he has meant by 'a unity of purpose' and 'a change of heart and spirit'. It would appear that these do not go beyond the effort that may be required to create a new physical environment. Certainly when it has come to speaking on the subject of political evolution, of communal relations, the Prime Minister's statements and those of his ministers have been much more muted. Co-operation between Protestants and Roman Catholics has rarely been spoken of explicitly: the stormy question of whether Catholics can be Unionists has been carefully kept out of sight. One could draw the conclusion that the government has been content to take the line that only a raising of the standard of living is required to keep the minority quiet.

Recent events have shown that that is a mistake. It is a fair reading of the situation that Nationalism has become more impatient because it has found that the new government offers no early action on what is called discrimination but which is often better called segregation. Even on so simple a matter as public appointments the past year has shown no response to the pleas that Catholics should be encouraged to take a more active part in public affairs.

The unanswered question is how liberal is the Prime Minister's mind. His social background possibly suggests that he is not the man to bridge a gap that so long has been so wide and so deep. One has to remember, of course, that he is the leader of a party with a powerful instinct for preserving unity, for closing ranks. This entails a constant deferring to the views of the Orange Order—some would even say a yielding to the intimidation of factions that are far more extreme. I would say too that Captain O'Neill is not yet sure of his hold on the House of Commons itself. The Unionist Party does not strike one as being enthusiastic in helping him to wield a new broom: the threat of a rebellion is always there if he should move too far or too fast. The fact is that the whole official party has no identifiable element pledged to back the Prime Minister in a real effort to reform the Unionist thinking. It's plain that here too progress can only be long-term: that the new image hides the conservative reality.

To those who observe politics and who hope for better things it has been rather disillusioning that some attempt at least has not been made. I hesitate to say that at the moment Ulster is in a ferment, but it can hardly be denied that there is now a feeling for tolerance and a freedom of expression among a great many people on both sides of the politico-religious fence, and that the Unionist leadership has done little or nothing to come to terms with an intellectual upheaval of this kind which could have far-reaching consequences. This is particularly true of younger generations to whom the Prime Minister is not yet fully addressing himself in the language of their times. The effect of that may not be seen in this year's general election, but it well could be in the first election he has to fight for parliament at Stormont.

Despite concluding that O'Neill had made 'an impressive beginning', this was a challenging critique from a friendly source, which lunch with Jim Malley, O'Neill's private secretary, had done little to mellow. In the next month he again asserted his independence when he highlighted (3 April 1964) how letters to the Prime Minister from two prominent Catholics critical of the failure to appoint more Catholics to government bodies had not even merited a reply. It is true that one of the two was his friend from the 'Your Questions' panel, J. J. Campbell, but Sayers published because he believed that the survival of the Unionist state depended on the integration at least of the Catholic middle-class. Consequently, under a front-page banner headline, 'End Apartheid—Catholics' and supported by a strong leader, he publicised their case and left the government acutely embarrassed.

Letter to Conolly Gage, 10 April 1964

Dear Conolly,
I was quite relieved to have your letter, written after what you read in the paper last Friday. I knew that publication of the letters was not likely to improve the situation, but Campbell and McGuigan obviously had to do something, and I could not blame them for coming into the open.

I was disappointed with the way they had been kept at arm's length for so long that I wrote rather more vehemently perhaps than I normally like to. It is good to have a cause, but I never like it to become a crusade and we have always to preserve some sense of detachment.

I am sure you are right in saying that Terence should have seized the opportunity. Robert Gransden wrote to say the same thing. If only there were more people who could see us as you do. It is not that one expects the PM to make some revolutionary statement. He need not necessarily get himself into trouble with his own right wing. A few appointments would not cause undue remark, and they would go a long way to encouraging the better Catholics to come into the open. Now we shall all have to wait 'for a cooling-off period', as was said after the fracas with ICTU. The trouble here is that cooling means frozen, and I am not very hopeful of a thaw.

I am sure Sir Alec [Douglas-Home] has done the right thing in waiting until October, but I doubt it will make much difference to Conservative fortunes. The articles and letters in *The Times* I thought a symptom of malaise, and, disloyally perhaps, I have an idea that the party needs a sojourn in opposition. The odd thing is that quite a few people here are prepared to believe that Northern Ireland would benefit from a Labour administration. Certainly the aircraft industry could wish for nothing better!

Ever,
Jack

P.S. Delighted that Oliver Lyttelton gave you so much pleasure.

Within a fortnight O'Neill had responded with his historic visit to a Catholic school—being photographed beneath a crucifix for his pains. Moreover, by the summer the government had at last resolved the tortuous negotiations concerning the recognition of the Northern Ireland Committee of the Irish Congress of Trade Unions. Thus when Sayers wrote to Gage describing his reactions to the Prime Minister's first cabinet reshuffle, his mood was decidedly optimistic.

Letter to Conolly Gage, 12 August 1964

My dear Conolly,
. . . As always, life is strenuous here, and I grieve that I read so little outside newspapers and the weeklies. Even on holiday I failed to keep up my average, partly due to the fact that we spent a good deal of the time with some very talkative American friends, the kind who assured me that Goldwater hadn't a chance of the nomination! They are not so sure now that he won't be the next President.

You will have seen Terence's choice for Governor, and perhaps asked yourself the kind of question people are asking here. If Erskine was a bit younger, I would think his appointment wholly good. Government house, and no fault of dear Lady Wakehurst's, needs to get much nearer to people outside, and I have always held that a Governor who was an expert mixer could do a great deal for us. I just hope that Terence won't find himself with a rival runner of the country.

His reconstruction made pretty good sense, apart from the fact that Craig [as Minister for Health and Local Government] has altogether too much to do. But I dare to say that Terence is becoming something of an autocrat, and not being Winston Churchill, that is something that Ulster people do not take kindly to. He makes a lot of these decisions without consultation, either with other ministers or the civil service, and it is not the best way to ensure that he has the right support.

I am sure he was right to leave Brian Faulkner in Commerce, but, of course, it is being said that this was a slight. The fact is that Brian will not take on anything which might earn him unpopularity, and that is why Craig always has to be the battering-ram. He is a bit punch-drunk and is, perhaps, more ready to force issues through than to apply the right kind of grease.

86

My graduation last month was a very happy occasion indeed, and everyone at Queen's was exceedingly kind. I had a secret feeling that the Dean of the Faculty did not quite explain why I should have been chosen for such an unusual honour, but again people have been good enough to say that his omissions were generally realised.

I really can't deny that there is a very different feeling here nowadays, although I would not overestimate what the *Telegraph* has done in bringing this about. Certainly things are said that even a few years ago would have been unheard of. Whether they are being done is another matter, and I have Martin Wallace at work on a study of the depth of the new tolerance. . . .

Ever,
Jack

The 1964 general election and the riots in Divis Street provided ugly reminders that progress in Ulster was unsteady and rarely assured. Paisley, ironically alerted by a report in the *Belfast Telegraph*, threatened to remove a tricolour flying over the Republican Party headquarters in Divis Street if the police did not act to enforce the Flag and Emblems Act. This left the police with little alternative but to intervene, and the result was four nights of rioting. Even the RUC suspected that the Unionist Party had encouraged the affair to swing a tight election in West Belfast. If so, they were soon to discover that the party hadn't 'hired' Paisley. Unaware of all this, Sayers deplored the sectarian violence in a leader entitled 'Ulster's Seamy Side'. Intriguingly, he viewed Protestant extremism as primarily a religious problem and looked to the churches to overcome it. On the morning after the first rioting Sayers rang his friend, the Methodist minister Eric Gallagher, bluntly demanding what action the churches were taking. When Gallagher informed him of a meeting due that morning between the Protestant church leaders, Sayers pleaded for Catholic participation. Such joint ventures were then unknown. However, Sayers even went so far as to find a Catholic representative willing to attend the meeting in Church House at an hour's notice. Thus, driven on by what Gallagher called 'the sheer compulsion of the Christian ethic', Sayers attempted to stir the institutions into taking the lead. He also, of course, got his own lead story and arranged publicity so that the church leaders could make a joint appeal on television. In his leader of 2 October 1964, although calling for the outlawing of the Republican Party if it continued to flaunt the authority of the state, the main assault was directed against 'the political blackmail' of the Protestant extremists, arrogantly threatening to take the law into their own hands.

Belfast Telegraph, 2 October 1964

GUILTY MEN

No defence whatever can be made for those who took part in last night's lawlessness, and little more for those on both sides of the political arena whose ill-thought and provocative actions have created a situation infinitely harmful to their city and their native land.

Religion and education have much to answer for when the mob can re-emerge so quickly and men and women and children attack the police and abandon themselves to an orgy of blind destruction.

But passions are well known to run deep, and no one in Northern Ireland should be unaware of a personal responsibility to see that primitive emotions are not aroused, and that peace is protected at all times.

People who have so little control of themselves that they are drawn into rioting in the streets do not deserve the name of patriots. They can only rank with the riffraff who have been ruled throughout history by the brutal instincts of the herd.

But what can be said of the men who are so righteous in not striking blows but do their damage by the striking of attitudes? These are also the guilty ones, and it is time that they were arraigned for their crimes against the community. . . .

In opening an emergency debate on the riots, O'Neill refused an inquiry, preferring to view it as the last flicker of the disorders of the 1920s and 1930s. Instead he chose to focus on the Ulster of the future and made his commitment to 'build bridges between the two traditions within our community'. A week later, with the election safely negotiated, O'Neill left for Nottingham and the first of the 'Ulster Weeks'. The following month saw him in London promoting Ulster's cause with the new Labour government. If Harold Wilson proved to be in too much of a hurry, O'Neill at any rate had a profitable meeting with an ebullient George Brown at the Department of Economic Affairs.

Letter from Terence O'Neill, early November 1964

> Glebe house,
> Ahoghill,
> Co. Antrim
>
> Saturday

My Dear Jack,
If I may say so, your leader last night hit just the right note and should do nothing but good.

My visit to Downing Street was very pleasant. He [Harold Wilson] looks grey and tired and considerably older than when I last met him. George Brown is an extraordinary character. I had to consume rather more whyskey [*sic*] than I wanted to, but it was worth it in order to draw him out.

He is interested in 'Shorts', which is a great thing. He also knows and likes Denis Wrangham. So I think we can take it that we will not be forgotten. On the other hand, I presume there may be some 'Concord[e] sufferers' to be appeased.

With renewed thanks for your statesmanlike approach.

Yours,
Terence

But Sayers had not forgotten so easily an election in which Terence O'Neill had declared the opposition to be no more than 'republican anarchists'.

Letter to Conolly Gage, 17 November 1964

TSS Caledonian Princess

My dear Conolly,
I'm London bound for a conference at Thomson House and have a chance to write my promised letter. I'm in the mood too, having earlier today attended a memorial service for Tom Finnegan. Would you have known him? President of Magee University College and a saintly rebel. Derry proved too much for his socialist idealism and efforts at reconciliation, and he resigned. A very fine address by Moore Wasson, the BBC's staff parson here, and I thought it brought out the best of Presbyterianism in its old liberal form. Anyhow, it was good to feel that there are some people concerned about our condition, and that one belongs to their company. By the way, on Wednesday next week I'm on 'Viewpoint' on BBC TV talking about an editor's work. Now that I'm near the date of the recording, I'm nervous of what I've undertaken—I think I did it in the hope that I can communicate something of what the paper is trying to do and why. Please God I won't be pious!

The election depressed me. Not Wilson winning—I think he had to have his chance, and he'll do things the Tories will be glad not to be able to undo. We made a muck of it here. Odd to think that Pat McLaughlin [the former Unionist MP for West Belfast] might have turned the scale. Certainly she would not have allowed Paisley to take over her campaign. Odd to think also that that's the constituency dear old Sir Douglas Harkness [formerly head of the N.I. Civil Service] had a thought to hang his hat in! There seems to have been a panic all round, with Glengall Street ready to use every means to get out the vote. Result: Paisley left lording it, and a very general impression that the party is now dependent on the support of his faction. Terence failed pretty miserably. Either he simply hasn't got it, or he was shaken by the backbenchers who proved to be all for the drum. It's the old story—no one will make any stand that might cause even one splinter. And, for all that I tried to do to let the party out with honour, there was no backing anywhere that mattered. Phelim [O'Neill, cousin of the Prime Minister], not for the first time, is baffled. Terence has a lot at risk. The planning legislation will have a rough passage, and there is far too much public talk about the friction between him and Brian Faulkner. Brian has behaved badly, but I have advised that he must never be able to say that he was not consulted. It could all come to a sacking or a resignation, and that would mean personal statements and a thoroughly bad taste. Do wish they would behave like adults, but the incompatibilities are probably too many. Not that Brian has the following to challenge for the leadership, though that could come later.

I had a note from Robert Gransden worried about how we will be treated by the Labour govt. But Terence and the others have made a good start, and I don't fear for them. Strangely, I heard from Frank MacDermot (what a good tale he tells of fighting West Belfast against W. E. D. Allen) that Cecil King told Lemass that when Labour arrived he'd see that they did something about partition. I'd say on the contrary that they will have to show that regional planning must work in N[orthern] Ireland as well as the North-East.

Thank you again for spurring me on at the time of Divis Street. I was wrong to say no one backed us: lots did, but Ulster doesn't have anything like a public opinion. In retrospect, the riots were only incidental: most people behaved well. How can we put them to the test with a straight choice between Paisley and tolerance?

Now to Asquith: he'd be amused to think that his life was written by a Minister of Aviation [Roy Jenkins].

Ever,
Jack

Gossip about the animosity between Faulkner and the Prime Minister had been rife from the early days of O'Neill's government. As early as 16 September 1963 Conolly Gage feared a 'collision', confiding to Sayers that 'Faulkner would be a disaster and might put us in the South African category with knobs on'. Ironically, it had been O'Neill that had persuaded Faulkner to enter politics in the first place and , as with many political enemies, they had much in common. Both firmly believed in 'the independent sturdy Ulsterman' and in Unionism as a classless movement in which the Orange Order stood as a guarantee of tolerance and social order. Politically they agreed wholeheartedly on the need to revitalise the Ulster economy and boost Northern Ireland's image abroad. Perhaps Faulkner's experience in the family firm with its mixed workforce made him more appreciative of working-class Protestantism and less sympathetic to courting the Catholic vote before 1965. But the real difference lay in personality. Faulkner, ambitious, energetic and fiercely determined, always found O'Neill aloof and remote. There was nothing that he resented more in O'Neill than the chill of the 'Big House', displayed even towards Faulkner himself, who, after all, had hunted with the best. Sayers viewed their disintegrating relationship with despair, but increasingly found himself siding with O'Neill. For this he came under attack from another source.

Letter to Shirley Bourn, 3 December 1964

. . . After the recording [on BBC's 'Viewpoint'] I was anxious for what I had said—one's mind is blurred after talking for twenty minutes—and even after the showing I realised the opportunities I'd missed. But so many people like you have been pleased, and I am relieved and encouraged too. Looking back, I think it was right not to slip down to a political level on which I could have spoken more forcibly. If only we could marshal all decent people, we'd soon put the extremists to shame. Sometimes I do get impatient because so much is left to me—Paisley attacks me all the time, and the *Irish Press* joined in today! . . .

His New Year leader reflected this mood with its early echoes of John Hewitt's 'Coasters' (1969).

Belfast Telegraph, 1 January 1965

HOPES AND FEARS

. . . The lesson of 1964 is that parties, government, church, even the man in the street, are still preyed on by factions who fear the light as other creatures fear the dark. Not yet has Northern Ireland thrown up men with the conviction and authority to break the bigots' spell.

When will it? When will our democracy find its saviours? When will this community discover its humanity and a common ideal? When will the New Ulster begin to have soul as well as body?

President Johnson has said: 'all will be hurt, none will be helped, if responsible citizens sit on the sidelines regarding the stability of our society as a spectator sport.' There are at every level here people who can bring the day of emancipation nearer, and nothing can be more profoundly hoped for at the start of another year than that they will step forward and let their voice be heard.

If any event was to inspire political action, it was O'Neill's shock invitation to Lemass to visit Stormont. Shrouded in secrecy and often close to farce, the event caught the imagination of the western world. It also came as a considerable shock. If O'Neill had not even consulted his cabinet colleagues, it was hardly likely that he would have consulted his friends in the press. Intriguingly, Sayers seemed to have shared the same sense of pique at the lack of trust that was to prove so corrosive to cabinet loyalty in the troubled years ahead.

Letter to Conolly Gage, 27 January 1965

My dear Conolly,
I have been saving up a letter, but the pressure is so great at the moment that it must wait a little longer. . . .

I cannot be sad about Winston [Churchill, died 24 January 1965] either—except that I am full of remorse that I cannot remember more of my service with him. But I did see enough to be able to say that everything that is being written now is true. God knows what would have happened to the country without him in 1940.

I will write about Terence and Lemass soon. Terence actually got ahead of me, and he had the grace to tell me, when I lunched with him last week, that he does not know where it will all lead. I would rather that than a pretence that it is all calculated. It has certainly put the political situation here into a state of flux.

Yours ever,
Jack

In the face of such an opportunity, Sayers began to play a more overt political role, devising a strategy that would transform Unionism. This involved the mobilisation of the widest possible moderate opinion in order to establish a consensus of the centre including Catholics, thus forcing Unionism to be non-sectarian and socially progressive. In a torrent of articles the *Telegraph* talked as if this popular movement already existed, and so encouraged many into politics for the first time. This was less wilful deception and more an unrestrained enthusiasm to read great significance into minor episodes; but the effect was to further the cause. Secondly, the *Telegraph* lost few opportunities to boost the standing of O'Neill within the party, whether it be editorials entitled 'Follow the Leader' (20 April 1966) or Sayers, in *The Round Table* describing the Prime Minister, two months before he was to face a vote of confidence within the party, as 'the master of the Northern Ireland situation'. Conversely, by speaking in its editorials as if he was O'Neill's mouthpiece, Sayers sought in effect to define 'O'Neillism'. Thus O'Neill's famous Corrymeela speech (9 April

1966) was heralded as the ultimate statement of Unionism and, of course, a vindication of the *Telegraph*'s line. It would be absurd, of course, to suggest that Sayers ran O'Neill or vice-versa. Rather, with the triumvirate of Ken Bloomfield, Jim Malley and Harold Black, Sayers also constructed a concept of O'Neillism and felt free to push it further than O'Neill would naturally have gone. The final element in this strategy was a relentless attack on all opponents of liberal Unionism and the establishment of Paisley as a *bête noire*.

Needless to say, O'Neill's strategic ambitions were not so expansive. Indeed, that the Prime Minister had not thought the purpose of the Lemass invitation through—save as a gesture of goodwill—was to prove all too apparent in the years to come. He remained content in his belief that nationalism would simply wither into irrelevance. Sayers, however, felt it crucial to win over the Catholic Church into assuming a role in the elimination of sectarianism. As O'Neill remembered, Sayers was particularly worried at the timidity shown by the Protestant church leaders in coming out publicly in support of the visit. In this, his friend Eric Gallagher, who denounced the Paisleyites as 'Protestant fascists', was the exception that proved the rule. While others hesitated, Sayers wrote to Cardinal Conway.

Letter from Cardinal Conway, 6 February 1965

Ara Coeli,
Armagh

Dear Mr Sayers,
Thank you so much for your letter, which I appreciate very much. I do agree that the atmosphere has lightened in the past year in a way that we would not have dared hope for. Human nature is eventually reasonable.
   With every kind wish,

Yours sincerely
✣ William Conway

Signs of this there were aplenty. Four days previously the Nationalist Party had accepted the role of official opposition in Stormont, and within a week O'Neill was in Dublin. For Sayers the former was of greater significance. He had called for this for a decade, believing it would strengthen the legitimacy of Stormont, and now was at his headmasterly worst. After according goodwill to Mr McAteer [the Nationalist Leader], he then urged on the Nationalists 'the sense of responsibility proper to a party which bids to be an alternative government . . . they must be builders, not wreckers' (*BT*, 2 April 1965). Yet without the chance of office, such symbolic gestures would count for very little, especially as the Nationalist decision was followed by the siting in a Protestant heartland of the new university at Coleraine and the naming of a new town near Dungannon as 'Craigavon', after Northern Ireland's first Prime Minister, infamous for his proud boast of 'a Protestant parliament and a Protestant state'. Sayers wanted Armagh for the new university, but felt that 'in ten years' time so great a gesture to national understanding might have been possible; 1965 has been, alas, too soon' (*The Round Table*, 1965). But such were the speed of events that anything seemed possible, though Wilson's call after the Lemass visit for tripartite talks raised Unionist hackles.

Letter to Conolly Gage, 19 May 1965

Dear Conolly,

At long, long last I have a moment to bring you up to date with events here. They have been so many that I fear you have given up remarking on them! I certainly thought to have heard from you after Harold Wilson started playing his game with the Ulster members. I'm pretty sure that a game it is, and was sorry that at first Terence tended to take it over-seriously. The best rejoinder was Rathcavan's—Willie Orr and Robin [Chichester-Clark] were too pompous. The trouble is, of course, that Knox [Cunningham] is a real old Blimp and that nobody would be responsible for the behaviour of Currie [Westminster MP for N. Down], who is deceiving himself and everybody else with his talk of Indian shipbuilding orders which, as Denis Rebbeck [Chairman of Harland and Wolff] could tell him, if he took the time to ask, have been hawked around British yards for years.

I am writing after yesterday's budget, which with some reluctance I allowed to take second place to [Dr Robert] Nixon's [N.I. MP for N. Down] retraction. In fact the budget is more significant than we have allowed in recent years. The big increase in revenue seems to me to prove that our progress is well-founded, and that there is no need for people to be apprehensive about financing the government's programme.

This is very relevant to the current situation as what with the new city, new university, the concordat with Dublin and Wilson, people have been feeling out of their depth, and correspondingly insecure. Terence has not helped things by continuing to be rather an arrogant PM working too much over and above the cabinet. I hope he has learned his lesson after the departure of Ivan Neill [2 April 1965]. If the cabinet had been at one with itself, this need not have happened, but I don't dispute that Neill had to go because he was a pocket Mussolini as Leader of the House.

It is luck that Brian Faulkner should now be Leader, as it brings him closer to Terence. He is playing a straight bat lately, and seems content to bide his time. He was right to stay at Commerce, where he is most successful, instead of going to Finance.

94

You will have seen the line that we have taken about Derry and the university. I came to the same conclusion as Lockwood about Coleraine only after a great deal of thought. Queen's could well take care of all our needs for a long time to come, but I think that if we must have a second university, we are best to start now. I was against a federal system, and had to accept that Armagh with the new city and the motorway is too much in Belfast's sphere of influence. Derry's has been a death-bed conversion, and I am sure that neither it nor Magee itself deserved full status. Coleraine is in many ways a considerable place, and I like its relative freedom from politics. It could indeed prove to be a great point of growth. We have to pray now for a first-class Vice-Chancellor who will give it prestige from the beginning. But it will not be easy to recover from the controversy of the last few weeks.

Today we shall be writing something about the present state of the Unionist Party. You will have seen how dismal a performance was put up by the annual conference, and I fear that no one has emerged who can educate it any more rapidly. The backbenchers themselves are laggards, and too many of them are rogues in both a criminal and elephantine sense. Nixon is a sheer exhibitionist, and poor Edmond Warnock [N.I. MP for St Annes and a former Attorney General] has to express himself to keep himself 'treading on the boards'.

Altogether we have lost too much of the better 'party men' spirit we have had for so long. I suppose we have to accept that the general freedom includes a freedom from the old discipline, so that people talk too loosely, and without a proper regard to the party's interest. The idea of throwing out Danny [Lord] Glentoran when he was the Speaker of the Senate is typical of their carelessness of the loss of dignity all round.

But we mustn't grumble. Terence has succeeded in putting over tremendous changes without putting too great a strain on the party, and if he will remuster his confidence and consolidate a bit, we should be on a good wicket by the time he has to go to the country. Do wish he would do something about Glengall Street—he's done nothing since beheading Billy Douglas, who still pervades the place 'with his head tucked underneath his arm'.

I was talking to Lord B[rookeborough] the other night (he is wonderfully well, after all) and was pained to realise how much of a backwoodsman he still is. Save us from Fermanagh! . . .

Ever,
Jack

However, backwoodsmen were not simply a characteristic of Fermanagh. Basking in the limelight after the Lemass initiative, O'Neill had found himself in early April facing calls for his resignation from two MPs, Dr Nixon and Edmond Warnock, over the secrecy of the visit. Their call for Faulkner to succeed was rejected by him and easily crushed at a meeting of the Unionist Parliamentary Party—but only after two hours of what Faulkner called 'straight talking' and his criticising O'Neill for 'lack of consultation'. None of this, however, could deflect O'Neill, whose confidence in 1965 was irrepressible and indeed infectious. In the March edition of *The Round Table* Sayers had showered him with praise for 'thinking internationally' and for his 'power of decision' and had claimed that O'Neill was 'the master of the Northern Ireland situation'. Ironically, it was over his perspective beyond the province that they came briefly into conflict. Given that to O'Neill the prosperity of Northern Ireland depended on foreign capital, it was only natural that he should look to the United States for potential investors. The sight, early in his premiership, of the Irish Republic fêting President Kennedy and emphasising the essentially Catholic nature of Irish-American links offended his own sense of Irishness. Undoubtedly, in the vehemence of his efforts to get into the White House there was more than an element of offended pride, but, with Ulster Protestants forming the majority of Irish in America, O'Neill was determined to establish this strong historical link and with it the attractiveness of Ulster to American investment. At home O'Neill's forays in international diplomacy occasionally attracted ribald comment, especially as O'Neill made it only too obvious how he loved to be seen in the company of the great. However, it was the assertion of Ulster as the homeland of the 'Scotch-Irish' in America that provoked the greater storm, for this portrayed an Ulster community with no room for the nationalist tradition. When Dennis Kennedy pointed this out in a *Belfast Telegraph* leader, Sayers was the recipient of a sharp rebuke from the Prime Minister.

Letter from Terence O'Neill, 24 June 1965

. . . Having been a minister since 1956 I am used to being criticised; nor is it on a matter of the first importance that I write. Nevertheless, I feel compelled to drop you a line upon your leader 'Potent Brew' which appeared on Saturday 19 June.

I have been to America on five occasions. On all of these I have taken part in industrial promotion work. I have also been struck—as were both Ken Bloomfield and Bill Taylor, who together spanned some five years of Ulster representation in New York—how often one met the Scotch-Irish in leading industrial positions.

When the National Trust decided to manage the Wilson and Arthur homesteads I informed President Kennedy, who wrote back and said that Mrs Kennedy would very much like to have information, photographs etc., of the restored cottages when they were ready, so that the White House information could be more complete. Dean Rusk's first words to me when I went to the State department last year were 'I'm Scotch-Irish'. Last month when I met him at the American Embassy he said to David Bruce: 'This is *my* PM!'

96

My Christmas card was of myself and L.B.J. chatting in his study at the White House, a posture we have seen on other occasions as well. He had no idea I was going to give him a book on the Scotch-Irish before I went to the White House, but when Dean Rusk heard about it he specifically asked to be allowed to have one too. . . .

A Prime Minister who knew nothing about America and had failed to get into the White House and had been unable to meet the Kennedys and the Rusks might perhaps be open to some slight criticism. . . .

Obviously the emphasis one puts on the Scotch-Irish story is a matter for discussion. For me it is merely one of several American approaches which I favour. A retired Scotch-Irish tycoon said to me in Philadelphia: 'You know what . . . the Scotch-Irish own America and the Southern Irish run it.' Obviously an exaggeration, but it is useful to keep in with a people who hold leading industrial positions in the States.

Incidentally, if we are going to get down to a denominational discussion, I am, as you know, an ardent Anglican! . . .

Sayers tried to restore the balance. In April he had briefly performed the role of go-between between Harold Black, the Cabinet Secretary, and Cardinal Conway. However, his efforts to subject the question of denominational education to rational debate backfired and only served to provoke numerous letters from lay Catholics critical of their narrowly clerical schooling.

Letter to Conolly Gage, 17 August 1965

My dear Conolly,
I expect you have been reading our articles on catholic education. This began as a study of what I believe to be a serious problem, but I was embarrassed to find that it seemed to unleash a great volume of criticism of the church in general.

There was also the suggestion of anti-clericalism at the Catholic social study conference, and the two together made me apprehensive lest the *Telegraph* should be thought to be exploiting the situation. For that reason I was glad to accept G. B. Newe's article which gave the moderate line.

Looking last night at a Telefís Éireann programme, I was again struck by how vocal Catholics are becoming. Cardinal Conway has been called to Armagh at a time when great statesmanship is obviously needed. Remembering all that I was brought up to believe about the church, I realise that no one can afford to have too many preconceptions nowadays. . . .

Ever,
Jack

Notwithstanding this, the Stormont election of November 1965 proved a resounding success for O'Neill and by implication his policies. In the static electoral system, he managed to make two gains and boost the Unionist vote by 6 per cent. Much to his surprise, Faulkner found himself benefiting from significant catholic voting. Such a triumph, however, had been won by directing the Unionist attack on the fledgling Labour Party. To many observers of O'Neillism it was simply pointless to destroy a party whose four seats hardly threatened the Unionist hegemony but whose presence on the opposition benches offered some hope of non-sectarian politics. Whether such a strategy ever had a chance in a society determined by communal politics was a moot point. Yet it was not one which concerned O'Neill. In many ways an unnatural unionist leader, the only way he had of establishing himself was to win his electoral spurs, and the only opportunities for that lay in the Labour constituencies. Nor was he above dubbing the NILP as anti-partitionist in order to win these seats. To Sayers this was regrettable, but in the euphoria of the moment he preferred to rejoice in the vindication of 'tolerance'.

Letter to Conolly Gage, 3 February 1966

My dear Conolly,

I have no excuse for not having written for so very long. I have been off duty for the past three weeks, including eight days in the clinic being 're-stabilised', but even then I confess I did not seem able to get down to writing you the letter you deserve. I am finally forced to do it by yours of 27 January, with which I agree so much.

There are times when Terence is disappointing, even though since the election he is in an impregnable position. He really should have corrected that rustic Unionist on the subject of Catholic membership. You will see a very good letter to the same effect in Wednesday's paper.

I do think he has the right idea, and he answered my questions so well at the election that I came out on his side. But he is still very windy about the Orange Order. Of course, he has to be reasonably circumspect, but he can lead the party without necessarily disappearing from its sight.

I hope you read my leader of Tuesday. Boal uses his lawyer's skill to denigrate us at every opportunity. I came to the conclusion that we must challenge him before he gives too much impression to the feeling, which I know does exist between some people of no great intelligence, that the *Telegraph* has gone over to the other side!

This man annoys me because he takes the government whip and is the Attorney-General's devil, but all the time he is strictly at variance with the Prime Minister's policy.

You would have been heartened by the reception I got on Monday night at the annual dinner of St Malachy's Old Boys' Association.

When I was the 'Methody' president last year, I brought St Malachy's for the first time, and this was the reciprocal invitation. Everyone was extremely friendly, and I myself got what I can fairly call 'an ovation' when I was called on to speak.

It all proved to me that what we are trying to do is not just idealism, but meets with a very real response from Catholics who are longing for acceptance.

You will know best, but I would have thought that at the dinner you mention it was possible to show Terence that there are other people who take the big view of things. More and more my fear is that the Unionist Party organisation will end up as a rump.

The election really was tremendously encouraging because Terence's success was such a vindication of tolerance.

I hope that with this you will forgive me. Please be sure you are often in my thoughts, the question being 'What would Conolly think of it?'

Every good wish to you both in 1966.

Yours ever,
Jack

Boal survived denunciation from the *Telegraph* ('Where We Stand', 1 Feb 1966). And Sayers deriding of his Unionist opponents as 'rustic' and 'people of no great intelligence' revealed a few blind spots of his own that later would prove quite telling. However, in the meantime Sayers was more preoccupied with courting the 'other side' in the run-up to the fiftieth anniversary of the Easter Rising. Describing himself as an 'emancipated Protestant', he attended dinners for the old boys of St Malachy's and the Belfast Christian Brothers' Past Pupils' Union. There he could only have been encouraged by the speeches in favour of O'Neill and widespread talk of the transformation in public opinion in which the *Telegraph* had played a major role. Compared with such achievements and the possibility of further advances, the affair of the naming of the new bridge in Belfast seemed only a minor, if rather tasteless, irritant. The rejection of Belfast's Council's provocative choice of 'Carson Bridge' led Paisley to entice Carson's son over to the province to lead the protests. If such stunts were bound to be embarrassing, the near-panic this caused among the Unionist hierarchy was more disturbing. The *Telegraph* firmly defended the Governor's judgement in pressing for 'The Queen Elizabeth II Bridge' (12 Dec. 1966) and in subsequent leaders heaped ridicule on the hapless Ned Carson. But the strongest language was reserved for the Protestant hardliners: 'Not even terrorism is likely to produce a throwback in Ulster as the rise of the malignant anti-Catholic forces exploiting the psychology of the mob. . . . It is time indeed for any who are not with [O'Neill] to declare themselves and go' (*BT*, 16 March 1966)

Letter to Conolly Gage, 24 March 1966

Dear Conolly,

. . . You must have seen all that we have had to report about poor Ned Carson. It has been rather pathetic to see how this poor man has been ill-used by his so-called friends. We had to be rather severe with him, but we were really attacking his masters, and I think we succeeded.

Terence and the others, having made their stand in private, were wide open for the charges of making a deal. It was only after pressure from me on Glengall Street and Stormont that I got them to approve my telling of the story, which appeared in Tuesday's issue. I think Robin Chichester-Clark was the leader of the resistance, and thank God for him. But poor Stanley McMaster put his foot in it by speaking to Paisley personally.

I needn't tell you that the demands made on Glengall Street by Paisley were quite grotesque. The trouble was they were being backed by too many of the right-wing members of the party. I do think they should be pushed out, even if they form a party on their own.

After the election I'll try to continue the story.

Ever,
Jack

In the Westminster elections, the loss of West Belfast to Gerry Fitt and Republican Labour did little to lessen the tension on the eve of the Easter anniversary. In this context, O'Neill's speech to an inter-denominational conference at Corrymeela on 8 April 1966 made an enormous impression on Sayers. The Prime Minister's description of 'the Ulster Community' as 'a place in which two traditions meet', his 'frank' defence of the constitutional position; and the coupling of this with an appeal for all to unite 'in working together—in a Christian spirit—to create better opportunities for our children, whether they come from the Falls Road or from Finaghy': all this had, for Sayers, the stamp of statesmanship.

Letter to Ray Davey, Head of Corrymeela, 10 April 1966

My dear Ray,

What a moment for all of you who created Corrymeela! I was thrilled that [it] should have fulfilled its purpose so soon—and at this of all times. You gave the PM the best of all platforms, and I was deeply impressed by the way he rose to the occasion. This was the bravest speech he has made, and it takes us a long step forward, but only if he gets support. There is more for Corrymeela to do!

Every good wish to you all.

Ever,
Jack Sayers

Sayers was determined that O'Neill's olive branch should be publicised to the full. After all the talk of bridge-building, the Prime Minister had, as the *Telegraph* leader acknowledged, at last traversed 'over the bridge'. The Paisleyites were to make much of those who build bridges only to go over to the other side. But it was the Catholic response that was all-important and therefore all the more disappointing when it came. Cardinal Conway's spirited defence of Catholic schooling and his blunt rebuke over discrimination were not what O'Neill and Sayers had expected, and the allusions to *Alice In Wonderland* in connection with their naïve assumptions regarding Catholic grievances undoubtedly hurt. But with hindsight the Cardinal had little alternative. Northern Catholics were beginning to express considerable frustration, as O'Neill's new Ulster appeared to be confined to Protestant heartlands. Yet in return for more fine words O'Neill was now demanding a 'minimum duty of allegiance' to the Unionist state. Even Sayers recognised that a meeting between the Prime Minister and the Cardinal was now 'outside the bounds of practical politics'.

Letter from Terence O'Neill, 13 April 1966

Stormont Castle

My Dear Jack,
Very good of you to write. I have no doubt that the speech will be much criticised in certain circles, and I'm only sorry that it does not seem to have had favourable comment in the South.

The way of the reformer is not easy, and it is a great encouragement when the press are enthusiastic in their support.

Yours gratefully,
Terence

It is easy to dismiss O'Neill's obsession with the press as mere vanity. His autobiography is littered with quotations from friendly editors in justification of his actions, and he was never slow to correct even the slightest error in the record. Nevertheless, his preoccupation with public relations necessitated a close relation with the press. Moreover, the support of the *Belfast Telegraph* and the *Belfast Newsletter* not only protected his policies from the 'noisy minorities' but also gave him access to a crucial medium in his attempt to shift opinion. If the real influence on his policies came from his coterie, especially Ken Bloomfield, who wrote many of his speeches, O'Neill did use Sayers as a sounding-board for these ideas and not merely as the instrument of their communication. As Harold Black's letter shows, to keep the press on side required the carrot and the stick. Sayers all too obviously treasured his lunches in the Ulster Club with the Prime Minister. But it worked both ways, and Sayers was assiduous in cultivating his sources. Thus a month after this letter Black was Sayers's guest at the Jutland dinner on HMS *Caroline*.

Letter from Harold Black, Secretary to the Cabinet, 13 April 1966

Stormont Castle

My Dear Jack,
Thank you for your letter of the 7th. I certainly look on you as the most responsible of editors in *any* context, but if I seemed over-assiduous in pressing a particular point of view, it was because editorial policy and outlook are not always evident at working journalist level. And there must be difficulties in an editor trying to control all the minutiae in his paper!

The PM, as you know, was tremendously pleased with the treatment given to his Corrymeela speech. I hope, as he does, that the immediate response will not be just the end of it, but that it will generate further discussion and ultimately a more constructive approach at the grassroots.

Yours ever,
Harold

P.S. We still have a luncheon appointment awaiting a day suitable to you. I know what a busy life you lead, so will not press you—but when you have a free hour maybe you would let me know. H.

In June Sayers was due to address the General Assembly of the Presbyterian church—a considerable honour, he felt, for a Methodist. He had in the previous year spoken warmly of its resolution asking Catholics to forgive Presbyterians for 'attitudes and actions . . . unworthy of our calling as followers of Jesus Christ' and had supported the Assembly's investigation into discrimination within the province. But to Protestant fundamentalists such ecumenical gestures threatened to 'sell the pass'. Ever the publicist, Paisley led a few hundred demonstrators to the General Assembly, which resulted in a riot in the

Catholic Cromac Square. Laying siege to the Assembly Room, they jostled and jeered the dignitaries as they emerged. The prime target was the Governor of Northern Ireland, Lord Erskine, who had denied them their 'Carson Bridge', and such was their hostility that Lady Erskine required treatment for a heart complaint two days later. To Sayers the lack of respect by these loyalists for the Queen's representative simply appalled him. Yet it also inspired him in his address the following night to the General Assembly.

After condemning the 'fanaticism' that sought to 'thwart . . . every ecumenical gesture' and the 'forces who would destroy religious freedom', Sayers outlined the role of the churches in a society racked by social change and separated 'from old anchorages'; a society where paradoxically 'social security' has only produced a 'new psychological insecurity'; a society in 'need [of] landmarks and . . . clearsightedness—and faith'. In so doing he showed how far his perception had changed from his Protestant assumptions of the 1950s.

Address to the General Assembly of the Presbyterian Church, 7 June 1966

Communication of the Christian Faith through the Printed Word

. . . The churches speak readily of the Ulster people; I write of them no less readily. It is salutary to ask what one means by the people of Northern Ireland. Do we think of a select community, the church-goers, those who think politically as we do? Or do we mean everybody—the unchurched, the sects, the Roman Catholics? We can *only* mean *every living* soul and think totally of their situation, their needs, and say what is of universal application. . . .

This is where I can say that the experience of an editor reinforces the mind of the Christian.

I have to look towards all the people of Northern Ireland; observe all the factors by which their lives are ruled. Again and again I have to conclude that there is much in our society that is wrong and that only the spirit of God can really put right.

The wrongs are not only in moral weaknesses and antagonisms in individuals. They exist in the system, in divisions and inherited prejudices and practices that we must confess are at variance with God's law. As such they call for the churches to condemn them and to lead the way towards their correction. In the province, as it is to-day, it is impossible for the Churches *not* to be aware of conflicts that are harmful to everyone of us.

It is only by recognising the problems of separation and hostility and the Christian responsibility for solving them that we can establish that the churches still have a mission. But it is not enough that church authorities should make pronouncements, important as it is that their official voices should be heard. *The* church is . . . a body of Christian citizens with a commission to bring about all the reforms that may be necessary.

This can only mean a quickening of the Christian's conscience. If we do not have that, I am afraid that in the changes which are forcing themselves on Northern Ireland today the churches may find themselves excluded.

I say that because what we are witnessing, especially among those young people, is a new democratic urge, a natural feeling for equality of status, for fair play for all, for the rights of the individual, for the ending of double-thinking and two levels of privilege. The worst of these things *are* going, but I want to see the church doing *its* part in seeing that they are ended. *We* don't want to see a state of things that is brought about only in the course of a revulsion. If there is to be fairer and happier society, a society based on the best foundations, it can only be created by us and of God.

I am not a dreamer. I know full well that we are facing a tangle of history and geography and emotions deep-writ on the human heart that has made good men despair before now. But I believe that we are called today, on every religious and political ground, to try again, and that this time we have a real hope of making this island at peace with itself.

Two things will be commanding, and will compel the newspapers and every other media, to take their part in the churches' communication. One is an utter compassion for all humanity; the other is courage: courage to think, courage to speak, not only in face of the mob, but to our own friends; courage to face *all* the issues without exception, and to declare ourselves on every conflict between Christ and the World, most of all the world on our doorstep.

May I evoke the name of John Wesley, a man who saw his society of the eighteenth century in revolution, much as we can see ours of the twentieth century.

> Perfect love is the great medicine of life, the never-failing remedy for all the evils of a disordered world, for all the miseries and vices of men.

And let us remember what perfect love does also: it casteth out fear.

No one who knew him ever doubted what Eric Gallagher called Sayers's 'sheer Christian integrity', and in this talk Sayers revealed that combination of religious commitment, social consciousness and moral energy so characteristic of Methodism. Nevertheless, it was inevitable that in many ways this essentially religious address would become part of Sayers's campaign to rid Unionism of what he insisted was a 'lunatic fringe' of 'bullies' (*BT*, 8 June 1966). With the dismissal of Boal and O'Neill's widely applauded denunciation of Paisleyites as 'Nazis', the showdown that Sayers had called for seemed imminent. Brian Faulkner's speech two weeks later however, arguing that Protestant anxieties were not restricted to a 'small group of agitators' (*BT*, 7 June 1966) suggested otherwise. In reply, the *Telegraph*'s editorial, 'Breadth of View' (20 June 1966) rejected calls to apply the 'brake' to reform and insisted that 'the party now had no course open to it but to press on'. Significantly, the Malvern Street murders were taken by both camps as a justification of their case ('Dragons's Teeth', *BT*, 27 June 1966). In such an atmosphere, even the anniversary of the Ulster Division's sacrifice on the Somme was not beyond a political point, with Sayers wondering aloud if it would 'take another fifty years to bring to an end the paradox that so many men who will face the enemy on the field of battle are gripped by an unreasoning fear of their own neighbours' ('Fifty Years On', *BT,* 1 July 1966).

Belfast Telegraph, 1 July 1966

FIFTY YEARS ON

... To the province 1 July 1916 was a day of mourning, but ever since an inspiration. No one can doubt that while Thiepval was one small sector in a gigantic confrontation across the face of Europe, it helped to shape the history of Ireland. And in part that is how the memory is being royally celebrated this weekend.

Of idealism, determination, discipline and bravery what more can be said? Put to the test, the Ulsterman never fails to show soldierly qualities. If needs be he will go to war again and not count the cost.

Yet this is a time to ask when the race of which the Ulster Division was an elite will set itself to cultivate in earnest the arts of peace? Must it take another fifty years to bring to an end the paradox that so many men who will face the enemy on the field of battle are gripped by an unreasoning fear of their neighbours.

While O'Neill prescribed the Ulster Volunteer Force, Sayers also called to account all those who for too long had 'winked' at sectarianism. The heightening of sectarian tension necessitated some clearing of the decks, and accordingly the *Telegraph* announced its refusal to accept Paisley's advertisements any longer. These, unlike most church notices, had given the title of the sermon to be preached and frequently referred to the Pope in disparaging terms.

Sayers too had for a number of years been the target of Paisleyite abuse. Journalists, in general, were regarded with loathing—'pestiferous, scribbling rodents'—but Sayers in particular was bracketed with O'Neill in the pantheon of the most detested. The *Telegraph* was regularly picketed, and hate-mail, threats of violence and even a copy of the Douai Bible were pushed through his letterbox. His courage in the face of these assaults encouraged many who had had a glimpse of such thuggery.

Letter from Edmund Gordon, Headmaster, 4 July 1966

Dalriada School,
Ballymoney

Dear Mr Sayers,
I think it is important for some of us who believe in the things you stand for
to make it clear how much we admire the courage and firmness and clarity
and moderation which you have shown in dealing with the present problems, and particularly that of Paisleyism. Over the last couple of years, one
has come to regard you and the *Telegraph* as the spearhead against racism
and bigotry and the ugly anachronisms which befoul Ulster life. Without
you, indeed, one would at times have almost given up hope, because there
was no other voice to speak [the] truth and not be afraid.

The resistance to Paisleyism probably started in Ballymoney, several years
ago, and that's why Paisley is determined to come back here tomorrow, to a
town which is ninety-nine per cent against all that he stands for. He is a very
astute politician, and unfortunately he has a certain courage too, though this
may partly depend on the four strong-arm men who go about with him to
protect his sacred person. I think that most people in Ulster still don't realise
the frightening atmosphere of these demonstrations and 'rallies', the obsceni-
ties, the muck-raking, the foulness of speech, the 'Mods and Rockers' atmosphere of regressive and degenerate adolescence: the man and his supporters do seem like corrupt and retarded adolescents having a private orgy.

Wylie [a minister of Paisley's Free Presbyterian Church] has just issued a
statement saying that 'teenage hooligans' from Dalriada School were ejected
from his last Ballymoney meeting for jeering and cat-calling, and squeezing
tomatoes into the collection-plate! If my pupils did this, I admire their courage, as well as their sense of humour. Alas, I gather from eye-witnesses that
the tomatoes were squeezed into the plate by a wealthy group of local busi-
nessmen.

I cannot imagine anywhere else in Ulster where the people (Protestants)
would treat the Devil with such cheerful contumely, except perhaps Queen's
University! The interrupters were forcibly ejected. Generally speaking, people in the province are perhaps wise just to stay away, as almost all Ballymoney
did, from Paisley meetings, but perhaps much of it is due to lack of physical
courage.

Anyway, I never forget your once saying 'Ballymoney is the *soul* of Ulster.'

At the moment one feels that it is you who would in all seriousness deserve this title, for you seem to remain at the centre of the resistance to the
forces of darkness.

Yours v. sincerely,
Edmund Gordon

In turn, such mail reinforced his own beliefs. For the Paisleyite assault on him had the effect of focusing and narrowing his perspective

of the Protestant revolt, almost into one of personalities. At the same time, in the heat of battle, he came dangerously close to losing his journalistic detachment as he rallied to O'Neill's standard.

Letter to Edmund Gordon, Headmaster, Dalriada School, Ballymoney, 8 July 1966

Dear Mr Gordon,
I couldn't but be touched and stimulated by your letter. People are being very kind to us on the same score at the moment, but I must say that it is very seldom indeed that a tribute to the paper is so splendidly phrased.

We are not all the only centre of resistance, but we do have the keenest sense of our responsibility, and it is really most encouraging to find that people like yourself appreciate our policy so much.

That you should have written at the moment makes it especially so. I won't say that we ever despair, but we do have some gloomy moments. The answer really is that people who are capable of thinking for themselves should make a stand in every way possible and give the Prime Minister some of the support that he ought to be getting from his colleagues!

May I say that I continue to revere Ballymoney and all the liberal instinct that it stands for? I fairly cheered when I knew that the Urban Council had voted not to let the hall [to Paisley]. In Belfast the Corporation is neither so wise nor so brave. . . .

Sayers's belligerence with the onset of the Twelfth did not go unnoticed in Catholic circles.

Letter from Cardinal Conway, 11 July 1966

Armagh

Dear Mr Sayers,
Thank you so much for your kind letter of congratulations. It was nice to be back again at Queen's in such a very happy atmosphere.

Recent events have been painful, but they have certainly not wiped out all the good work—with which you yourself have had so much to do—of recent years. History does not go into reverse. In many ways they have done good. I thought the Prime Minister's speech at Armagh was excellent.

I said a few words yesterday asking for calm. I deliberately pitched them at a low key in order not to heighten alarm, and I thought this the most opportune time to make them. We all appreciated very much your noble tribute to Catholics in 'Viewpoint' last Friday.

Perhaps it would be useful for us to have a talk some time when you are free. . . .

The leader the Cardinal so admired was 'Ulster on Trial' (*BT*, 8 July

1966), but it was the leaders of 11–12 July that really caught the eye. For all the references to 'Mad Mullahs', they were less a declaration of war than an appeal to what O'Neill called 'those decent, sensible Orangemen who have long been the backbone of Ulster'.

Belfast Telegraph, 11–12 July 1966

FACTS OF LIFE

[11 July] Winston Churchill was thinking of two world wars when he wrote of 'that long, dismal catalogue of the fruitlessness of experience and the confirmed unteachability of mankind'. If the words should have an aptness for Northern Ireland today, let it be remembered that their author's faith was, in fact, the opposite.

A year ago the Orange Order, reflecting the province's peace and prosperity, was giving a new emphasis to its own precept of charity towards all. Tomorrow it takes the field under a threat from men, some unscrupulous, some merely deluded, who would usurp it and the government as well, and in so doing pull down the creative work of fifty years. . . .

The unteachables today are those who will not see that Northern Ireland, for all its parliament, is not a law onto itself. Nor is it the master of its fate – except by an act of suicide. It must exist within the comity of nations; it must observe the Charter of Human Rights; it must have stability and dignity. If it does not, it will surely fall in ruins.

Nothing is so wrong, politically as well as morally, as the extremist dogma that to survive Protestants must actively dominate Roman Catholics. Ulster's position today is simply that the more fairly it treats its minorities the longer it will endure.

That is true not only of the attitude of an increasingly watchful British parliament, but of the response of Catholics, who are enabled to enjoy the privileges of British citizenship to the full. The signs of this are plain if purblind people would open their eyes long enough to see them. . . .

After forty-five years it is not too soon for us to learn this lesson. And tomorrow is hardly soon enough for political leaders to begin in earnest the task of educating ordinary people about the facts of their existence, their security and their well-being. Most of all about the tumour in the constitution represented by the zealots who brag that they are its strongest defenders.

[12 July] Not long ago speeches on the Twelfth of July were the dullest part of the proceedings. But not today. What the Orange platform have witnessed is a critical round in a struggle not only for control of the Order but for possession of Northern Ireland's soul.

Is that statement too strong? We do not think so. Orangeism is again in a key position. It is the first to have to make the choice between responsible government through the present Unionist leadership or a form of dictatorship through a religious war led by a latter-day 'Mad Mullah'.

No self-respecting Ulsterman should be confused by such an issue. But many of simple mind are troubled by the shades between. It is they who have to be saved from error. As for the mob, it spawns in all ages, and to-day's mob is a very terrible cross to bear for the failure of Christianity and education at this level of our society. . . .

If the brethren are not to be persuaded that in isolation the province could become a religious jungle, they may at least ponder a situation in which the Protestant churches will continue to go forward—and Orangeism will go in a different direction, one that at this moment leads only to a kind of Klu-Klux-Klan.

To look further, they may give thought to what will happen if Unionism also reaches a parting of the ways. There is a central body of opinion deeply convinced that any compromise with the extremists means a tragic end for Northern Ireland. This body will stand fast, and it will be the rest who are the independents and who may die in the last ditch if they choose to.

What is at stake is not Protestantism, though its good name is in the direst peril. It is the British connection itself, and with it all the honour Northern Ireland ever had. Today more church and Unionist leaders are coming to this realisation, but until all take courage and start to teach reason and the meaning of tolerance the whole of Ulster could be put to shame.

This was no less than an appeal for 'the soul of Ulster'—a phrase he first used in a letter to the *Sunday Times* in riposte to its blunt exposure of 'John Bull's political slum'.

Letter from Bishop Buchanan of Clogher, 14 July 1966

Private and personal

My Dear Mr Sayers,
Again I congratulate you on all your 'leaders' and also on your letter to the *Sunday Times*.

I agree it is a battle for the soul of Ulster. We have two clear duties. One is to oppose the extremists with all our might, and the second is to convince the ordinary Ulsterman that his fears are groundless. I think we are seeing our way more clearly about the latter. But, apart from you, are we doing enough about the former?

It is hard to know at this distance whether many RCs have left their homes. I was able to protect people in 1935, and my own parishioners told me they would look after their neighbours. If there is any fear of eviction, I would be glad to write a stronger appeal.

God prosper you.

Yours very sincerely,
Alan Clogher

With the Twelfth passing off without any serious trouble, Sayers seized the respite to bring his friend up to date.

Crying in the wilderness

Letter to Conolly Gage, 15 July 1966

My dear Conolly,

So much has been happening that I hardly know where to start. The right place is where I thank you for your last letter—all the time I feel you are watching Ulster and , like us, feeling intensely for it. I did have some despair after the shootings, but the government's strong action seems to have stopped the rot, and it has been a vast relief that the Twelfth is over without any further violence.

I must confess that my mind is still rather divided on the question, what next? One can only fear that, with the temper as it is, Terence will have to slow down, but he has some big commitments, and Harold Wilson and others are not likely to let him renege on them. On the other hand, there is just a chance that he can consolidate and be in a stronger position than he has been.

There is admittedly a lot to be said of the view that the party, after coming so far so fast, should now take a step to the right, possibly under a man like Faulkner, but it would be a disaster if Terence were to be displaced in the near future, and in any event Faulkner, while the epitome of much solid Orange and Unionist thinking, does not yet command a real personal following in the parliamentary party.

Nevertheless, he is lying handy all the time, and if Terence were ever to be unseated on the grounds of too much liberalism, he would take over almost automatically.

I do think that under the pressure of events Terence is getting more open support from those, particularly in his own cabinet, who have been very reticent in the past. It is fortunate for him that the parliamentary party, aghast at the murders, rallied to him as they did. Otherwise he would be in a distinct difficulty in being made a scapegoat for every ecumenical gesture from Dr Ramsey's visit to Rome to the very proper objections of Bishop Elliott to the Second Resolution!

In perhaps a rhetorical moment, I spoke of 'a classic struggle between the forces of progress and reaction'. I was thinking, of course, of the confrontation with Paisleyism, but strictly it is between the official and the sluggish elements in the Unionist Party itself.

All the writers have been having a great time at our expense, but as I have said to them as they walk out, don't forget those of us who are left, and who really have to deal with the problem. Hence my leaders of 11 and 12 July, in which I tried to persuade and educate, the thing that all of us must do more and more. I would that you were here to give a lead. There is a great need for men who can be on good terms with the average Ulsterman and bring him along in the right way.

There is a good deal in our make-up which I feel inclined to turn against, but I am always brought back to the point that these are all my fellow-countrymen, and that one has to persevere.

It has been a bad time, and I fear we shall take years to live it down, but a showdown was inevitable for Terence, and I hope that this is it. The policy will be to make the government as a whole bear more of the responsibility, and to show that the constitution is not in danger. As for the ecumenical movement, I would be very much afraid that the Orange Order is heading for a split with the churches, for one of the most encouraging signs is that these are now far more conscious of their Christian duty than they were in days when they were either aiding or winking at the things done in the name of Protestantism and loyalty.

Your mind must be full of it too—do tell me how it looks from the outside. . . .

Ever,
Jack

O'Neill also shared in the buoyant mood. However, his note of caution revealed a perceptive appreciation of the strength of Paisley's appeal.

Letter from Terence O'Neill, 15 July 1966

Stormont Castle

My dear Jack,
How kind of you to write. The Twelfth went better than I had dared to anticipate. At Cullybackey no visitors—and there were many—would have known that Paisley existed! We had 'Cassandra', the editor of the *Irish Times*, NBC, BBC, ITV and perhaps many others I did not see.

John Nixon [notorious D.I. in RUC and later Independent Unionist MP, 1929–49], the Rev. Coffie [?], and even Tommy Henderson [Independent Unionist MP for Belfast Shankill 1925–53]—not to mention [Rev] Godfrey MacManaway [N.I. MP Londonderry City, 1947–51]—were all extremists in their day. But they had no organisation behind them. *The Protestant Telegraph* was selling well in Ahoghill on the Twelfth morning, and by lunchtime most of the brethren had one sticking out of their pockets. In Cullybackey, where three Orange Districts assembled, two Ballymena men were doing a roaring trade at 6d a copy.

More and more Free Presbyterian chapels are starting up all over the country, and they seem to attract a more affluent type than the street mob which follows him through Belfast.

I only mention this because so many people have said to me since the Twelfth 'You've settled Paisley now.' I fear this is not so. The battle must continue despite the fantastic gap which exists between the 'Establishment' and the back streets of Belfast.

Yours in gratitude,
Terence

P.S. I thought your letter in the *Sunday Times* quite excellent.

Three days later Sayers and O'Neill found themselves in danger of being called by Paisley as defence witnesses in his trial for unlawful assembly outside the General Assembly in June. This was averted, and Paisley was jailed, provoking two days of rioting by his supporters. In the *Telegraph* Sayers renewed an earlier call for greater police powers, observing tartly that 'there is no other faction in Northern Ireland which could have succeeded in straining the Government's toleration so far' (*BT*, 22 July 1966). Claiming the law was being humiliated, he called for the government to be resolute—which it was on 24 July, banning all marches for three months within a fifteen-mile radius of Belfast. Letters of support flooded in, though none was more welcome than that from his old chief of the Map Room days.

Letter from Richard Pim, Formerly Chief Inspector of the Royal Ulster Constabulary, 28 June 1966

My Dear Jack,
My first thought on returning from a sailing holiday on the West Coast—during which I missed few 'NI News' on BBC and press accounts of our sad story—was to tell you how very impressed I have been by your wonderful stand for strong government and appeals for sanity in the populace.

The *Telegraph* was the first to take a strong line, and the leaders were excellent—even if they resulted in Paisley not feeling you were Top of the Class—and hoping to make things awkward for you in court—if he got you there.

Your letter in reply to the *Sunday Times* was so much to the point, and the government here should be grateful to you, as they couldn't write it.

The *Telegraph* is showing just the strength of leadership shown—in not dissimilar times in 1921–24—when we had Derry prison fairly full of the 'Ulster Protestant Association'. In short, Jack—you have got 'guts', which some others have not, and I for one am grateful and proud. . . .

As ever,
Dick

With Paisley behind bars, ironically it seemed as if O'Neill was more on the defensive. The growth of the Campaign for Democracy in Ulster among Labour backbenchers in Westminster had resulted in Harold Wilson summoning O'Neill to London. If, as according to Sayers, this represented 'a constitutional departure', it was not without its value, enabling O'Neill to state that if the liberalising of Ulster stalled, 'the British people will want to wash their hands of us'. In fact Wilson had little intention of getting involved in Ulster's affairs. Sayers spotted the real issue in bemoaning 'that so much of this appeal to his followers is devoted to what is not changed when the Downing Street meeting is so concerned with what must be changed' (*BT*, 3 Aug. 1966). With O'Neill making firm declarations on the constitution and meeting Free Presbyterian delegations, the initiative seemed to lie elsewhere.

Letter to Conolly Gage, 19 August 1966

My dear Conolly,

My good secretary is just on the point of leaving for her holiday, so I am rushing this note to say how much I was heartened by your letter. Indeed, I hope with your permission, I have shown it to Harold Black, who is also in need of encouragement at the moment.

The PM has asked me to call on him next Wednesday, so I may be able to mention it to him.

My buoyancy is rising in the natural way, but I am bound to say that Terence is left with an enormous problem, and if he does not get more positive support from the party and the public, I doubt if he can solve it. We really are in grave danger of seeing the Unionist Party infiltrated and demoralised. This is why I am so anxious that the extreme protestants should be cut loose and made to fend for themselves. If they ever get any of the official nominations, I fear we could be lost. . . .

Ever,
Jack

Others shared his fears, and by late August Major Chichester-Clark, the government Chief Whip, had organised a 'Back the Government' group to counter the spread of the Paisleyite 'O'Neill Must Go Campaign'. However, they were soon to discover that the real threat to O'Neill came less from his avowed enemies as from his supposed friends. Early in September, when the Prime Minister was holidaying in England, Desmond Boal, the MP for Shankill, began to collect names from within the parliamentary party for a resolution calling for O'Neill's resignation. Later that month a meeting took place in Brian Faulkner's home at which Boal and his fellow-conspirators tried to persuade the Minister of Commerce to lead the revolt. Whatever the temptations, Faulkner recognised the dangers. His close friend and cabinet colleague, Harry West, advised him to wait another six months. After all, he had been closely involved in all the government policies, so ringingly endorsed by the electorate less than a year before, and in any case Boal had failed to secure a majority. Still, Faulkner's refusal lacked the stamp of finality. Were O'Neill to fall, he left no doubt that he would stand. Quickly he covered his tracks. Not only did he not go into the room with the rebels, but he also saw fit to warn Chichester-Clark. This was just as well, as the O'Neill camp had known for some time. When the news leaked to the press, O'Neill 'threw down the gauntlet' fully aware that no one would pick it up. The first Sayers knew of this leadership crisis was when his lunch with the Chief Whip was hurriedly cancelled. But he was soon into the fray. Under the banner of 'No Time for Change' (*BT*, 24 Sept. 1966), he ridiculed those who were 'deluding themselves utterly if they think they can present Captain O'Neill's downfall as anything but a triumph for Paisleyism, even while its arch-priest is behind bars'. Barely able to disguise his contempt for these 'covert' dissidents ('what one of them has spoken in public?'), he reminded them that 'Ulster has no use for revolutions, palace or otherwise'. To a party 'preyed upon . . . by ultra-Protestantism' he defiantly asserted that 'Unionism is broad and wide; it consists of far more people than are found in Orange and gospel halls. Its body is the great mass of voters who believe in the constitution and good government and can keep their heads.'

On the eve of the crucial meeting of the parliamentary party the *Telegraph* sustained its relentless attack ('Teaching a Party', 26 Sept. 1966). Taking his cue from a headline in the *Irish Times* which asked 'Is Unionism digging its own grave?', Sayers warned the rebel MPs 'that their party's funeral will be Northern Ireland's funeral also'. That it was in such a parlous state was because some in government preferred to make the Prime Minister 'walk the plank' rather than 'set themselves honestly and bravely to tell the party the way it has to go'.

With Faulkner absenting himself to fly to America on government business, the result was inevitably a unanimous endorsement of O'Neill. And yet it was a result that even for the *Telegraph* lacked conviction. Its leader was aptly entitled 'Coming to Terms' (*BT*, 28 Sept. 1966) and predicted a revival of the 'restlessness' on the back benches if the cabinet did not rally wholeheartedly to the cause of reform and O'Neill.

By contrast, O'Neill was euphoric.

Letter from Terence O'Neill, 29 September 1966

Stormont Castle

My Dear Jack,
The '*Tele*' has been magnificent. 'Not an inch' has been your motto through-out and mine as well. . . .

We have come through unscathed.

Yours with thanks,
Terence

Sayers recognised that it had been a close-run thing. Without a leader and an alternative set of policies, the revolt had little chance. O'Neill's Old Etonian hauteur riled many already disgruntled by his refusal to consult widely, if indeed at all. But these were old complaints. What now gave them greater weight was the growing unease over O'Neill's 'ecumenical' gestures towards the South and the minority within Northern Ireland. What probably saved O'Neill was that these gestures had not yet graduated into what may be called policy, so denying the rebels a specific target. Even so, Boal's 'list' was only one short of a majority; and with the British government arguing for the acceleration of reform, O'Neill needed all the allies he could get.

Letter to Conolly Gage, 4 October 1966

Devonshire Club,
St James's SW 1

Dear Conolly,
Your letter was a treat. . . .

I was most agreeably surprised by the way people rallied to Terence, and we do know now that he has a solid basis of support in his own right. But I must tell you that this was a plot that went off at half-cock, and that if the people concerned had had a bit more intelligence and more resolution, they could have spilt the party wide open. Now it is up to the PM to try to mend it, and he will need more than power of command to do it. Brian F[aulkner] hardly played the game—he ought to have backed his leader and he didn't. I pray that it is not too late for him and Terence to come to terms. Together they are invincible. The PM's strong point is that he is the only defence between N[orthern] I[reland] and intervention by the British government. . . .

I am here for the night and will be attending my first meeting of the executive of the British Council as N[orthern] I[reland]'s representative—wished on me by Terence, I think with the best of motives!

Ever yours,
Jack

P.S. There is a fruit machine in the bar here—what would Gladstone and Hartington have said!

O'Neill did attempt a reconciliation of sorts with Faulkner, appointing him Deputy Prime Minister and assuring him that he would retire before the next election (expected about September 1969); after this the co-operation between the two was 'wonderful' for six months. However, by now even O'Neill's sympathisers were deploring the situation into which he had got himself.

Crying in the wilderness

Letter from Sir Robert Gransden, 14 October 1966

Dear Jack,

As you can realise I have been following with much interest and sympathy the recent convulsion in the Ulster Unionist Party.

I am glad to see that O'Neill has weathered the storm—for the moment—but the tragic thing is that with all the efforts the PM has made—supported and encouraged by the Telegraph—for a better and more fruitful co-operation in our community, there are still so many backbenchers in the party (with a few cabinet ministers) fighting against any rapprochement with the minority.

I have written to you earlier about the O'Neill–Lemass meetings and how I felt that O'Neill was particularly maladroit in arranging them. He gave a shot in the arm to the Paisley movement, which got an added impetus from the progress of ecumenism.

I don't think there was any change of heart or conversion amongst the right-wing dissidents in the party. They were in disarray, and to my regret I can't see O'Neill having sufficient diplomatic skill to forge ahead with any practical plans for 'ecumenism' in Ulster. His flag was lowered when he agreed to the name of the new city—and will he have the courage to face the people who wanted the Lagan bridge named the Carson Bridge?

The problem which faces O'Neill is the preparation and strategic unfolding of a plan which will command the support of the constituencies.

I have had sufficient experience of politics in Ulster to appreciate the immensity of the task.

With every respect I know you will keep on to the end of the road. Being wholeheartedly with you, I would value your comments on a few points.

Can we ever have collaboration with the South in fields where the Southern Irish government presume to speak for 'Ireland'?

On one occasion I told the S[outhern] I[reland] Ambassador in London that I personally couldn't talk to people who were dishonest. (Incidentally, he and I became great friends.) I was irritated at the time by the advertising by the Southern Development Association, in a map of the whole of Ireland, of the inducements offered to new industries: 'Apply to the Association in Dublin'.

This leads me back to the fundamental point of collaboration between North and South on specific issues. No political problem arose when we joined forces on fisheries, transport, electricity and drainage.

But where political overtones are present, how do we deal with the problems without denying the right of the S[outhern] I[reland] govt to speak for 'Ireland'?

I'm sorry for all this diatribe, but can O'Neill deal with these matters without giving a handle to the right wing to wield the arguments that we are on the road to a united Ireland?

Regards,
Ever,
Robert

Nor was Sayers any more optimistic.

Letter to Conolly Gage, 27 October 1966

Dear Conolly,

... Once again I was struck in reading your letter by your good judgement about events here. You see a broader sweep than I am able to do, living so close to men and events. I am happy enough about Terence as the representative of the best of Unionism, but he is weakest at the point where the cabinet may be divided, both on his policy and its liking for him, and where the backbenchers are a good deal less than statesmen.

I have been doing my best to make Terence and Brian Faulkner see eye to eye, but I doubt if there has been any great improvement.

In fact I am oppressed by the thought that if these two cannot give the right lead to the cabinet, and thus solidify it, the Unionist Party will not be able to do the things it simply has to do. History will have much to say about the disparate personalities of these two men in particular.

Terence now seems to be leaning more and more on James Chichester-Clark, who is a nice man, but not a politician. Some see in C.-C. the next Prime Minister, but he is no Brookeborough, and I am inclined to think that the gentry's hold is not going to last.

Thank God Paisley does not seem to have made much impact on his reappearance. He will be looking for trouble in order to get himself back into the headlines. ...

Ever,
Jack

Writing his (now) biannual report for the *The Round Table* gave Sayers the opportunity for sombre reflection. With his friend O'Neill caught between the expectations of London and Londonderry and the 'false fears' of Protestant Ulster, Sayers feared for the party and the Union. He continued to view the uncertainty of the backbenchers as the product of extremist pressure and not personal conviction. In this portrayal, the fate of Ulster and O'Neill came to depend on a gladiatorial contest with Paisley—'a man whom he [O'Neill] must succeed in discrediting if he is to resume his forward motion' (*The Round Table*, Nov. 1966). However, for the first time Sayers seems to have appreciated the sheer scale of Protestant frustration. 'The dangers of Paisleyism', he now recognised, 'are not only that it provokes communal strife, but that the belief in its leader's "fundamentalism", in politics as well as religion, colours as much as half of the working-class backbone of Unionism.' (ibid.) This impression was confirmed by David Lindsay Keir on his return to Belfast.

Letter from David Lindsay Keir, Former Master of Balliol College, Oxford and Vice-Chancellor of Queen's University, Belfast, 6 November 1966

Dear Jack,

. . . It is a pleasure to read what you say about *The Round Table*. And reassuring too. Northern Ireland does need access to such a forum. The world of journalism doesn't seem to find it easy to report impartially or even accurately—too many Southern Irish journalists perhaps! Now more than usual, our case can be misrepresented, and silence as reply is not always sound tactics. Terence O'Neill can do with friends on this side of the water. I read the *Telegraph* with interest and sympathy, also not with[out?] anxiety. What struck me when I was over was that while middle-class support for him was general—and confident—it was nothing like so certain at the lower-middle and working-class levels. And nothing by way of compensation from the Nationalist side. . . .

I enjoyed being at Lennoxvale again—but for those Residential Towers. Oh my!

My doubts about the New University do not, I fear, get less. But of course I haven't seen Derry or Coleraine of late.

Yours ever,
David

With O'Neill still having to be 'his own reconnaissance party', the year of decision had ended gloomily indeed.

6 The Press Militant, 1967–8

That the events of 1966 had severely shaken Sayers, there can be no doubt. If his press campaign had won plaudits from friends and rallied the faithful, it had not created the atmosphere necessary for much conversion. Indeed, it had served only to provoke O'Neill's opponents into further challenges to his leadership, while at the same time publicising Ulster's problems, so arousing the attention of English opinion and Labour backbenchers. Thus by November O'Neill had found himself in a two-way squeeze from which there appeared no obvious reprieve. Not surprisingly, Sayers's first editorial of 1967 dwelt on a 'grim' year past 'with chilling moments of revelation of hatred and thuggery hidden not far below' (*BT*, 2 Jan. 1967). None of this killed off his optimism, which still rejoiced in the emergence of 'a braver and fairer-minded consensus'. Sustaining this was the world-wide ecumenical movement. For Sayers this was an essential ingredient to the liberalisation of Ulster politics, and he had sought continually to encourage dialogue between the churches. In late January he was again on television promoting this cause, anxious that such progress had yet to involve the laity. On the same programme Cardinal Conway took up this theme by pointing out that with their 'very deep sense of social and economic grievance . . . to some [Catholics] the ecumenical movement seems like asking them to shake hands with someone who still has his boot on their neck' (BBC's 'Viewpoint', 25 Jan. 1967). Yet the programme's opening shot of the 'Paisley riots' showed where the real political challenge to ecumenical movement lay. That week the visit of the Bishop of Ripon, Dr John Moorman, to Belfast to talk at an ecumenical meeting in the cathedral had to be cancelled when Paisleyites and the Orange Order threatened to march on the cathedral. The Dean of St Anne's, Cuthbert Peacocke, was determined to defend the principle of free speech. But O'Neill feared a fresh outbreak of disorder and over dinner with Peacocke pondered aloud on the possibility of desecration.

Letter to Conolly Gage, 31 January 1967

My dear Conolly,
A month of the year gone before I have wished you and Nancy a happy one.

Your letter has been waiting for a reply all this time, and I can only plead work, work and more work—and the arrival of a new managing director from the *Scotsman*. A financial mind, but none the worse for that, provided he doesn't squeeze my space quotas too far.

You are getting this partly because I've hurried away from lunch and partly because I know you will have read about the Bishop of Ripon in our paper last night. No harm to him, but was there ever an Englishman with less understanding of the (Northern) Irish! I'm sorry for Cuthbert Peacocke, who shouldn't have given the cathedral in the first place. Events have had Stormont very worried, and they can't be any more content now with the prospect of the Bishop being kept away altogether. It makes any story for press and TV all over the world. I confess I would rather Dr Moorman had never been asked—we are getting on well enough with inter-church co-operation without straining after unity, however that may appeal to heart and intellect in those who are most aware of the need. But for all this, Paisley was reasonably quiet, cooking up something for the municipal elections in May.

We have three articles on the Mater [Hospital] this week, partly designed to put a stop to the all-or-nothing thinking of Ardill [N.I. MP for Carrick] and other backbenchers close to Morgan [Minister for Health and Social Services]. Terence did well to get the cabinet behind the electoral reforms, but he [has?] education grants and family allowances still to come. He *is* a trier—with the significant aid of Ken Bloomfield. I hope you noticed the PM's speech at Ballymoney with the accent on the radical tradition in Unionism. Do tell me what you thought of Wilson's remark at Strasbourg. Stormont very suspicious, of course, but I didn't attach too much importance to it. It's the old story—and very much your own—that we only have to do the reasonable things and stay together and there is naught to fear. Bless you again for all your faith and encouragement last year—I'll need it again this year too!

Ever,
Jack

It has to be said that Moorman was an inflammatory choice. He led the Anglican delegation to Italy for talks with Roman Catholic theologians. Moreover, on his return he had declared that the Pope would have to be leader of any reunified church. Sayers's retort in *The Round Table* (Feb. 1967) that 'the intellectual processes by which he reached this conclusion are not, alas, given to the average Ulsterman' reflected a few lacunae of his own. These sprang from the fact that Sayers chose to interpret events in Northern Ireland as 'a classic struggle between the forces of progress and reaction'. In the 1960s in particular, reactionaries were viewed with especial contempt, and certainly their opinions were rarely deemed worthy of serious consideration. Consequently, rather than try to understand Paisleyism, it was simply discussed as 'rabid', for ever invoking the 'egregious bogey of the Romeward trend'.

At a Council of Europe meeting in Strasbourg, Wilson, in answer to a delegate from the Irish Republic, had simply repeated the official British view that if the North chose to reunify with the South, Britain would not resist. To suspicious minds this was deemed ambiguous. The reluctance of the Catholic Mater Hospital to surrender its independence and come under the aegis of the welfare state in return for government funding raised equally traditional hackles at home. Soon, however, Stormont would have a genuine crisis to agitate over. In late April O'Neill sacked Harry West, the Minister of Agriculture, for contravening the code of conduct O'Neill had established for cabinet ministers in 1963. Concern particularly centred on West's purchase of farmland which Fermanagh County Council was considering acquiring with financial support from Stormont for an airfield. However, the affair soon grew out of all proportion to the issue by the public declaration of support for West by many of O'Neill's critics. Foremost among these was Faulkner, who declared that West was 'certainly absolutely blameless'. This had been an off-the-cuff remark made as he was being hounded by journalists, but immediately Stormont was thick with rumours of plots. To Sayers, increasingly fearful of British intervention if the reform programme stalled, such displays of disunity seemed to him the height of irresponsibility. 'Historians will not fail to remark', he noted disparagingly, 'that on the day Mr Harold Wilson proclaimed Britain's will to enter Europe the parliament of Northern Ireland had nothing better to do than grub in the muddy fields of Co. Fermanagh.' ('Single Standard', *BT*, 3 May 1967) After quoting *The Times* that West's actions were 'of a kind which would be held to be incompatible with the tenure of ministerial office in London', he openly despaired at 'an elderly statesman like Brookeborough allow[ing] a personal loyalty to come before what should be his highest loyalty of all'. What this squalid affair brought into stark relief was that for some Unionists their Britishness was less a way of life than a flag of convenience. 'They . . . tend to see Northern Ireland in isolation, a law unto itself, who are British when it suits them, and who refuse to play any part in bringing the Unionist Party out of the past and into the present.'

As talk of British standards seemed to cut little ice in Fermanagh, Sayers looked to his friend Conolly Gage for moral support.

Letter to Conolly Gage, 3 May 1967

My dear Conolly,

. . . Tonight's news is that Terence is likely to dispense with Brian Faulkner, and difficult as Brian has been, I do consider this a great tragedy. It would signal the end of my hope that he and Terence could form a common front, without which I fear Terence will never really reach the rank-and-file of the party.

He had to act over West, and the Fates were against him that it should have caused such a storm. Brookeborough for one was stupid in his attitude. My feelings you will have read, particularly in the leader tonight. Ulster is failing to rise to the challenge of the times.

I suppose the truth is that if we had a Stanley Baldwin, he would be the man to take over from Terence. There is no one else, so with all his faults we have to support him. I do wish that his personality would allow him to bring together a really liberal 'band of comrades'.

I grieved for the death of Brian Maginess, although he was long since spent as a political force. I do wish he had kept his mission alive instead of becoming Attorney-General.

Ever,
Jack

P.S. Glad you liked *The Ulster Crisis*. I was relieved when the *Irish News* held it not to be offensive to Nationalist opinion.

In the event Faulkner stayed. If anything, the crisis harmed him more than O'Neill. Daily he found himself subjected to press demands (particularly from the *Belfast Telegraph*) for assurances, as he angrily put it, the like of which 'he couldn't give to the Archangel Gabriel'.

In some ways O'Neill was his own worst enemy. Sayers was furious at O'Neill's refusal to press the flesh after his speech to the Unionist Party conference, with the West controversy then at its height. On those occasions when the Prime Minister did allow himself to be buttonholed by one of his own backbenchers, his boredom could be only too obvious. Nor was his relationship with his cabinet colleagues much warmer. The lack of consultation over major initiatives affected his sympathisers as much as Faulkner. On top of this, more out of shyness than anything, he developed a cold, aloof manner in cabinet that did little to win friends. At the same time, for all that he became the victim of Faulkner's ambitions, he was no less ambitious himself, which the later tones of moral superiority could never erase. Moreover, he could be quite feline in his personal rivalries: 'If you like me, you like my policies', he once told Rafton Pounder, when querying his friendship with Faulkner. Consequently, he came to rely on a kitchen cabinet of civil servants—Harold Black (Cabinet Secretary), Ken Bloomfield (Cabinet Office) and Jim Malley (Private Secretary)—who were like-minded and respectful. In contrast to his coolness towards his party colleagues, his relationship with his advisers became quite intimate, and they in turn became highly influential. Indeed, the increasing hostility from Unionist Party ranks only intensified O'Neill's dependence on their companionship and advice. This obviously was no way to run a party, and the Prime Minister sought to overcome this by elaborate presidential displays and walkabouts in which the image became a substitute for consultation. Yet O'Neill lacked the charisma to appeal over the heads of the party to the Ulster people. While he took great heart from what he called the 'Bobby Kennedy-like receptions' that greeted him in his forays into the province, this counted for little in comparison with institutional support. In this respect, the attempt to expel his cousin, Phelim O'Neill, and two other prominent Unionists from the Orange Order for attending Roman Catholic services boded ill for his reform programme.

In the end, judgement was delayed for a year. Sayers chose to escape from such intolerance by retreating into nostalgia. This had been encouraged by two works: A. T. Q. Stewart's *The Ulster Crisis* and a manuscript copy of the Holmes Memoirs (which Sayers felt had shown that Gladstone had been 'honest about Ireland').

Letter to Conolly Gage, 5 July 1967

My dear Conolly,
I hope you will not have been anxious for the safety of the manuscript [of the Holmes Memoirs]. After I read it I thought John Horgan would like to see it. He has been ill, and it struck me that it was the kind of reading that would go with his convalescence. . . . I liked both the Irish and London atmospheres, and I must say that it left a good impression of Gladstone.

If there are any historical disclosures I am afraid they escaped me. This is a pity because my own picture of Irish affairs in the decade before the first Home Rule Bill is far from clear, particularly as to the North. How little mention we get as such in the Memoirs!

We have been talking to A. T. Q. Stewart, the author of *The Ulster Crisis*, about the *Telegraph* centenary which falls in 1970, and I hope he will do a broad survey of the whole period. He is casting around for another subject for a major work, and the most I could do was to suggest that he might try to trace the liberal thread from the early eighteenth century. Have you read the two volumes by MacKnight, who was editor of the [*Northern*] *Whig* in the last thirty years of the nineteenth century, and who, beginning as a Liberal ended up very much the Unionist? This kind of experience seems to make it all the more necessary that someone should show that the liberal lode [star] was not entirely lost at that time. . . .

I must say that since the West episode Terence seems to have crossed a watershed, and is now more secure than he has ever been. I just wish that he felt strong enough to tackle the party organisation and the Orange Order, and to try to ensure that the new harmony produces results.

For your private eye, we had the Cardinal to lunch last Friday, and he asked, with no little justice, when the promises of legislative reform are to be accompanied by more jobs and houses and appointments to public positions. I must say that from this point of view Terence's policy is slow to have practical effect.

Ever,
Jack

In such a mood, Sayers sought to concentrate sympathetically on the Orange tradition in his eve-of-the-Twelfth leader ('Remember 1967', 12 July 1967). Later that evening, after the Belfast parades had passed off peacefully, Peter Moeller of *The Times* found Sayers in high spirits at the *Telegraph*. 'This is Ulster. You can't ignore it: the uniforms, the bands, the parade—they are all part of what we are.' After the West affair, there was now a sense of confidence among O'Neill supporters. The near-lynching of the Unionist MP George Forrest by anti-O'Neill Orangemen in Co. Tyrone should have served as a warning against complacency. But metropolitan assumptions that the west was always wild invariably prevailed. Hence when Brookeborough suffered a serious illness in the autumn, Sayers's precautionary obituary was generous indeed of a man who had lost few opportunities to distance himself from his successor's policies.

Draft Obituary of Lord Brookeborough, BBC, 7 September 1967

I can't believe that anyone ever had a greater hold on a political party than Lord Brookeborough had in the first ten years of his premiership. Of the Ulster leaders before him, Carson was idolised and Craigavon was admired and respected. But Sir Basil, as everyone knew him then, was extraordinarily well liked—and by people of all kinds. *And* this wasn't only for his charm and humour, quite overwhelming as they could be.

His lineage made him a natural leader, and as a Unionist and as an Orangeman he, almost effortlessly, inspired complete confidence. He was the first to say that he wasn't a *politician*, and I rather think that if he had been, his popularity would have been far less.

When he went to Canada and the United States in 1950, I went with him as press officer. The tour was a great success—I remember that he even charmed the Irish-American pickets outside the Waldorf-Astoria—but he could never stick to his scripts. These were speeches prepared in advance, but after the first paragraph or two he nearly always went off on his own. Afterwards his apology would be: 'I like to say exactly what I feel, so that, at least, they can't accuse me of insincerity.'

And, of course, that is entirely true. He was a countryman, and he was shrewd, but he was always himself, and no one could ever say that he was devious. He was not a political thinker, and in most governmental matters he leaned heavily on his advisers.

But he knew he had the party behind him, and he would hardly ever do anything to disturb its unity. . . .

I just wonder how much more he could have done for the Unionist Party, and Northern Ireland, if he had thought in the broader terms of today, and had made full play with that famous personality and authority.

All this proved premature and only served to infuriate the 'Young Turks' at the *Telegraph* who deplored these wistful reflections on effortless leadership and blue blood. But more pressing matters would soon claim their attention.

Letter to Conolly Gage, 11 September 1967

My dear Conolly,

. . . Our three weeks in Malta passed serenely, but the heat was rather too severe for me at times—from a high BP I fell so low as to be faint, an odd condition indeed. . . .

I only missed the R[oyal] N[avy]. One frigate and one minesweeper was all that Britannia could muster. And when we left, the Grand Harbour had been taken over by the US 6th (?) Fleet carrier and all! The Knights must rub their eyes! While I was there I heard of the death of my dear friend, John Horgan, in Cork. He was eighty-six and in full possession of his wonderful mind until the end. If only there had been more Irishmen like him! Perhaps you saw Dermot Morrah's appreciation in *The Times*—I persuaded him to write it as the former editor of *The Round Table*. Into which I have more and more difficulty in getting a piece about Northern Ireland. Not that there is so much to say—Terence is lying very low. The meeting with Lynch seemed set for last week, but again he drew back, and the hope now is that it can take place among the Christmas festivities. You will have read Glengall Street's fury with the Labour lawyers—the enquiry can hardly fail to find that not enough is being done, certainly in the way of public appointments, to my mind the easiest sector in which to show some goodwill. We had the Cardinal to lunch earlier in the summer, and he was strong on the point that there is much talk and little action. I fear this is too true. The striking thing is that McAteer has become so philosophical about it. I am spending tomorrow at the Foreign and Commonwealth Offices with a party of provincial editors and hoping against hope that I shall hear something that will restore my faith in what we stand for in the world. . . .

At home we are all past the stage of preaching. The talk begins to be hollow, and we need to find positive courses of action. If we don't, I could see many good people on both sides becoming frustrated and cynical. . . .

Ever,
Jack

The Society of Labour Lawyers had launched their inquiry into religious discrimination in April 1967. While some Unionists saw it as outside interference in the province's affairs, others feared that the raising of such a controversy could only endanger fragile improvements in community relations. To Sayers the sensitivities of the latter view were fast becoming a luxury. Catholic frustrations and a growing British concern for 'normal democratic standards' would ensure that the issue would not conveniently disappear. Instead he looked to the report 'clarifying' the issue and compelling the fulfilment of Catholic desires for 'greater social recognition and equal citizenship' (*The Round Table*, Aug. 1967). Given this, it was not surprising that he should dismiss as 'sublime stupidity' (*BT*, 30 Sept. 1967) recent appointments to government boards which saw eleven Protestants appointed to every one Catholic. On the other hand, Unionist attempts to improve the grant to Catholic schools ironically backfired.

Letter to Conolly Gage, 26 October 1967

My dear Conolly,

... I think you will have liked Jenkins's speech on Wednesday—I was drawn to his historical approach. The Ulster members are inclined to think that he was against them, but I thought it a reasonable statement. How far it will get us is another matter, now that we face another conflict over the schools. Wilfully or no, Philbin 'couped' the White Paper even before it was issued, and I can't see how the Cardinal can get him out of so entrenched a position. The trouble is that so many Unionists, even some near the top, are pleased and the rest of us are left wondering how we can make any gains while the schools are the scene of so much bitterness. I don't blame the cabinet, although it might have been put more winningly. You must be sure to read all the letters to the editor—they give a lot of support to the ministry view that the laity, not to speak of a fair number of priests, would welcome the maintained status. We uphold the principle (Martin Wallace's leader made the point strongly), but what I wrote last night (Wednesday) I believe to be the most politic course. ...

Ever,
Jack

What had aroused Bishop Philbin's anger was the government's demand for representation on the school management boards in return for the increased grant. This he saw as a ruse to win control over Catholic education. Sayers thought this far-fetched, particularly as 'four-and-two' committees guaranteed a Catholic majority. He put the bishop's outburst down instead to fear that an increasingly obsolete system of clerical control could give way to lay management. However, he recognised that Philbin's disastrous intervention was also the product of ministerial reluctance to be seen hobnobbing with the Catholic hierarchy. By not allaying clerical anxieties and 'smoothing the advance' of the White Paper (*BT*, 25 Oct. 1967) a gesture of good-will had only stoked up the flames of ancient controversy. When the atmosphere improved after the visit of Jack Lynch, the Irish Taoiseach, to Belfast on 11 December 1967, it took G. B. Newe to ensure that there were no further mishaps.

Letter from G. B. Newe, Secretary, Northern Ireland Council of Social Service, 29 January 1968

Personal and Confidential

My dear Jack,

I know you will be, personally, most interested to know of a small part I was able to play in getting discussions going again between the Cardinal and the Minister of Education on the Education Bill. I also feel that the knowledge may help you in any editorials. . . .

Cardinal Conway—and Dr Philbin—each sent me copies of the bishop's statement. After much thought I wrote to Bill Long, who is an old friend of mine, urging him not to do or say anything which might result in putting the climate of relationships back to pre-Garron Tower Conference days. I also reminded him that, three years hence, Northern Ireland would be celebrating fifty years of statehood and it was my earnest hope that the event would be celebrated with the utmost goodwill and understanding on the part of all sections of the community.

I sent Cardinal Conway a copy of my letter and, in a covering note, urged him to make similar approach.

One of the factors which impelled me to so write was the fact that the Cardinal had invited the Catholic MPs and Senators to meet him. I foresaw the danger that the approach to the principles involved would be reduced to the level of a Catholic–Protestant slanging-match, with consequent disastrous results for all concerned.

It happened I had to be at the Ministry of Education on Monday 22 January for discussions about our request for grant-aid to enable us to appoint a full-time officer for our Junior committee. Bill Long rang me and asked me to see him.

We had a very frank discussion, as only friends could have. It was clear to me that the Cardinal was making a grave error in showing little interest in discussing the form of the instruments which, in the shape of Statutory Rules and Orders, would give effect to the Bill's provisions. Long had assured me that it was more than likely that 60–70 per cent of the fears expressed by the bishops would be taken care of in the rules and regulations to be made under the Bill.

Before I went up to Dundonald House, Cardinal Conway phoned me to thank me for my intervention and said he would be glad to have a discussion with me. He phoned me before I knew I'd be seeing Bill Long.

On my return to the office I phoned the Cardinal and at 5 p.m. went down to see him.

Again we had a frank exchange of views, as between friends. I think the Cardinal was glad to have someone like myself to talk to in the way we did talk.

As I suspected, he had shown no enthusiasm for discussions about instruments resulting from the proposed legislation, because he felt that to do so would perhaps be taken as weakening his primary position vis-à-vis the Bill.

To make a long story short, I was able to persuade him to

(a) frame suggested amendments and put them to Long directly, inviting him (Long) to introduce them as his own, if he should find them acceptable. Only if Long felt he could not accept them should the Cardinal circulate them to the opposition;

(b) enter into discussions with the Ministry as to the shape and content of the instruments – the S[tatutory] R[ules] & O[rders] – to be forged to govern such matters as the duties, function and responsibilities of School Management Committees.

I persuaded him further that the discussions should be with him directly, and not with any 'lesser fry' on the Catholic side. This not alone to save time, but also because—as I told him—he was the only churchman I knew who could rise above prejudices of one kind or another and was as well the *only* man who could talk the same language as the officials! I agreed that my views reflected rather badly on his fellow-bishops and the clergy generally!

He somewhat grudgingly admitted that his legal training as a canon law lawyer gave him an advantage and enabled him to see the whole edifice rather than isolated rooms and corridors.

He agreed I could tell the ministry of his readiness to talk in depth about the instruments which would give flesh to the proposed legislation. He made one proviso—namely that the minister should speak, in introducing the second reading and in replying to the debate, in conciliatory tones, 'closing no doors'.

I got back to Belfast at 11.45—dead beat! It had been an exhausting exercise, for I had to try to interpret the minister to the Cardinal and be sure I could interpret the Cardinal to the minister, without damage to my own integrity.

On Tuesday morning I telephoned Benn [Permanent Secretary, N.I. Ministry of Education], and my message introduced a new atmosphere and fresh hope that, perhaps, reasonable agreement could be reached without loss of face on either side. I also spoke to Ken Bloomfield and asked him to put the PM in the picture as well as urge that the government's approach should continue to be conciliatory. Naturally Bloomfield was very pleased, and what I was able to report coloured the attitude of both the PM and the minister in their meeting with the Catholic MPs.

Benn, of course, agreed to drop everything and meet the Cardinal on the Friday and, if needs be, on the Saturday. This because the Cardinal had to leave for Rome on the Monday until Wednesday. He (the Cardinal) explained that he had to go since he already had had the meeting postponed twice because of the White Paper, etc. etc.

That's the position as I left it. I have had a letter of appreciation from Long, and I pray that the discussion will have a favourable outcome.

Long has, of course, to placate his 'extremists'; equally, the Cardinal has to bring his 'diehards' with him. As I recognised when I read it, the 'Bishops' White Paper' was written by the Cardinal, and written in tones which were much more friendly than some of his colleagues would have them!

We, all of us, are fortunate that a man of the Cardinal's temperament and outlook is where he is, and we must go as far as possible to strengthen his hand.

I did tell him of the most unhappy atmosphere created by Dr Philbin's statement when the White Paper was published—a statement I felt to be inspired by Monsignor Mullally and the shades of the Dr Mageean regime. I told him too that the Northern bishops badly needed a good 'P[ublic] R[elations]O[fficer]'! He was kind enough to say that the job was mine if I wanted it, and on my own terms! . . .

It has just struck me to wonder if another meeting between you and the Cardinal might not be opportune? What do you feel?

Yours ever,
G.B.

The next day Newe wrote again, this time to congratulate Sayers on the latest recognition of the *Telegraph*'s efforts to confront sectarianism, the New Ireland Society's Community Award. 'Often', he wrote, 'in the past ten years (since the Garron Tower Conference!) your light has been a beacon, to guide us past the rocks thrown up, now and again, by feelings of frustration if not almost despair.' (G. B. Newe to Sayers, 30 Jan. 1968)

In contrast, the *Protestant Telegraph* ridiculed the award as the 'greatest joke yet'. That was of little consequence to Sayers (although he kept the press cutting). What was of significance were two speeches by O'Neill rejecting the charge that Unionism was sectarian. In both his speeches, to Carrick Unionists (31 Jan. 1968) and the Irish Association (19 Feb. 1968), his olive branch to the minority consisted of an invitation to share the spoils as 'Northern Ireland Ltd' reaped the economic rewards of the link with Britain. Once again he repeated his call made at Corrymeela for 'minimum duty of allegiance' from the minority and rejected arguments for 'reciprocal emasculation' as 'like trying to solve the colour problem by spraying everyone a pale shade of brown'. Intriguingly, Sayers, who had been fulsome in his praise for the Corrymeela speech, had now come to doubt if such a vision would be sufficient.

Having heard O'Neill's 'admirable speech' to the Irish Association, Sayers was left pondering on why, after all his own efforts, 'the democratic process does not yet reflect fully the broad area of middle ground . . . occupied by reasonable men'. Accepting his award from the New Ireland Society two days later, Sayers signalled a tactical retreat. Stressing that political obstacles 'were not to be overcome by frontal attack but by wide outflanking movements', he called for a 'transition from a political to a social approach'. In practice this meant not only the acceleration of modernisation (motorways, new towns, economic planning) but also the greater involvement of the minority in the administration of at least health, education and social welfare.

Letter to Conolly Gage, 5 March 1968

Devonshire Club

My dear Conolly,
At last a chance to assure you that I still exist! As you say, it isn't always apparent from the look of the *Telegraph*. Your feelings about the wretched [J-]cloth were exactly my own—but I lost the struggle to have it refused. I fear the truth is that the management side will always carry the day in issues of that kind. Am I spoilsport to say that we are—on grounds of morals as well as of date—overdoing 'Find the Ball'? I've tried to have it restrained, but it presents a ready way to bring in a mass of money: indeed, it now forms an essential part of the paper's revenue. It is vain for me to point out that all these things inevitably detract from our editorial standing—a stronger editorial director in London would take my part, but among the Thomson regional newspapers only the *Scotsman* is able to rely on its character.

This is my apology, such as it can be. I continue to have authority in my own department but the paper is being changed by other means, and what with this and the burden of administration, production, promotion, budgeting, personnel management and the rest, I'm glad I can look forward to my retirement. In any event, I think that perhaps my job has been done and that newspaper-making if not politics is now for younger men to grapple with. The New Ireland Society award was gratifying, but I had an impression that it marked the end of an era. Not that there isn't more to be done in the atmosphere that now prevails (where it does prevail), yet again it is younger people who must do the exemplifying.

Since Terence talked to the Irish Association—a venturesome thing to do even now—my mind has been occupied with a problem of which I've always been conscious. Community relations are all the thing—the term is in danger of becoming a bore—but in their better form they are only a beginning.

The PM sees this and no doubt the political disadvantages; he doesn't or won't see that the movement needs a more inspirational basis, that you can't ask Catholics to forget their nationalism in favour of civics and good works. We should be looking for more of a sharing of the Irish heritage. Perhaps for St Patrick's Day I'll develop this in an editorial. Terence fled from the mention of Wolfe Tone—and I wouldn't plug it—but the answer is that any rapprochement he is looking for can't be confined to a glorification of Ulster alone. That Red Hand should only be one of two.

As PM he continues to worry me by his loneliness and insecurity. The Irish Association speech had a most plaintive note. No wonder. Even the Belfast housing controversy is being used as a threat to him through the Minister of Development. It's said that he can count on not more than four backbenchers—with Phelim [O'Neill] unpredictable! He keeps advocating devolution for the rest of the UK, but to me it's folly for the country to subdivide itself any further.

I was at the Foyle College O[ld] B[oys'] dinner in Derry on Saturday and must say that I was immensely impressed by the new spirit there—as between Protestant and Catholic and in a rediscovery of confidence in the city. The area plan is a great thing—why don't you support its showing at Guildhall on 29 March. All Ulster notables in England will be there! You will have seen that Teddy Jones and Ambrose McGonigal have got the new judgeships. There was to have been only one appointment—McGonigal—but a point was stretched in Teddy's favour. He'll be very good even if the Bar is left to put up with an Attorney not to its liking by any means. Porter was too junior to succeed—and without Queen's behind him may not get another seat. He is very much a man after your own heart, and significantly enough he's from Derry of all places.

I really have been tied down by work and public duty of one kind or another and am sorry to be so undependable a correspondent. Please be sure your letters—even your reproaches —are as welcome as ever.

> Every good wish to you both,
> Jack

P.S. The education system will not be so bad as it may look.

If he too was sounding plaintive, it was as much due to developments in the press as it was to the limitations of government policy. The absorption of the *Telegraph* into the Thomson organisation was proving increasingly painful. While there was no interference with editorial policy, Sayers resented the attempts to poach his best reporters and the intrusion of whiz-kid economics with its obsession for cost-benefit analyses and 'bottom lines'. The promotional supplements he found pure vulgarity. As for the insistence, on grounds of cost, of less (and less late) editions, it seemed to him a denial of his journalistic instincts. Nothing symbolised the new regime more than the fact that it was the advertisement department that first sorted out the layout before sending it up to Sayers and the journalists to fill in the spaces. With each day littered with minor humiliations and his health worsening, it was not surprising that he began to consider the future. What followed was a memorandum that represented something of a journalistic last stand—proud and defiant —and no doubt was filed away as such.

Internal memorandum, Editorial Department, Belfast Telegraph, 8 March 1968

Memorandum by Editor-in-Chief

By July 1968, when I shall be fifty-seven, I shall have edited the *Belfast Telegraph* for fifteen years, and from every point of view the right course will be for me to retire from the editorship at the age of sixty. In this way I would be able to take part in our centenary in 1970 and to complete forty-one years with the paper. (My father joined it in 1896, and our family association would run to seventy-five years, a matter of no little pride to me.)

For these reasons I welcome a plan of succession, and having regard to the long range planning now being initiated I think this must involve consideration of the kind of paper we expect to publish in the seventies.

The *Telegraph* aims to give as comprehensive and responsible a local coverage as is usually found in the medium-sized provincial mornings. In recent years it has actually assumed the functions of a morning, treating the news in the widest sense and giving the strongest leadership to public opinion. Our editorial policy (and the vagaries of the *News Letter*) has enabled us to become the source of a broad range of information indispensable to Northern Ireland.

While this has proved a sound basis for our success as a business, I doubt whether it can be fully maintained in face of many changes that are now making themselves felt. These include commercial and production policy, competition from television and possibly local sound radio.

They all point to a trend towards the evening paper prototype, concerned very largely with the liveliest news stories, pithiness, colour pictures and high-speed methods. And it is true to say that in the future our readers generally may look for a more sophisticated offering.

I am none the less certain that we have a duty to try to preserve the standard of intelligence and social outlook we now have in mind in our assessment of the importance of news, in editorials, magazine page articles, criticism, etc.

The hold we have on the best public opinion should be kept, although this may not be so easy with new formats and against the developing 'argumentativeness' of television and the other papers. I see our main campaign of reform already rewarded and future situations in which we will seem to be rather less radical in our views.

Yet his leader on the eve of St Patrick's Day was probably too 'radical' for most Unionists. Not for the first time, constructive Unionists in pursuit of common identity took refuge in Ireland's pre-reformation past. Rejecting the 'colleens, begorrahs, leprechauns, Celtic mists, and all other stage props', Sayers stressed the modern relevance of St Patrick lay elsewhere. 'Somewhere the community that badly wants to become more close-knit has to rediscover its common heritage. And that can only mean that all must be ready to look back beyond the Scots settlements and the Plantation.' Taking his cue from Estyn Evans, he argued that 'only when more acknowledgement is made of these origins of all our life today can the present movements in Ulster find their truest expression'.

But such an evolutionary approach would at best take a generation to win over the constituencies, and in the short term it was simply unrealistic for O'Neill to adopt. By now any criticism in the *Telegraph* of O'Neillism was so oblique as to be almost imperceptible. Certainly O'Neill had no complaints with Sayers or his chief political correspondent, Roy Lilley.

Letter from Terence O'Neill, 20 March 1968

Stormont Castle

My dear Jack,
I hope to see Roy in the House—meanwhile as Harold is lunching with you I thought I would drop you a line.

I found Roy's articles last week both interesting and excellent. We could not have done as well ourselves in this office! I am very grateful.

Yours,
Terence

In the political lull there was time now for a holiday on the continent and even for a quick note to Gage to bring him the latest news as the year-long process to expel Phelim O'Neill from the Orange Order came to a head.

Letter to Conolly Gage, 25 May 1968

Devonshire Club

My dear Conolly,
It's odd that I never seem to write until I get to London. We are off to Austria tomorrow, and it's a mark of holiday that I have a few minutes to think of things other than *BT* and its ever-increasing weight of administration, the

most exhausting being a negotiation with the NUJ that would frighten Barbara Castle herself. A fortnight ago I might have told you of our fears for Terence, but since that episode on the Shankill Road, minor as it was, there has been a reaction very much in his favour. The fears are ever present because West, Craig, John Brooke—no longer Brian Faulkner—lean towards the argument that the party would be happier with a leader from the centre. I fear Brooke in this regard. The Orange looks to be giving nothing away on the issue first raised by Phelim [O'Neill] and really brought into the open by Robin [Chichester-Clark] and Drennan in attending your kinsman's funeral. This puts Terence in a new difficulty, for he mustn't have it said of him that he presided over a split between the party and the order. I've given up trying to persuade him to do more to combine his friends in one phalanx—he is forever operating on his own. By the way, we paid a tribute this week more to Ken Bloomfield than to T[erence]. Bloomfield is the speech-writer and to a very large extent the ideas man, and he makes a brilliant hand of it. Wish we did more justice to his scripts in our columns.

I must fly— . . .

Ever,
Jack

As he left, the increased grants to the (Catholic) voluntary schools became law, and Cardinal Conway wrote in appreciation of Sayers's support.

Letter from Cardinal Conway, 27 March 1968

Dear Dr Sayers,
Thank you for your kind comments on the bishops' statement, and I need not say that I share your hope that the operation of the scheme will be undertaken in a spirit of harmony and goodwill. I was glad to learn from your letter that you felt that more might have been done to relieve our anxieties; the 'Not another inch' policy pursued after the publication of the bill was indeed a grievous disappointment.

May I say also that I am sure that any Catholic school would be very happy to have you as public representative on its committee or board of governors.

Yours sincerely,
✠ W. Cardinal Conway

Sayers returned from Austria to the news that his friend Phelim O'Neill had indeed been expelled from the Orange Order for attending a Roman Catholic service during a civic week in Ballymoney. Never one blessed with the instincts of a diplomat, O'Neill had refused to disguise his contempt for his accusers, let alone attend the crucial meeting. Yet if O'Neill had not helped his own cause, the judgement of the Orange Order was nevertheless, to Sayers, 'a fateful decision', given the Prime Minister's recent assertions of a non-sectarian Unionism. 'Either the Order alters its outdated rules or surrenders its influence in party affairs'. (*BT*, 11 June 1968) But that, of course, was not the alternative. Sayers was dismayed to see the Chief Whip, Brian McConnell, preside over a meeting of a country lodge which reasserted these anti-Catholic regulations. Worse was to follow when in Twelfth of July speeches Faulkner, West and Roy Bradford strongly defended the Orange Order's position in Ulster Unionism.

Letter to Conolly Gage, 11 August 1968

My dear Conolly,
This is more than usually late when I think that your letter in June told me the good news that you are to have another Irish holiday. . . .

You must come in time to experience our extraordinary drought—I have never known the weeks after the 'Twelfth' to be so very dry. In the country today everywhere had a burnt-up look and it might have been France. Fortunately we are not having the atmosphere that goes with a 'long, hot summer', although I am still more concerned that Terence does not have more reliable support. It is disappointing to see John Brooke proving so antagonistic—of all people he has allied himself with Boal! The Grand Lodge post Tony Clark seems to be in the wrong hands. Phelim [O'Neill]'s was not the best of test cases but it will be really serious if the same action is taken against Robin [Chichester-Clark] and John Drennan following your kinsman's funeral. For the first time at the Twelfth I felt out of sympathy with the Orange [Order] and tended to write accordingly. Did you read the leader of yesterday? It referred to our report of the previous day that Brian McConnell—such a time-server—is to be president of the Industrial Court. This is not so much a reward for past services as the Ulster equivalent of a peerage, complete with salary. However, I don't think Terence is justified in using patronage to remove him, undependable as he is. Thank you again for the heartening things you said in your last letter in response to my woes about journalism. As for that and other crosses, it is a case of 'say not the struggle naught available'. . . .

Ever,
Jack

The atmosphere changed soon enough. On 24 August the first major Civil Rights march took place from Coalisland to Dungannon, where it found its path blocked by the RUC and 1,500 loyalists. But it was the events of 5 October that transformed the situation utterly. The defiance of a ban on all processions in Derry led to a violent confrontation between Civil Rights marchers and the police. If riots were not exactly a rarity in Ulster politics, what made this occasion significant was its capture on film. In *The Round Table* (Nov. 1968) Sayers ruminated on a 'sidelight of history' whereby a shortage of world news that weekend ensured that Derry became a focus of international attention. But there could be no denying the power of television to 'highlight, not to say over-illumine, such local situations'. Notwithstanding this, to Sayers 5 October served to make the issue crystal clear. The Civil Rights movement may have been 'a coat of many colours', but its protest against 'outrageous' discrimination in Derry was 'authentic enough'. 'The diminishing Irish volcano', he wrote with tragic lack of foresight, 'has had an eruption, but something says it could be one of the last.' (*The Round Table*, Nov. 1968) Such confidence was founded fatally on the politics of rational self-interest. Almost to the end he had assumed that most Unionists would respect 'the forces of destiny' (*BT*, 8 Nov. 1968) and rejoin O'Neill's 'decent, sane, orderly march towards social and economic progress'. Now with Wilson under pressure to intervene, Sayers feared that Stormont would be lost through Unionist bloodymindedness. Ruing Brookeborough's failure to educate the party, he wrote a series of leaders (*BT*, 8, 23, 25, 29, Oct. 1968) urging sweeping reforms. All was to no avail, as the cabinet continued to quarrel.

Letter to Conolly Gage, 1 November 1968

My dear Conolly,
I knew you would be intent on all that is happening here. Like the Prime Minister himself, my mood fluctuates, but perhaps after his visit to London on Monday he will be in a stronger position. Nothing is needed more than that he should be as fully in command as [Sir James] Craig.

It will have struck you, too, that the Unionist Party has come to a pretty pass when its top men are divided among themselves, and the best of the community is beginning to stand aside from it, certainly in so far as the churches and many others are backing the PM against all the diehards.

I have to admit, however, that there is still a lot of education to be done in the party before it really sees the light. Am I right in thinking that this is the last chance? It seems to me that if Wilson goes even a little too far, it could be the beginning of the end.

I am really staggered that we should be in the present position all for the lack of a united cabinet. If they would all stand together, I feel perfectly sure the country would stand with them. I have a mind to make this appeal when I write again on Tuesday next.

This is in haste. I do hope I shall manage to give you a longer bulletin next time.

Ever,
Jack

At Downing Street Wilson privately insisted on civil rights reforms and made ominous references to the future of Treasury subsidies to Stormont. Far from strengthening O'Neill's hand, this only stirred up a furious debate within the Unionist Party over Westminster 'interference'. In his Tuesday leader Sayers's counter-attack was stark in the extreme:'The threat to Northern Ireland's future is not Mr Wilson or Mr Lynch or the IRA, or even nationalism. It comes from Protestant Ulstermen who will not allow themselves to be liberated from the delusion that every Roman Catholic is their enemy.' (*BT*, 5 Nov. 1968) After 5 October it had become increasingly difficult to pass resolutions in favour of O'Neill at Unionist meetings, especially west of the Bann. Wherever the Prime Minister spoke he was accompanied by hostile demonstrations. At Maghera he had to preach his brand of liberalism behind locked doors as the mob bayed outside. The televising of the Derry riots had not only served as the signal for the 'Catholic revolt', but had also ensured the final collapse of Protestant deference. At one stormy meeting, as they waited on the platform to speak, Faulkner turned to Rafton Pounder and warned him 'to watch that guy in the third row'. When his colleague asked why, Faulkner explained:'You don't expect a cloth cap in the third row.' It was Paisley's ability to encapsulate the pent-up rage of the Unionist rank-and-file at their 'betrayal' by their 'betters' that enabled him to give cohesion to this Protestant revolt. In the light of this, the intellectual smugness of the *Belfast Telegraph* was bound to infuriate, particularly since—as this piece from the *Protestant Telegraph* suggests—the battle to win over public opinion seemed to be going the way of Royal Avenue.

Protestant Telegraph, 16 November 1968

... For many years Ulster people have been fed on a poisonous diet concocted and served by the press, radio, so-called Protestant churches, the Roman Catholic church, political parties of all shades and, of course, those unkempt and vociferous vassals from Queen's University who are presently misled and manipulated by a callow and self-opinionated boor.

Dr Ian R. K. Paisley has, for a long time, borne the brunt of this vicious and sustained spate of abuse. Never before has such a vile, constant and mighty torrent of hatred and malice been levelled at one man. . . .

Foremost in the fray is that fivepenny falsehood known as the *Belfast Telegraph*. For sheer lying and dishonesty, this fifth-rate excuse for a newspaper deserves special condemnation. . . .

This alleged newspaper once commanded respect. The advent of Sayers and Wallace has altered that. . . .

Nevertheless, the smear-sheet has accomplished its evil work. Having for years presented Dr Paisley as a bigot, lawbreaker, hatemonger and vicious extremist, it has convinced certain people that this rubbish is true.

The *Belfast Telegraph* has set Dr Paisley up as a target for every evil-intentioned thug. . . .

If every reader of the *Protestant Telegraph* determined not to buy the *Belfast Telegraph* and influenced his friends to do likewise, the scribbling serpents of Royal Avenue would have their fangs drawn. . . .

However, Paisleyism posed a more serious problem to Sayers. Invited to Sayers's office, Canon S. E. Long countered the editor's appeal for the Orange Order to restrain extremists by pointing out that it was the *Belfast Telegraph* that was giving Paisley maximum publicity. In a recent issue a Paisleyite rally had made the front page, while nationalists, who had on the same day opened their yards to provide parking space for the opening of a new county Orange hall, barely got a mention in the main body of the paper. Not surprisingly, such arguments left Sayers 'perplexed'.

No more so than his friend Terence O'Neill was. With Wilson's stay of intervention hanging over him, the Prime Minister was struggling to find a package of reforms acceptable to his cabinet, let alone his party. Since many of the reforms had never before been seriously considered by most Unionists, it was virtually impossible to overturn long-treasured assumptions in a matter of weeks. Nor, even if the parliamentary party had succeeded in doing this, would they have been able to win over the constituencies. Denied recuperation through a period of opposition, the Unionist government stood transfixed awaiting the crash. Characteristically, it took yet another leadership crisis to get things moving. Lunching at Aberfoyle with Sir Basil McFarland after attending an armistice service in Derry, O'Neill was called to the telephone to be told that some of his cabinet were plotting to oust him. Determined to resolve the conflict, O'Neill forced through a compromise with his five-point plan of 22 November. Yet he baulked at introducing 'one man, one vote' in local government elections. Despite the fact that it would have enfranchised more Protestants than Catholics, it had become a 'sacred cow' to the former, livid at having to make concessions to an alliance of, in the eyes of some, crypto-communists and the IRA. This package could never have stilled the civil rights momentum, and the vicious cycle of march and counter-march continued unabated. For Sayers himself, the sight of all that he had worked for being cast aside in an effort to resist 'the force of destiny' began to tell on his health. On 2 December his doctor ordered him to convalesce for a month.

Letter from Terence O'Neill, 5 December 1968

Stormont Castle

My dear Jack,
I was very delighted to hear from you and to learn that although you are having to take it a little easy you nevertheless remain at the helm. This is good news for all of us who owe so much to your influence over the years.
   I do hope you will soon be completely fit again. I only wish that we could find some remedy which would have an immediate effect upon the health of the body politic, but at all events we are doing our best.

Yours,
Terence.

O'Neill's 'Ulster at the Crossroads' broadcast on television four days later, while it was not to prove a lasting remedy, certainly had an immediate effect. Sayers, attending a Christian Brothers' Past Pupil Dinner the following night, took great heart in the enthusiastic cheering of every reference to O'Neill. Such a response reflected the near-universal praise that greeted the speech. Not since the early years of his premiership had O'Neill struck such a chord across the sectarian divide. Yet, as Sayers was witnessing the fruits of O'Neill's triumph, across the city Bill Craig, the Home Affairs Minister and longstanding ally of O'Neill, made a speech directly challenging the latter's acceptance of Westminster's right to intervene in Ulster's affairs. The sacking of Craig threatened to shatter the Unionist movement. In the light of these developments, Sayers returned to his office and, as well as writing the usual articles of support, he printed 'I back O'Neill' coupons in the *Telegraph* which his readership could cut out, sign and return. As a consequence of such instant polls, O'Neill received 150,000 messages of support in a matter of days, and Craig's challenge evaporated. With a decisive vote from the parliamentary party on 12 December, O'Neill ended the year firmly in office.
   Ironically, Sayers despite commissioning Alf McCreary to write an

article on 'The Fifty Day Revolution', was no longer so sure. The fact that at this critical moment in Ulster's history it had taken the cabinet six weeks to agree a policy on local government—an issue that was 'nakedly sectarian' (*BT*, 8 Nov. 1968)—depressed him enormously. He recognised that, in agreeing to shelve local government reform for three years, the government had in effect abdicated—and all, he noted bitterly , 'for the sacredness of Londonderry, the belief that to give away what King James could not capture in war was to give away all that William of Orange had ever stood for' (*The Round Table*, Nov. 1968). Still, for the moment the talk was all of triumph. Denis Hamilton, the editor of *The Times*, wrote to congratulate Sayers on O'Neill's performance and on the *Belfast Telegraph*—'an outstanding paper'.

By associating himself so openly with O'Neill's cause, Sayers had compromised any pretence to journalistic detachment. Indeed, 'Cromlyn' in the *Church of Ireland Gazette* entitled his article on the crisis 'O'Neill and Sayers', going on to declare that 'no one in our day in this country had done as much (not even Terence O'Neill himself) to enunciate and promote ideals of tolerance, justice and peace' than Sayers. Others spoke in even higher terms.

Letter from Bishop Buchanan of Clogher, 16 December 1968

My dear Dr Sayers,
Last week may prove memorable. If so, it will be largely due to you and to your paper. I realise there may be hurdles in front of us, but I think we may have turned the corner. I write to offer you my warmest appreciation. You have made history. . . .

Your very sincere friend,
Alan Clogher

Such optimism was to be short-lived, and in the new year others would show how really to make history.

7   Post-Mortems

The Irish magazine *Hibernia* (3 Jan. 1969) began the new year with a searching analysis of the *Telegraph*'s political muscle. This made much of its extensive readership, its pretentions to 'national' coverage, and the moral authority it had acquired under Sayers's editorship. Nevertheless, the true source of the *Telegraph*'s influence lay in its relationship with O'Neill, which appeared to be so close that 'at times, indeed, it is as if Capt. O'Neill has a doppelgänger flitting through the offices of the *Telegraph*'. It was a bond, of course, that worked to mutual advantage, but they also shared some weaknesses too. Both, *Hibernia* felt, believed it 'only necessary to state their aims in order to have them immediately apprehended and ultimately realised'; although it is hard to see how Sayers could have avoided adopting this attitude without turning the *Telegraph* into a political organisation. Equally telling was the criticism that for all their victories in the battles over principle, they were no nearer to winning the war over policy. That this was so was because the *Telegraph* had not yet achieved its chosen task of convincing enough of the public of the need for change.

Within twenty-four hours the justice of this charge seemed irrefutable after the ambush of a Civil Rights march at Burntollet. With the television screens providing, in the images of violence in Derry, the first sight for many of a traditional enemy, the moderate opinion that Sayers had cultivated so assiduously quickly succumbed to baser instincts. The next day he received a letter which appeared to extinguish any lingering hopes for a progressive, non-sectarian Unionism capable of winning significant Catholic support.

Letter from Mrs AW, 4 January 1969

Dear Sir,
I have just read 'Viewpoint' and wish to say thank you for understanding the situation so very well. I am a Catholic, a Civil Rights supporter (Civil Rights for *all*) and until now a law-abiding housewife with two young sons—I am also married to a Protestant! Anyway, after all this display of non-protection of Civil Rights marchers during the past few days, and of the blind eyes shown to the militant Protestants, I am beginning to feel stirrings of great anger

141

within myself at the injustices towards Catholics. I realise there are many non-Catholics who know what Civil Rights really means, but it's beginning to look to us now as if the government, RUC and most Protestants are against us when it comes to the crunch. I've even come up against it with my very good Protestant neighbours. Their attitudes are so changed, and I was grossly insulted in a neighbour's house the other night (the man of the house is a vice-principal in a leading school in Derry) and had to leave. They later apologised, and later still I discovered that they did so mainly because they were afraid of the other Catholic neighbours finding out. I don't know what they thought we would do or say, but this is the attitude all the time. You know we are not against Protestants, only against injustice and unfairness. We are taught by our church to love our neighbours and try to be good to them, especially if they are not of our faith, but now I find I have to ask God at intervals all through each day to give me patience and not to let me hate, and it is so very difficult not to, especially when we see Paisley and [Major Ronald] Bunting and realise how many thousands of Protestants openly *and* secretly support him. I now feel [suspicious?] of all Protestants, and I've never been like this in my life [before].

Now, I'm sorry for being so long-winded to such a busy man, but I'm really full up right now after things I've just seen down town. Those police hosing innocent women coming home with their shopping, even babies, old and young men and women and bus queues. My sister and I went down late, thinking it was all over, and walked right into it, and in one shop when we complained of the drenching a Protestant girl said: 'What are you all doing out anyway?'—now what do you say to a person like that? I saw young teenage boys being very badly beaten and manhandled by several policemen at a time, and my brother-in-law was told by an RUC man to f— off when he said he should go over to a place where Protestants were attacking young students. A Radio Éireann man was there also, but unfortunately his sound was not on and so it has not been recorded.

Now, what I really wrote to you about was this. It is people like yourself and Martin Wallace (who are probably Unionists and Protestants) who give the rest of us hope and the will not to despair. There was a time when I would not have bought your paper because it had such a bad name for sectarianism; now I buy it every night and just look for your words and think, especially tonight: 'Well thank God you [are] one decent man who sees things as they really are.'

So will you both continue to be as fair as you are today (I am sure it is far from easy, and it takes guts). You are doing untold good. As well as helping to calm us down and letting us see we are not completely alone and misunderstood, you may also help other Protestants who see only one thing in Civil Rights, [the] IRA.

I am a Nationalist and have always been in favour of settling everything with discussion, but today I think I understand the feelings of the IRA people and am afraid if I were a young boy or girl, that is where I would give my support. Maybe it's only after the sights I've seen that I feel like this, but honestly it's awfully hard not to feel bitter when you know that all these things are being done all because you love and worship God in a different building, all in His holy name. Can you imagine how He must be feeling now? . . .

For Sayers too, Burntollet was to prove a turning-point. He admitted to Dennis Kennedy (now working for the *Irish Times*) that he was 'badly shaken because my faith in so many ordinary people has not been realised. Having used the word 'atavistic' so often in the past, I fear I lost sight of its undying meaning!' (6 Jan. 1969)

Just as depressing was O'Neill's bad-tempered condemnation of the organisers (of what admittedly could only have been a provocative march), without dealing in equal measure with their Protestant assailants. The mobilising of the B Specials only intensified Catholic outrage and led to vigilante groups patrolling in 'Free Derry' and fresh riots in Newry. And yet O'Neill's announcement of an independent inquiry under a Scottish Judge into the recent disorders proved one gesture to the minority too many for Brian Faulkner, who on 24 January resigned at last.

For Sayers, incarcerated in hospital and in no mood to be generous, Faulkner's departure also provided the opportunity to pass judgement on O'Neill. Not surprisingly, given his perspective, the failure of O'Neillism was, he felt, a failure of leadership. A personality conflict between an ambitious, abrasive Faulkner and the feline Prime Minister had eroded the authority of the government, packed as it was with too many with no more courage than to 'wink' at the excesses of the extremists. Moreover, it lacked ideological commitment. It was not just that O'Neillism had too few supporters in the party, but also that even close friends were not sure where the PM stood. That Sayers should look instinctively, if only fleetingly, to the 'Big House' for a new leader suggested that he had not yet appreciated the temper of Protestant Ulster.

Letter to Conolly Gage, 26 January 1969

My dear Conolly,
At long, long last. And, I must confess, chiefly because I am a prisoner in the Musgrave Clinic. You will know the strains I have been under, but they ought not to have prevented me sending even notes in answer to your ever-wise observation of our calamities. I take it all to heart. Your encouragement is constantly needed, and your warnings no less. I am here because my blood pressure got out of hand again, and now I am right up against the question of retirement. At this time it smacks of treason. Nothing has been decided yet, but I like to think I could keep a political oversight—writing the leaders

when necessary—and hand the rest of the paper and its administration to Martin Wallace. All this until September next year, when we have our centenary. I can't possibly miss this, but when it is over I would expect to go, possibly keeping my directorship, not that that has any effectiveness. If Ulster has found itself again by then, I would be [happy] to turn to other things, public service in not too exacting a form. I have to own that the drugs I've been taking for so long can't any more fit me for the daily onslaught—an evening paper can be a madhouse at times! Really, I have been a [medical] case for twelve or more years, so I can't complain. If only there was more to show for my campaigning—one does feel a hopelessness sometimes, and Brian Faulkner's resignation has left so many of us with a sickening and sinking sensation. Later today I mean to write an editorial for tomorrow—the party must be called back to a sense of duty.

Brian's action looks cynical to me. Nor has he been completely honest in his statements. Terence is not free from blame. He has never worked well with his ministers—he has been suspicious of some of them, and all of them suspicious of him. I have said from the beginning that he must beware of an autocracy, and it is true that too much of government has been on a presidential basis, with the secretaries, Black, Bloomfield and Malley, as the aides. In general, the policy has been right, but coming from a divided cabinet it has lacked authority, the authority always necessary in Ulster, and all the more so when we have such undependable backbenchers. I have never yet been able to satisfy my mind about the PM's liberalism—it's far more intellectual than emotional, and even then much of it originates with Bloomfield. I dearly wish we could discuss this in the paper—it is so much the root of current history. But I can't let them down, not now! Once again I think Terence must battle on—but how much more battering can the party stand without flying apart? Of course, it is a classic situation for another man to take over. But think on it as we may, there isn't one. If Brookeborough was younger? Yes, but he is a Bourbon, and young John is worse. . . .

I must say that many people have, like you, been extraordinarily kind about what I have written since 5 October. I have been collecting the series for reference and like to believe that I have been at least on the side of the angels. If the party had paid more attention to the dangers I pointed to, it would not be as it is today.

A word on Newry. I agree we ought to have said more on the lines you indicate. But ever-present in my mind is the threat to liberty represented by Bunting. This man and his organisation is the greatest threat of all, and I am sorry to say that he intimidates the police and the government as well as everyone else. The story of the Derry march is a terrible scandal, and the man is still at large! I am convinced that we shall never emerge from the shadows till we have freedom of assembly and the tolerance that goes with it. Newry is a town where I thought it might be guaranteed. It wasn't and mainly because the government bowed to that frightful reaction Protestants have to the sight of any large body of Roman Catholics. It is compounded of fear and a bad conscience. Let Catholics keep to themselves and say nothing, and they can be at least indifferent to them; let them join together to make a legitimate protest, and they are rebels and even, in Paisley's word at St Paul's, 'scum'. Sometimes I lose my romantic notion of the Ulsterman and his love of liberty.

I'm reading John Drinkwater's life of Charles James Fox, and find a remarkable parallel between the loss of the American colonies and the loss we look like making of the friendship of the Catholic minority. Fox and Burke were so supremely right in urging a liberal settlement, but they were swept away. Why are we always so long and so late in being generous? As if it wasn't a Christian virtue taught from our earliest years. It's the corruption of power and the weakness of men who, knowing full well what must come, haven't the courage to tell their own followers. I think these are more to be scorned than those whose minds are shut. . . . But this is merely being moralistic—my experience of liberalism is that we pay lip-service to it but have little idea of practising it. . . .

Ever,
Jack

As promised, Sayers delivered his Burkean oration. For all the polished phrases and the sheer force of his political vision, there was now an unmistakable note of despair. Even allowing for the irritation that his quaintly Victorian moral tone could arouse, it was now the very powerlessness of the written word that so floored him.

Belfast Telegraph, 31 January 1969

LOSING ITS HEAD

Alas! Alas! When will this speculation against fact and reason end? What will quiet those panic fears which we entertain of the hostile effect of conciliatory conduct? Is it true that no case can exist in which it is proper for the sovereign to accede to the desires of his discontented subjects? Is all authority of course lost when it is not pushed to the extreme? Is it a certain maxim that the fewer causes of dissatisfaction are left by government the more the subject will be inclined to resist and rebel?

Burke's eloquence did not avert the War of Independence and the loss of the American colonies through the blindness of George III and Lord North. Can it say anything to an Ulster tottering on the brink of another act that could find a place of its own in the history of national folly?

This weekend the Unionist Party stands in grave danger of cutting off its own head. Never before has one section set itself so implacably against another; never before has it courted the disaster of putting personalities before prudence, politics before principle, provincialism before patriotism. . . .

If the time is past for the best of Ulster's leaders to command the natural obedience of all the rank-and-file, the time is also past for people of intelli-

145

gence and vision to deny themselves for the good of the cause. That kind of bowing in the direction of Sandy Row has gone. Political and social conscience . . . has reawakened and become the powerful and uncompromising liberal force that Ulster once knew.

It is well that the Guy Fawkeses at Stormont know this. The removal of Captain Terence O'Neill will not remove the thousands who have seen in him the hope of a new era imbued by a spirit of emancipation. Between those who are already Unionist and those who are not, there is the making of a centre party that could be the most significant development that Northern Ireland has yet seen. . . .

If his resort to crude jibes and talk of centre parties smacked of throwing in the towel, he nevertheless picked himself up for what was to prove the decisive battle, when O'Neill in a 'desperate throw' to protect his position called a general election. With the Unionist Party splitting into pro- and anti-O'Neill camps, he won a 'reasonably convincing victory at the polls' (*The Round Table*, Feb. 1969), winning, indeed, 44 per cent of the vote for his brand of moderate Unionism. Yet this achievement was undermined by the 'utterly surprising' narrowness of his victory over Paisley. Facing for the first time in his life a challenge in his own Bannside constituency, O'Neill was soon out of his depth. With the media turning the election into a high-profile, gladiatorial contest, his meagre majority became to him a very personal humiliation. Thereafter he could think of nothing else and was to be found forever seeking to justify the result to his friends. As always, in his review of the election for *The Round Table*, Sayers was sympathetic to O'Neill's plight. However his concluding description of O'Neill as 'this somewhat lonely and sometimes arrogant and awkward man, stamped by Eton and the Irish Guards', who nevertheless 'inaugurated so great a revolution', had all the hallmarks of an obituary. Others, equally sorrowful, could only agree.

Letter from David Lindsay Keir, Former Master of Balliol College, Oxford, and Vice-Chancellor of Queen's University, Belfast, 11 March 1969

My Dear Jack,
I have for some weeks felt the need for putting on paper my thoughts about what has been going on in Northern Ireland, and for sending the result to a sympathetic and well-informed friend. . . .

The *Telegraph* has been of the utmost interest and value to us here. Never have we both been more grateful, both for the reporting and the commentary. These issues will be indispensable to all who in future have the task of writing Ulster's history today. To keep one's head when all around . . . How often have I wished that the press on this side of the water had gone into questions as judiciously and with such detachment. They didn't find things at all easy to understand. And when they and the pollsters predicted a big win, even a landslide, for O'Neill, I felt sure they were wrong, and your cautious assessment was realistic. I've been wondering how surprised you were by the overall result. We ourselves got it nearly right. Belfast went less to O'Neill than we had hoped. It was surprising, however, that in Derry County there was so much support, though not enough. And North Down and North Armagh were somewhat odd. However, we were only three out about the general result, though not quite right on the detail. The general theory was to assume support for O'Neill east of the Bann and not west of it—and in the towns but not in the countryside.

Anyhow, even if not unexpected, the outcome was disappointing. Perhaps it was too much to hope that all Northern Ireland would choose to remain British-Irish, and at the first time of asking. Yet surely the value of the election, however disappointing and inconclusive . . . was that for the first time in generations it got Ulster to the polls, to think about votes and issues on which to decide (however confusingly presented), and to behave properly. It was really a well-conducted exercise and great experience.

Why did we get less than we hoped for? Some of the lessons are too obvious to need discussion—though the reporters and pollsters (who had a bad time!) didn't seem to have spotted them. The most interesting problem, I think, is whether O'Neill went about his task the right way. It's all too easy to criticise: a rather remote manner and lack of ease in getting in contact—partly reflected [in] Bannside's weird result, which we here didn't at all expect, and which is the gravest blow our cause sustained. Again, a tendency to act too personally—it's one thing to act against the wishes of one's colleagues, quite another not to tell them one is going to do so. Moreover, the appeal direct to the electorate, over the head of the party and without any clear indication of how popular support of a plebiscitary kind could become electorally effective, belongs more to presidential than to parliamentary government (Harold Wilson has damaged himself in the same way.) Further, the reliance on the material benefits accruing from the British connection, whereas men do not in the last resort vote on such grounds, whatever their relevance. And once again, the implication that Ulster depends on the 'subsidy' which might be cut off, and that a breakdown of government might lead to direct rule from London, both being unlikely to happen and, even if they were threatened, more likely to put Ulster's hackles up than make for submission. He might have organised and displayed his case better. And yet—and yet—he does stand out as the only man who was ready to put his career and reputation in peril for what he believed in, and such men, who are rare, get their reward, in personal trust and respect, even affection. In this way he stood, and still stands, alone among the leaders. Even among those who purport to agree with him, none shows such candour and courage. Some show none. There seems to be no progressive policy about which most Ulstermen could unite as loyal citizens and subjects of the Crown other than his.

Yet the centre on which he relied failed him. He won the Unionists of the towns, but not of the rural areas—the middle class, but not all of the working class, and few of the farming class. As to the Roman Catholic Nationalists, where were they? The election was fought on an old register. I suppose one could take a look at the registration lists, remembering that the registration of voters is a more significant stage than any election. So one might try to make out where the support O'Neill had hoped for really went. Hardly at all Unionist, I suspect—not very greatly Labour in any of its many guises—not Nationalist, I fear. The defeat of Eddie McAteer was a sad event, even sadder than Bannside. My guess is that if it could vote P[eople's] D[emoracy] or something similar, that's what it did—otherwise it stayed at home. But I may be wrong. Certainly, however, the Roman Church might have done better than fire a wink and a nod.

So I begin to think—like Blaney [TD for NE Donegal] and Lynch—that the border is still the great virus and that nothing that has supervened in recent times has produced a fundamental change of attitude about it. The task, still unfinished, indeed hardly begun, is to bring about that change. That Unionists should see the border as an ordinary frontier and not as a twentieth-century version of Derry Walls, a refuge for Protestants only. That Nationalists should be something more up to date than old-world Fenians. That Civil Righters and Labourites should like Gerry Fitt seek [only] true rights as British subjects and true allegiance to the queen. It all seems a long way off still. . . .

Harold Wilson cannot risk adding one more to his list of failures—dearly though he might like to tackle Ireland, it would be even harder than Rhodesia.

I go on too long. I have wearied you, I am sure. But you'll forgive, I'm no less sure. Ulster gave me some of the very happiest years of a happy life.

Yours ever,
David

By now Sayers's continual ill-health had finally taken its toll and sapped him of the will to fight on. Gone were the days when Malcolm Brodie, the *Telegraph*'s sports editor would be summoned to Sayers's hospital bed with a dinner jacket and ordered to drive his chief out to preach the cause of constructive Unionism at public meetings and 'old boy' dinners.

Letter to Conolly Gage, 17 March 1969

My dear Conolly,
I owe you a long, long letter—one to repay you for all the good things you have been writing to me these last few months. This can't be it, but you shall have it later. I do want you to know before you read it in Tuesday's paper

that my retirement has been fixed for 31 March. After that I go on as a director, writing our official history and planning our centenary in September,
1970. That makes me not unhappy. I decided that I should not go on carrying
the responsibility if I could not exercise the fullest command. To my regret,
Martin Wallace is not to be editor. After a lot of frustration he has accepted
the post of political editor (and deputy). He will have exceptional autonomy,
and that is an insurance for our political policy and the more serious side of
the paper. The editor is to be Eugene Wason, from the group's *Evening Post*
at Hemel Hempstead. He is a fifty-four year-old Scot with a wealth of experience at home and abroad, and I have to admit that he can do more techni-
cally for the *Telegraph*—which it badly needs—than Martin. (I do have a
liking for Wason.)

I've been editing the paper since 1953, so I've had a fair run and no regrets. It was a satisfaction to get back for the election and to lend the PM a
hand. We got very wedded to him—partly for want of anyone better—and it
is well that Martin should start to take a more independent view. I don't
doubt his turn as editor will come. I'll write again as soon as I can. Don't stop
writing please!

Ever,
Jack

The announcement of his retirement precipitated a flood of appre-
ciations, but it was a tribute from his confidant of many years that was
particularly cherished by Sayers.

Letter to Conolly Gage, 2 April 1969

Ulster Club,
Belfast

My dear Conolly,
Yours was the kindest thought of all. I must have received more than a hundred letters and messages, all immensely kind, but only you wrote for publication. I must say there was great hesitation all round before action was
taken. But when it came to 31 March and something had to be written for
the record, I felt I could consent. And indeed, I could not be prouder than to
have that kind of tribute, most of all from you. It was beautifully put, and I
thought that apart from what it said about me it was good that it should be
read by others who live by the press. On such a wave of goodwill I am happy
to go—I never had an outstanding academic record, and it means a lot to
believe that I have served my profession and Ulster. The PM lunched Daphne
and me yesterday, and while it was a memorable way to spend the first day
of my retirement, I had the disturbing feeling of being a deserter. After the
Unionist Council vote [which O'Neill won 338 to 263] he needs all the defenders possible. I fear that for him the struggle is coming to another and

still more bitter crisis. The antis are organising, as is Paisley, and I can see storms to come. It will be hard for me to stay on the touchline when that happens.

Ever,
Jack

Retirement from the *Telegraph* and the political fray enabled Sayers to regain a detached perspective on what seemed a profoundly depressing state of affairs.

'Outlook', BBC Radio 4, 26 April 1969

It was one of Ulster's own MPs who said at Westminster on Tuesday: 'There never was born an Englishman who understands the Irish people'. And he could have been right. But the real tragedy is that the mass of the people of Northern Ireland itself simply do not understand each other, and have hardly begun to try.

Here we are in an area no bigger than Yorkshire, barely a million and a half souls, and we are again being driven apart—as if we want to lay it down that Protestants belong solely to one strain and Catholics to another, strains between which there is an ancient distrust, one that is biologically incurable.

We mix physically, of course, but at the end of this profoundly saddening week there are many of us, on both sides, who are tempted to despair of a meeting of minds . . . and the discovery of a common humanity that will give this province the gift of charity, and with it the peace we long for.

The last few months in Northern Ireland have made us heartsore. We have seen the Civil Rights movement rise like a gathering storm; we have seen politics hurled into confusion; we have had a bitter general election that decided little or nothing; we have watched a horrifying descent into violence in the streets and terrorism at large.

Now we have heard what the British government says we must do to save ourselves, but still the ruling party wars with itself, and a Prime Minister, who is constantly urging reform, hangs by a thread in parliament. And all the while the ordinary Protestants and ordinary Catholics are again being inexorably separated and segregated, in their beings if not in their bodies.

As recently as February the brave ones among them stood out for moderation, co-operation, friendship. We do not hear so many of their voices now. They have been shocked into silence by the riots and the sabotage. And I am forced to say that the silence is also due to a dread of the extremists and their power of reprisal. So much for those most precious things, our freedom of assembly and our freedom of speech.

I cannot tell you now all that is caught up in this conflict. But I want to say that I am one of those who believes that if there is to be unity among the Ulster people worth having, it can only be when all of them are equal. And that if there is to be no such unity, the future for all of us is dark.

You listened to the remarkable Miss Bernadette Devlin. I did too. And, a liberal as I am, I learned from her. I could not agree with all that she said, but I saw very clearly what I had imperfectly seen before, the depths of the hurts to the human personalities of so many Catholics, those who today are openly claiming their right to full citizenship, to the highest standards of social justice. With many others I can only ask God's forgiveness for the failure of our imaginations.

To be fair, he had already been closely involved in the setting up of PACE and had chosen as his swan-song at the *Telegraph* a major interview with Cardinal Conway. His imagination was again to the fore when, after O'Neill's resignation on 28 April, he began to reconsider his allegiance to the Unionist Party. O'Neill, as he himself later remarked, had quite literally been blown from office by the destruction of water-mains which reduced Belfast's water supply to standpipes. These explosions, later discovered to be the work of Protestant extremists, were at the time thought to herald the revival of the IRA. However, the death-knell of his 'crusade' had been sounded on 24 April 1969 when he finally persuaded his party to accept universal suffrage in local elections. But with the party—for whom unity had always been the touchstone—split with 28 for and 21 against him, this could only be a pyrrhic victory.

Writing to Robert Porter, O'Neill's Home Secretary, Sayers tentatively raised the possibility of a new departure.

Letter to Robert Porter, 2 May 1969

Dear Beezer,
. . . I would very much have liked to have heard your views at the small meeting in the country on Wednesday. It was necessarily inconclusive, but even I—for long a romanticist about Ulster—now gravely doubt whether cohesion can ever be restored. The issue therefore seems to me to be a very real one.
    Every good wish.

Yours sincerely,
Jack Sayers

This clandestine gathering was at Tom Caldwell's [N.I. MP for Willowfield] house outside Lisburn, where discussion centred on the future for the pro-O'Neill Unionists and the possibility of form-

151

ing a new party of the middle ground. With the prospect of having to change the loyalties of a lifetime, Sayers not surprisingly sought advice.

Letter to Conolly Gage, 2 May 1969

as from home
Ulster Club

My dear Conolly,
Can I have your advice—on the most confidential basis? I feel you are the one man I can ask. The movement towards a centre party has really begun, and I was called into a consultation this week—with a number of MPs and others who backed O'Neill at the election. The fact that James C[hichester]-C[lark] won yesterday—and what a 'close run thing'—will give more time for thought, but if he falls, as he could do after a few riots, and B[rian] F[aulkner] gets in, there will be quite a number ready to cross the floor. Quite a number? Well, who really knows, but say four to be added to the three unofficial Unionists already on the other side of the House.

You may guess that I am one who remains impressed by the power of the ticket, and I have pressed the question whether the liberals can still get control of the party organisation. The answer is said to be No—and I am prepared to believe the truth of it. Everywhere the Paisleyites appear to be taking over the associations and the better people are being turned out. So my faith in the unifying power of Unionism has waned. But you will agree that the formation of new party—a United Ulster Party, with Catholic backing also—would be revolution indeed, and the problem is whether it would have any real hope of success. Again I have said that it must have guaranteed support of many Unionist leaders if it is not to hold Glengall Street, a good organisation and lots of money. They say all this can be done and that the new party could face an election immediately if B.F.'s retort was to call one. This predicament for Unionists will be understandable to you, and as always I would be much guided by your opinion, especially in the historical context. It is also said that the new party in opposition to official or right-wing Unionists could let in anti-partitionists in only a few places and that our constitutional stability would not be in danger. As for Terence, nobody knows how he would stand—he is one of those who would run the greatest risk by leaving his divisional association.

Please tell me what you think—it will be between ourselves *solely*. And be in no doubt of the reality of it all—something *is* going to happen, I am sure. I am well and enjoying being out of the race against the clock!

Ever,
Jack

Gage replied by return on the difficulties of such a venture.

Memorandum from Conolly Gage, 5 May 1969

My mind has been moving along the lines of a new party in Ulster; so, having given it some thought lately, I can answer your letter quickly. I should emphasise that being out of touch I cannot answer specific questions, but I can give some broad considerations which may help.

1. The advantages of the moderates taking over the party machine of Unionism are obvious.
   (a) They would have a ready-made and efficient organisation to hand, with money to back it.
   (b) The official Unionist ticket gets automatically a large number of unthinking votes.

2. The difficulties are equally obvious.
   (a) The party would have to be infiltrated at all levels quickly by moderates, who before the next election would have to occupy such a commanding position in the party that only moderate-minded men or women would be selected as candidates.
   (b) I doubt if this is possible, except in the towns, and even there it is doubtful.

3. The disadvantage is that even if this were possible (and what you say confirms my view that it is impossible), such a party would be unlikely to attract a worthwhile RC vote, as the last election showed. There is too much bitterness to allow Unionism to attract a strong RC vote.

4. My vote, therefore, would be cast for a new party.

5. To enable a new party even to get off the ground, what is required is money, organisation and a backer, in that order.
   (a) Money is essential. Enough candidates, enough organisation and enough advertisement must be procured to convince the public that the new party is in a position to provide a viable alternative government. Otherwise people won't vote for them, however sympathetic. See the Liberals here. This costs money. Are there enough rich people or companies ready to back such a party? Pud Grosvenor [5th Duke of Westminster] and Christopher Lindsay would, but you will need more than that.
   (b) Organisation is most important. A new party will need a first-rate business mind as organiser. Woolton for the Conservatives after the war was the real architect of the Conservative revival. Can you find such a man? The new party will have to be organised from the top down to the grassroots, and electoral success will depend on his efforts. In the end it is the people who knock on the doors who win elections, and the workers must be plentiful and good.
   (c) A backer is of less importance, but he must be respected and a speaker. It would be better if he is a Protestant, as that is where the main appeal will be, but an RC No. 2 would be of inestimable value. The backer

should be a new man untouched by old bitterness. Apart from the fact that he probably would not do it, Terence O'N would not be a good choice. He would rob the party of its newness. Too many would say it was a ruse to get him back, and much as I like him personally and his policies, he has been a failure. That is too great a burden for a new party to carry. You need feel no regrets. Politics is a ferocious game, and no one should go into it who thinks of it as anything else than ruthless. Failure is never forgiven, and if one man goes down in an effort to build a new Ulster, it is sad, but worth it.

You and your friends will be in the best position to judge whether there are present in Ulster all the ingredients to build a new party. I pray there are. It is our only hope for salvation and bringing us to the point where there is a government with a strong opposition.

Do not burden the new party with the name of 'Liberal'. Too many people remember Gladstone and Home Rule. 'Radical' would be better. There are many radical reformists in Ulster once you get away from religion and partition. They are especially evident in Belfast. Paradoxically, 'radical' might alienate the RCs, who are conservative to a man. All the small RC shop-keepers and other RC friends of mine in Belfast were more conservative than I was, but you will know about this.

Finally, I do not now believe that there is much threat to our constitutional position, so I would be unmoved by the idea of letting in anti-partitionists. Even our newly canonised 'St Bernadette [Devlin]' seems to negate this. That mixed-up child (attractive as she sounds) is too near socialism for the small RC shopkeepers of the Falls Road.

By the way, some warm telegrams must now be passing between that ill-assorted trio of Harold Wilson, de Gaulle and T. O'N. Hope I've been of some help.

This effectively killed off any sentimental attractions Sayers had for inaugurating a centre party. For so long an establishment figure, he lacked an enthusiasm for the conspiratorial antics of opposition. Nor, any longer, had he the strength for them. Consequently, he went to hear the Ulster Orchestra rather than attend the next meeting at Caldwell's house on 9 May, sending Gage's memorandum in his place.

Letter to Conolly Gage, 29 May 1969

My dear Conolly,
I was deeply struck by your letter on the situation here—you could not have been nearer the mark in your analysis of events and your estimate of the current possibilities. Indeed I had a typewritten copy made (omitting all identification) and showed it to Peter Campbell when we lunched last week. He agreed entirely. What a nice fellow he is! His policy is to work on preparing

an organisation which can really take the field when James C[hichester]-C[lark] goes, or at some later date that would be fixed in relation to some happening that will bring all the moderates together again. Of the need for a new centre party he is in no doubt—and despite the PM's good progress to date, the party is still hardening. You will have seen the nominations to the Senate and the actions of the Young Unionists. Peter is fully aware of the need for management but like myself he doesn't know who could take the leadership. I begin to wonder if we could turn to an Ulsterman in London, not that anyone has come to my notice. After all we went to Dublin for Edward Carson!

The Campbellite Parliamentary Groups are now operating in some constituencies and there is agreement to leave the others to the New Ulster Movement. This is in much the same predicament, having to mobilise moderates who are mostly content to let the new government get on with it. I was taken to lunch yesterday by their treasurer, Basil Glass, solicitor, and asked to be chairman. But I simply cannot get actively involved in politics—it would be out of the frying pan into the fire! In any event, NUM tends to be nondescript in political terms, with leftist leanings more than radical ones. And it too is bereft of a public figure to give it real authenticity. Peter and I would estimate that a new party will not come about until there is another crisis of toleration and a mass movement across the House, including [Herbert] Kirk and other ministers. This *could* happen in extreme circumstances. For the moment Roy Lilley would say James C.-C. is secure but that the atmosphere is still very divisive. David Lindsay Keir paid us a visit last Saturday and remarked of the Unionist Party: 'The tide has come in, but the rocks are still underneath.' This is very descriptive of people who have been forced to accept so much of Terence's belief but still don't like it. I saw T. himself at lunch at Willie Johnson's—he is stuck both to Bannside and Glengall Street but seems to think that Glengall Street at least is irredeemable. The irony is that he is not the best of assets today—and he will say silly things when off the leash. . . .

As if I had not enough interests already, I have accepted nomination by the minister to the board of the Christian Brothers' Grammar School. It seemed the right thing to do, even though there has been no lay representation whatever in the past and the reform may not be easy. If the Mater Hospital negotiations are finally successful, I expect to go on the board there too. This is the most I can contribute now that I've had to lay down my pen. As I do again now. Enjoy your holiday and come back here soon.

Jack

Off the leash O'Neill had indeed said some 'silly', if rather revealing, things. Most infamous was this assertion in a radio broadcast given in the aftermath of his fall from office: 'The basic fear of Protestants in Northern Ireland is that they will be outbred by the Roman Catholics. It is simple as that. It is frightfully hard to explain to a Protestant that if you give Roman Catholics a good job and a good house they will live like Protestants, because they will see neighbours with cars and TV sets. . . . But if the Roman Catholic is jobless and lives in a most ghastly hovel, he will rear eighteen children on national assistance.' This was constructive Unionism at its most reductionist and insensitive. Like Arthur Balfour before him, O'Neill had come to grief because he had yet to grasp that 'break [ing] the chains of ancient hatreds' would require respecting different cultural identities and traditions rather than seeking to obliterate them through ameliorating economic griev-ances. And yet Sayers could easily have subscribed to this in the 1950s. Nothing could show more clearly how far Sayers had come ideologi-cally and how far he had left O'Neill behind, and also, after the fate of O'Neill's cautious campaign, how far Ulster still had to go.

A wedding in Sussex provided some respite from such thoughts and gave Sayers the opportunity to visit Chartwell and the haunts of his old master. From there he returned to London for a British Coun-cil meeting, where he found time to bring Gage up to date on North-ern developments.

Letter to Conolly, 21 June 1969

Devonshire Club

My dear Conolly,
I really thought that Peter Campbell was a near enough kinsman for you to know him quite well. He's still busy with his parliamentary associations and so are the N[ew] U[lster] M[ovement] in the constituencies they have been given a free hand in. Well they might, as Roy Lilley (do read his article of last Friday) thinks there will be another upheaval over the pattern of local gov-ernment and votes at eighteen. James C[hichester]-C[lark] has been nice to everyone, but the question is how long he can keep that up. Did I say that I had been asked to be chairman of the NUM? But active politics are cer-tainly not for me. I have enough to do, and having got good reports from my doctor I don't want to reverse the process!

I'm a bit sad about the 'Telly'. Martin Wallace has thrown in his hand and is becoming Northern reporter for Telefís Éireann—not the best of assign-ments for a man who is essentially a commentator and writer. He has a curi-ous reticence and tendency to sulk, and as political editor I don't think that he stood up to the new editor as much as he could and should have done. Roy will probably take charge of this field, and I am advising him privately that he must insist on his position. The real difficulty is that politics cannot be segregated—the whole paper has to be a setting for our policy, and the new man is responsible for a treatment of the news which I can only describe as 'hack' in the journalistic sense. Its also painful for me to see how we have allowed the demands of a mass circulation on production [to be] so easily met by neglecting the service to the reader.

I was on television (NI only) on Thursday in a discussion on the Éire election—and found in my more detached situation that the press does tend to over-write, certainly ahead of events. The dangers of expecting too much!

Love to you both—till August.

Ever,
Jack

The Twelfth of July saw a renewal of sectarian rioting and Sayers at a loss for words.

Letter to Conolly Gage, 25 July 1969

My dear Conolly,

This is to do no more than remind you to give us good notice of when you will be here. We shall want you to come and see us and to pay a visit to Tara Cottage. I am become a gardener—the work there has been the greatest relaxation I've known for a long time! And it does wonders for the waistline—with that (and dieting) I am one and a half stones lighter and feel all the better for it. I had hoped that Terence and Jean might be able to join us when you come, but they will be away for August. Perhaps you would like to meet Ken Bloomfield, who is still serving the PM, as is Black.

The Derry and Dungiven outbursts have distressed me, and I confess that if I was still editor, I should hardly know what to say. Both extremes are gaining strength, and the more they do the more I fear for Northern Ireland's ability to survive. This seems to me to be the great issue as we near 1971—whether we have really proved our capacity for self-government. The next few months will have much to say to that. Do write soon.

Ever,
Jack

As it was, August brought four days of continuous rioting in Derry and Belfast; and with the police unable to restore order, British troops were called in.

Extract from interview. 'Ten O'Clock', BBC Radio 4, 15 August 1969

Hunt: You talked a moment or two ago of great fires burning. Now, are large parts of Belfast in flames, or is it only a small part of the city that's affected by the violence and the burning, though, of course, being terribly badly affected?

Sayers: Well, I must make it clear, that perhaps one square mile would cover the area of the disturbance and fires tonight, and in relation to the whole city that might be an eighth or a tenth. It is a dusky night here. There is a great deal of mist, and not everybody would be aware that fires were burning and that the smoke was going so high into the sky.

Hunt: So that you could be in Belfast tonight, as perhaps a lot of people are, without really knowing that anything's going on?

Sayers: Yes, but there's a certain air about the city that is full of apprehension, the buses have all been stopped about now. Most people are taking the advice of the Prime Minister and have gone home early. There's a tension everywhere. . . .

Hunt: Major Chichester-Clark has called this the 'most serious and malevolent threat in the country's history'. Do you agree?

Sayers: I think this must be true. We have had attacks by the Irish Republican Army. The last one was about ten years ago. It was a campaign extended over about five years, but it consisted almost entirely of outrages committed every few weeks. Nothing like this scale of violence in the streets, this continual fighting over periods of several days, has happened since 1936, and even then it was nothing like so bad as it is now.

For Sayers, who as a young reporter had witnessed the riots of the 1930s, his life seemed rather strangely to have come full circle. A few days later saw him once again broadcasting on the overseas service. But the glad confidence of the post-war years had gone.

Radio Comment, BBC Overseas, 20 August 1969

It wasn't exactly a revolution, although to the world it must have looked very like one. But it *was* the most shattering week, and the most earth-shaking politically, that Northern Ireland has known in all the fifty years of its stormy history. The riots in Londonderry and Belfast spoke for themselves. Eight people killed and millions of pounds' worth of property destroyed by fires that brought back awful memories of the blitz. We were a province in utter turmoil, gripped by communal fears and on the very brink of civil war that might have involved the Irish Republic too.

And now the British government, after ordering the army into the streets to restore order, and sending 3,000 men as reinforcements, has intervened in the way it has long threatened to do in the attempt to bring Ulster's quarrelling to an end.

But many are saying today that the changes in the relationship between London and Stormont mean that things will never be the same again. The government here is to be supervised by the Home Office as it has never been before—all with the object of seeing that not again does it fail with reforms that, in Mr Wilson's words, should have been brought in ten, twenty, thirty, fifty years ago. . . .

Will it all work out? Is this the end of the great Civil Rights agitation that began last October? Can there really be peace and common purpose between Protestants and Catholics, Unionists and Nationalists? Is this the best way to hasten the political education so much neglected in the past?

We can only hope it will, and that first of all Ulster ceases to be an armed camp ruled by fright. . . .

Sayers was devastated by the sight of 'both sides . . . spoiling for a communal blood-bath'. Faced with what he found 'scarcely believable', he in his last report for *The Round Table* let his friend Tyrone Guthrie speak for him: 'We have shown, not just to the world but to ourselves, a frightening lack of logic, imagination, self-control, humour and Christian charity.'(*The Round Table*, Aug. 1969) To a close friend he simply confessed: 'I thought I knew my Ulsterman, but I was wrong'. About this time Sayers drafted some observations for the commission investigating the United Kingdom constitution. These echoed earlier doubts (*The Round Table*, June 1969) over the viability not only of Unionism but of Stormont and of the experiment in devolved government.

Submission to parliamentary commission, no date [c. August 1969]

Commission on the Constitution:

Submission by John E. Sayers, D.Lit.

Parliamentary reporter	*Belfast Telegraph*		1936–1939
Political Correspondent	"	"	1945–1953
Joint Managing Editor	"	"	1953–1961
Editor-in-Chief	"	"	1961–1969

While it is true that many of the difficulties of operating devolution in Northern Ireland are due to the presence unusually of a dual society, I would with respect submit that regional parliaments are not to be contemplated without careful study of the likely natures of the party systems that will go with them. It is not enough that local self-government may serve, as in Northern Ireland, to meet an urgent political problem, nor that it can confer considerable administrative advantages. Regional conditions require at all times to be conducive to the practice of a high standard of parliamentary democracy as the United Kingdom knows it. . . . In so far as party politics will determine the make-up and character of any new parliament, it is well to remember the saying 'God made meat, but the Devil made the cooks'. The obvious illustration in Northern Ireland is government by the same party over a period of forty-eight years. . . .

It was the Downing Street Declaration (19 August 1969), in which no amount of diplomatic language could disguise the emasculation of Stormont, that compelled Sayers to shed the last of the treasured assumptions that had brought him back to Ulster after 1945. Unexpectedly, his retirement had witnessed a remarkable series of reassessments, driven on as much by relentless honesty as by events. Yet, at the last, to be stripped one by one of cherished ideals could not but be a painful process.

Letter to Kenneth Bloomfield, Secretary to the Cabinet, 21 August 1969

. . . I feel I want to say something to you, but I hardly know what. I've been thinking that everything that has befallen us is what Terence warned the party against, and I couldn't but have a thought for you at Downing Street as a witness of the very breakdown and intervention you strove to avert. I am more than crushed by the human tragedy of it all—step by step I'm being forced to the conclusion that we are incapable of normal political development, and that without this we cannot sustain a parliament and system of our own. I've been asked to give evidence to the Commission on the Constitution, and ask myself whether I must be honest and say just that. I've come a long way from my inborn romanticism about Ulster and the inspiration that came from you. Forgive me for my failure—the extreme violence in Belfast was bad enough, but the communiqué and the declaration have hit me as an indictment of Unionism from which it can't recover. Could we meet once before October if you get a respite? I so much need to know your own state of mind.

In such opinions Sayers was not alone.

Letter from Terence O'Neill, 24 August 1969

Well Vale,
Alford,
Lincolnshire

My Dear Jack,
How sad it is. I read my papers and listen to the radio. We are, of course, quite out of touch; with Roy Lilley at your right hand, you are in the picture.

However I can read between the lines! An ex-ambassador [Oliver Wright, appointed British government representative in Northern Ireland on 22 August 1969] would not be content with some small back room where he can read last week's cabinet conclusions. Nor would a general of Freeland's calibre allow himself to be pushed around by Brooke and Taylor.

I do so hope that Ted will not allow himself to be used for any improper purpose. We really cannot have another 1912.

I flew back with Phelim [O'Neill] from London in July. He was so confident.... 'You know I feel a few genuflections to the right are required.' Has it really paid to receive Paisley at Stormont three times this summer? Perhaps it has—but I just could not have done it.

But what of the future? How will it ever be possible to remove the troops? Will unemployment rise this winter? Will the British people continue to subsidise a province of which they do not approve?

Jim Malley, on the telephone, tells me that so-called moderates (with the honourable exception of Dick Ferguson) are becoming hardliners from the basest political motives.

The choice would seem to lie between the present set-up as it exists this week—or DIRECT RULE. The latter may well be the *only* alternative.

I would hope—perhaps I am *now* out of touch—that if the minority were given fair treatment, they would want to stay in the UK.

It is all *so* sad. To quote Gandhi, 'at the moment I see no hope on the horizon anywhere'.

Yours,
Terence

Nor probably could Sayers. Whether even he would have retained his passionate concern for Ulster politics after the disintegration of all that he stood for in a matter of eight months must be doubted. As it was, he was not put to the test. On 30 August he suffered a massive heart attack and died. After a funeral service at Carlisle Memorial Church, he was buried at Carnlough, where his ancestors had first settled in the seventeenth century and in the county that was the heartland of his beloved radical tradition. By such ideals and myths had he lived, and with them he died.

'These years will become a famous chapter in Ulster history,' wrote Lindsay Keir on Sayers's retirement, 'and what is to take place in coming years, as in the past, will largely have been shaped by your influence over thoughts and events'. A year later, on the first anniversary of Sayers's death, O'Neill spoke in equally eulogistic terms but the tone was much more pessimistic.

Lord O'Neill. 'Proud His Name', Northern Ireland Home Service (Radio 4), 30 August 1970

Well, he was obviously a man of great integrity and great sincerity—I think that must have struck everybody who met him. He was a wonderful person in many ways—I should add, I think, to that, that he was also a man of great courage, because it took courage to adopt the policy which he adopted at a time when it was far from fashionable. And I have no doubt that like all people who had to—felt they had to—adopt this way of life, he had a lot of threats, which unfortunately is the sort of thing that happens to one in Ireland, and he was quite undeterred by these threats; he carried on in the way he felt was the right way. And I would go further than that and I would say that had Jack been listened to at the time that he was talking to us through his leaders in the *Telegraph*, some of the terrible things that have since happened might not have happened. To start with the obvious things, some people might be alive today who are now dead; some people's houses which have been burnt down might still be standing. But perhaps even more important than that, our position within the United Kingdom would have been much stronger had his opinion been listened to than it is today. This is one of the tragedies of this whole situation through which we have lived—that they didn't understand, that the message which Jack was trying to impart was not a message of treachery, as they thought, but a message of common sense, a message of goodwill, a message for improving Northern Ireland and (I hate to use this word) Northern Ireland's image throughout not only the United Kingdom but throughout the world.

In the end, Sayers had not made history in quite the way he intended. Few do. Yet in spite of all the changes that have taken place in Ulster since his death, the fundamental issues to which he addressed his life's work remain intact and, with them, the moral vision that inspired all that he wrote.

8   The View from the Wilderness

Yet Sayers's career was not simply another study in failure. 'Owlish, peering through his glasses, slightly swarthy, very neat dark suit and a tight knot to his tie in a hard white collar', Sayers had always looked a little archaic for the 1960s. Nevertheless, he was one of the most remarkable editors Ulster has ever produced. He gave the *Belfast Telegraph* an imaginative vitality and an authority that no rival could match. But for all his many talents, it was his ability to motivate and enthuse his younger lieutenants that was to prove his greatest attribute. If his manner was rather forbidding and the standards demanded severe, he nevertheless won their respect by leaving them relatively free to write and defending them through the ensuing controversies. In later years most were to speak warmly of him, although in practice the relationship had never been warm and they had at one time or another all resented his conservative restraint on their youthful idealism. His protection, to their dismay, of O'Neill reflected in part the personal rapport of two shy and formal men but also his recognition that the *Telegraph's* strength lay not in indulgent revolt but in its position at the heart of the Unionist establishment. Interestingly, he never once revealed to them the rawer radicalism shown in his correspondence with Conolly Gage, preferring to endure their occasional hostility and thereby ensuring that the *Telegraph* buzzed with a creative tension. With journalists of the calibre of Cole, Flackes, Wallace, Lilley, Waugh, Kennedy, McCreary and Brodie, he established a paper with the greatest ever sales in the North (over 200,000) and a readership that straddled the sectarian divide. That Paisley should adopt the title *Protestant Telegraph* was a fair indication, however unintended, of Sayers's influence.

At the very least, the *Telegraph* helped to sustain and mould a popular moderate consensus which, however fragile, remains a unique achievement in twentieth-century Ulster. While hindsight may mock a decade of community weeks and inter-church activities, they had a spontaneity and confidence that most community workers today can only envy. Nor was Sayers without his political successes. Through him, liberal Unionism was made acceptable, even fashionable, for the first time since 1903. By adopting an independent line he broke the stranglehold of Glengall Street on the media and revitalised political debate in the province. This development was a part of the wider collapse of the political press in Britain, but with the fierce control exercised by the party through the Hendersons at the *Newsletter*, the Cunninghams of the *Northern Whig* and Harry McMullan at the BBC, it took enormous courage. His description of the 'wasted years' under Brookeborough led to him being shunned and denounced as a traitor. O'Neill, irritated by one leader, simply cancelled lunch, knowing full well how much Sayers treasured their public *tête-à-têtes* in the Ulster Club. In such a closed society, these snubs could only have hurt one who so valued acceptance. But it never deflected him. With his constant emphasis on British standards and with the wide coverage given to all parties, he probably contributed to the Catholic strategy of seeking justice within the system, which was to so unnerve Unionism. And while the 1969 election was viewed as a defeat, O'Neillism won a very respectable poll and was within a few hundred votes of the resounding victory it needed—and that with little organisation or help from O'Neill. In a society in which, traditionally, few speak out, that so many chose to do so in 1968–9 was in no small part due to the leadership Sayers's *Telegraph* offered in the political vacuum.

'History does not go into reverse,' Cardinal Conway had assured him (11 July 1966), but he would have been better advised to have put his trust in de Toqueville. Still, for all the dangers that faced a reformer, Sayers undoubtedly contributed to his own downfall. To begin with, he exaggerated the power of the written word. At the height of the Civil Rights crisis in October 1968, Roy Lilley, the senior political correspondent of the *Telegraph* found Sayers in despair: 'Roy, we must find someone to write a piece that will bring Ulster to her senses. Could Quintin [Hogg] do it?' Lilley demurred, but later found that Sayers had left the editorial office for the seclusion of the library in order to write the article that would singlehandedly turn the tide. Such faith was hopelessly naïve. Sayers's writings could reaffirm or encourage reassessment of ideas, but they could not of themselves overturn basic instincts. Significantly, Richard Rose's survey taken at the height of Sayers's editorship found that half of the *Telegraph*'s leadership endorsed 'ultra' views. Sayers's liberal constituency was in spirit too professional middle-class, too suburban, and too east of the Bann. Above all, it was too 'British'. A fine example of the 'Ulster-British' tradition within Unionism, Sayers represented a social milieu for whom the United Kingdom was a reality, London the capital, and British ethos the ideal. At the same time, this tradition had never lost sight of an all-Ireland perspective. All of this emotionally detached them from the rank-and-file, for whom Britishness paled into insignificance in comparison with the emotional appeal of 1912 and, occasionally, UDI. Consequently, he failed to appreciate the fears of ordinary Protestants and the appeal of fundamentalism. Free from the necessity of having to attend constituency meetings 'in the sticks', he could indulge himself in the assumption that Paisley represented antediluvian reaction. His sharp retort during the Harry West affair that the Unionist Party should not be run at the behest of Fermanagh starkly reflected the contempt shown by those for whom 'civilisation ended at the Finaghy crossroads'. Despite years travelling around Ulster with the BBC's 'Your Questions' team, his 'Honest Ulsterman' assumptions had, almost to the last, remained unshakeable. He had no conception of the humiliation that was pent up in the Unionist rank-and-file and which Paisley transformed from an inchoate frustration into a powerful political movement. Indeed, as Sayers was seeking to spread the word, his very language with its elitist overtones aroused only hostility. Crucially, Sayers misunderstood the nature of Unionist leadership. Taken in by the image of the titans, Carson, Craig and Brookeborough, he failed to see how far they survived on populism and the 'distribution of the bones'. Sayers was not, of course, the only one to underestimate Paisley. But in addition, he never resolved the dilemma between journalistic values of fair reporting and his fear, as he stared glumly at Paisley's picture on his front page, of 'helping to create a monster'. Unable to prevent publicity-seekers from exploiting his paper by creating news, he was not particularly adept either at manipulating the politicians. He was, of course, too wedded to the institutions, the party and the world of the 'Big House'. Moreover, he did not have the means or the personality to play politics and be a kingmaker. Here was no Beaverbrook.

More hurtful to Sayers perhaps was the failure to establish a lasting tradition at the *Telegraph*. In his retirement he railed at the descent into 'hack journalism', but even he had been unable to stem the advance of the advertising department. He may have been one of the last great writing editors, writing for a public who knew of life before television, but as such he had outlived his time. When the crisis broke in 1968–9, it was television and radio and not the press that set the pace (and possibly the agenda) of public debate. Furthermore, the emergence of independent television (UTV) with its confrontational style of political reporting challenged the very essence of his own reflective, sympathetic approach that had been such a marked feature

165

of his journalism, especially on radio. Comparisons may be invidious, but one of the many reasons why Sayers's 'Ulster Commentary' never achieved the longevity of Alistair Cooke's 'Letter From America' was that Sayers spoke too much as an insider. Nor was there the time to reflect once the purchase of the *Telegraph* by Roy Thomson had inaugurated the unceasing search for profits. Gone were the days when a young reporter, reproached by Sayers for excluding on grounds of space all reference to the Imperial Contribution in a summary of the Stormont budget that had already run to two columns, was told bluntly: 'Damn it, man. Let it run on a bit!' There was also something rather dated, as he himself sadly recognised, in his anxiety on moral grounds over the decision to make 'Find the Ball' a prominent feature. Equally sad has been the retreat of the leader into the far depths of the paper—recently, indeed, to sit opposite an article on burgers. All these new developments were signs that the social revolution unleashed by the 'Troubles' had ensured, very suddenly, that these were no longer his times.

Wherein lies his significance? Undoubtedly at a critical time in Ulster's history he fomented and at times led public debate, and if he was primarily influential among the intelligentsia, the 150,000 pro-O'Neill 'coupons' and other *Telegraph* polls suggested a wider popular appeal. But by 1969 the great educational experiment to reverse centuries of bigotry had collapsed utterly. The moderate consensus that he sought to engineer had produced only a 'pick'n'mix' liberalism that involved no sacrifice of cherished prejudices. But perhaps this is to criticise him for attempting the impossible. In broadening opinion the *Telegraph* had helped to create an opportunity for change, but the paper could not of itself provide the political will to exploit it. Equally, learned persuasion from on high was not likely to prove decisive in a society that had been founded and on occasion successfully sustained by the defiance of mere reason and the odds. Perhaps instead his importance lies less in what he achieved and more in what he represented: firstly as an inspiration, through his courage, integrity and energy, of the power of idealism to challenge an intellectually repressed society. Historically he reveals the survival of the constructive Unionist tradition of Dunraven and Plunkett, which then, as now, exercised on governments an influence out of all proportion to its numbers. Moreover, just as in the 1890s, so in the 1960s, the impact of constructive Unionist reformers was to highlight the fissures within Unionism and its inability to develop beyond a mechanism for the monopolising of power into a philosophy of *government*. Unlike the controversies of the early twentieth century, the challenge of the 1960s proved too much for the Unionist monolith. In this Sayers played his part. His campaign to deny the hardliners respectability helped to delay the widespread mobilisation of Protestant extremism and to prevent Paisley from assuming what he craved—the mantle of Carson. In this Sayers was more a midwife than a maker of history, one whose role was vital at the time but was quickly forgotten thereafter. Ironically for one so constructive, Sayers's achievement was primarily destructive in contributing, however unwillingly, to the splintering of Ulster Unionism—which perhaps may prove an essential precondition for any political reconstruction in the province.

In the meantime the Sayers Lectures, held annually at Queen's University for up to a thousand schoolchildren, remain a fitting and lasting tribute to his faith in education and the force of the word. At the same time, his advocacy of the values of liberty, Christian tolerance and community have lost none of their relevance. 'It is an ancient practice', a former Moderator reminded him on his retirement, 'to destroy the prophet [rather] than to do what he says.' Maybe it will only be when (if ever) we emerge from our present wilderness that the reputation of the 'prophet' will be seen in its true light.

However, any hints that the political logjam may be breaking up are more a product of war-weariness than a belated popular embracing of political liberalism. Fittingly but significantly, that liberal Unionism retained any influence at all after the defeat of 1969 was due to the British and the establishment of direct rule. Whether through the Alliance Party, the higher civil service or through the numerous government quangos filled by the great and good, Sayers's natural constituency continues to exercise considerable sway. Yet the reliance on British governments to preserve 'British values' in Ulster invariably raises anxieties over the viability of the British commitment to Ulster; particularly as with every year of the Troubles the province's experience diverges more and more from that of the rest of the United Kingdom, and while the Protestant diaspora in Britain continues to grow. If he had lived, Sayers would undoubtedly have drawn the parallel between the events of 1969–72 and the loss of nerve in 1798 and the subsequent seeking of refuge in the Act of Union in 1800. Whether he would have gained any assurance from the outcome of that union in 1916–1921 is a moot point. After all, having been brought up as a 'child of the revolution', he had dedicated his life to the prevention of another revolution, only to die at the very moment when Ulster was once again staring into the abyss. Although late in life, he for one came to recognise the perils of nostalgia.

Index